Butterfly

YUSRA MARDINI

with Josie Le Blond

Butterfly

From Refugee to Olympian, My Story of Rescue,
Hope and Triumph

bluebird
books for life

First published in the UK 2018 by Bluebird
an imprint of Pan Macmillan
20 New Wharf Road, London N1 9RR
Associated companies throughout the world
www.panmacmillan.com

ISBN 978-1-5098-8167-3 HB
ISBN 978-1-5098-8168-0 TPB

1 3 5 7 9 8 6 4 2

A CIP catalogue record for this book is available from the British Library.

Printed and bound by CPI Group (UK) Ltd, Croydon, CR0 4YY

Visit www.panmacmillan.com to read more about all our books
and to buy them. You will also find features, author interviews and
news of any author events, and you can sign up for e-newsletters
so that you're always first to hear about our new releases.

The Boat

I dive into the glinting water.

'Yusra! What the hell are you doing?'

I ignore my sister and duck under the waves. The ocean roars over the drum beat of my pulse. The life jacket tugs upwards on my chest. I break the surface. Desperate prayers ring out from the boat above.

I grab the rope and glimpse the shore. Europe is in sight. The sun inches down towards the island. The wind is up. The passengers cry and shriek as the boat spins in the swell. The Afghan pulls desperately on the engine cord. It splutters but doesn't catch. The engine is dead. We are alone, at the mercy of the raging sea.

The boy's face appears between the huddled passengers on the boat. He grins. It's a game. He knows nothing about all the desperate people who died here. Mothers and their babies, old men and women, strong young men. The thousands who never made it to shore, who battled for hours in vain until the sea took them. I screw my eyes shut and fight the rising panic. Swim. I can swim. I can save the boy.

I see my mother, my father, my little sister. A parade of half-remembered triumphs, defeats, and embarrassments. Things I'd rather forget. Dad throws me into the water. A man hangs a medal around my neck. A tank takes aim. Glass shatters onto a pavement. A bomb rips through a roof.

My eyes flick open. Beside me, my sister stares grimly up at the next towering peak of angry water. The rope cuts into my palms. The sea drags and sucks at my clothes. My limbs ache under the weight. Just hold on. Stay alive.

Another wave rises, the dark water looms behind the boat. I brace as we rise and fall, drift and spin. The sea is not a swimming pool. There are no sides, no bottom. This water is unlimited, wild, and unknowable. The waves march on, relentless, an advancing army.

The sun sinks faster now down to meet the island's peaks. The shore looks further away than ever. The water glints dark purple, the wave's crests shine creamy yellow in the dying light. How did it get this far? When did our lives become so cheap? Risking it all, paying a fortune to climb onto an overcrowded dinghy and take our chances on the sea. Is this really the only way out? The only way to escape the bombs at home?

The surf rolls and surges. Choppy peaks of water knock my head against the side of the boat. The salt water stings my eyes, fills my mouth, my nose. The wind whips my hair around my head. The cold creeps down my body, working into my feet, my calves, and my thigh muscles. I can feel my legs beginning to seize up.

'Yusra! Get back on the boat.'

I grip the rope more tightly. I'm not letting my sister do this alone. No one is going to die on our watch. We're Mardinis. And we swim.

PART ONE

The Spark

1

I swim before I can walk. My dad, Ezzat, a swimming coach, just puts me in the water. I'm not yet big enough for armbands, so he removes the plastic grate from the gutter overflow at the pool's edge and plonks me into the shallow water underneath.

'Here, move your legs like this,' says Dad.

He makes a paddling motion with his hands. I thrash my legs until I work out how to kick. Often, I tire myself out and the water's lapping warmth lulls me to sleep. Dad never notices. He's too busy barking orders at my older sister, Sara. Neither of us chose to swim. We don't remember starting. We just swim, we always have.

I'm a cute kid, with light skin, large brown eyes, long dark hair, and a small, neat frame. I'm painfully shy and I rarely speak. I'm only happy when I'm with my mum, Mervat. If she goes to the bathroom, I'll wait outside until she's done. If other adults try to talk to me I gaze up at them in silence.

Most weekends we visit my grandparents in the city. My grandmother Yusra, who I'm named after, is like a second mother. I hide behind the long folds of her *abaya,* a floor-length, fitted jacket, as my grandfather Abu-Bassam tries bribing me with sweets to get me to smile. I never fall for it, so he teases me and calls me a scaredy-cat.

Sara is three years older than me and the other extreme. No one can get her to stay quiet. She's always talking to adults, even strangers in shops, babbling away in a made-up language. She likes to interrupt tea parties by standing on Grandma's sofa and talking nonsense, waving her arms as if she's making a speech. When Mum asks, Sara says she's speaking English.

We're a big family. Mum and Dad have eleven siblings between them. There are always cousins around. We live in Set Zaynab, a town south of Damascus, the capital of Syria. Dad's older brother, Ghassan, lives in the building opposite us. His kids, our cousins, come over every day to play.

Swimming is the family passion and Dad expects us to share it. All Dad's siblings trained when they were young. Dad swam for Syria when he was a teenager, but had to stop after being called up for compulsory military service. When Sara was born he returned to the pool as a coach. Dad has always been a passionate believer in his own skill. One day, before I was born, he threw baby Sara into the pool to prove how good a coach he was. He wanted to show the others he could even teach his baby daughter to swim. Mum looked on in silent horror as he fished Sara out again.

The winter I'm four, Dad lands a job at the Tishreen Sports Complex in Damascus, home of the Syrian Olympic Committee. Dad signs me and Sara up for swimming training. He arranges for another coach to take me on while Dad concentrates on seven-year-old Sara. I train three times a week in the creepy Olympic pool. The main sources of light are long, low windows that run along three sides of the building. Above the glass, fixed metal blinds block out the glaring sunshine. Mounted on one of them, next to the scoreboard, hangs a large portrait of Syrian President Bashar Al-Assad.

It's always freezing in the pool. But I soon discover that being tiny, shy, and pretty has its advantages. Before long, my new coach is smitten. I have him wrapped around my little finger.

'I'm cold,' I mumble, gazing up at the coach with wide, innocent eyes.

'What's that, little one?' says the coach. 'You're cold? Why don't you go and take your towel and sit outside in the sun for a little while? What's that, *habibti*, my dear? You're hungry too? Well then, let's get you some cake.'

For the next blissful four months of spoiling, I'm rarely in the pool. But I can't escape Dad. One day I pass him after training. The pool is empty, Dad is getting ready for his next session. Mum has come to pick us up as usual and is waiting quietly on a chair at the poolside. Dad spots me before I can reach her.

'Yusra,' he calls. 'Come here.'

I pull my towel closer around my shoulders and hurry over to him. Once I'm in grabbing distance he rips off the towel, lifts me up and launches me into the water. I battle to the surface and gasp for air. My arms and legs thrash around in panic. Four months lying in the sun and eating cake have left their mark. There's no hiding it from Dad. I've forgotten how to swim. His curses echo around the hall and ring in my ears. I struggle towards the edge and grab the side. I don't dare look up.

'What have you done?' he shouts. 'What the hell have you been doing?'

I haul myself out and get to my feet. I force myself to look at him. It's a mistake. He's marching towards me, his face flaming with rage. He reaches me in a few strides. I stare down at the tiles and brace for my punishment.

He bends down towards me.

'What's wrong with you?' he shouts. 'What did he do?'

Dad shoves my shoulders hard and sends me flying backwards into the pool. I slam into the water back first. I surface, nose full of chlorine, eyes wild with shock. I splutter and flap like a hooked fish. I thrash and scoop my way back to the edge and cling on, eyes fixed on the dancing water.

'Out!' he shouts. 'Get out now!'

I drag myself out of the pool and scuttle a little distance away. I watch Dad warily. He has the look of a man who is willing to do this all day. A third time, a fourth time, twenty times, until I can swim again. He advances again. I throw a pleading look at my mother. She's sitting motionless, staring at us from the poolside. Her expression is unreadable. She says nothing. The pool is his kingdom.

'Ezzat! Are you crazy?'

I risk a glance. It's my uncle Hussam, Dad's youngest brother. My saviour.

'What the hell are you doing?' shouts Hussam, striding around the pool towards us.

I look at Dad. His face is still bright red, but he now looks disoriented, cut off mid-rant. This is my chance. I scurry over to Mum and dive between the legs of her chair. I pull her long skirt down behind me. The poolside argument now sounds comfortingly far away. Mum shifts slightly in her seat. I'll be safe here until he calms down.

After that Dad doesn't let me out of his sight. He won't risk anyone else spoiling me. I'm his daughter. And I'll swim whether I like it or not. He stuffs me in inflatable armbands and puts me into the pool with Sara's age group.

I float around at one end of the pool while they train. The older swimmers show me no mercy. They push past and dunk me under. I soon learn to bat them out of my way or dive deeper down while they plough on over my head. Dad gradually deflates the armbands bit by bit until I can swim again.

That summer, my uncle Ghassan and his family move to Daraya, a suburb of Damascus eight kilometres south-west of the city centre. Mum and Dad decide to follow them. We move into a large house on a long, straight road that marks the border between Daraya and another district, Al Moadamyeh, to the west.

Sara and I get the biggest room at the front of the house. It's always flooded with light; the outside wall is made entirely out of glass. Mum and Dad's room is smaller. In the centre is a huge white antique bed, a present from Grandma and Grandpa. Sara and I ruin it by drawing on it with Mum's make-up. Another of our favourite games is to make a big pile of Mum's clothes on the floor and sit on top of it like queens of the castle. I spend a lot of time on the balcony, staring down at the busy street or gazing up above the rooftops, at the pointed minarets of the district's many mosques.

Our parents aren't the strictest Muslims, but I'm brought up to know the rules. They teach us to follow them and, more importantly, they teach us that a good Muslim shows respect. Respect your elders, respect women, respect those from other cultures and religions. Respect your mother. Respect your father. Especially if he's also your swimming coach.

Dad likes to separate the two roles. At the pool, we have to call him coach. At home, we can call him Dad, but in practice he's still coach. Training never stops. I come to dread Fridays, the first day of our weekend. Every week, Dad waits until we're relaxing on the sofa, then strides into the living room and claps his hands.

'Come on, girls!' he says. 'Go get your resistance bands and we'll work on your shoulders.'

We trudge off to find the long elastic bands. He fixes them up to the living-room window and puts us to work. The best part of Dad's training plan is when we get to watch sports on TV. We sit through the aquatics and athletics World Championships, all four tennis Majors and the UEFA Champions League. I become a passionate FC Barcelona fan. Dad doesn't waste a second of TV time. He points out the minute differences in the swimmers' techniques. He admires the soccer players' individual style. He praises the tennis players when they grind their opponents down and is scornful when they crumble under pressure. We sit and nod in silence.

The summer I'm six, we watch the closing races of the Athens 2004 Olympic Games. It's the men's 100m butterfly final.

'Watch lane four,' says Dad. 'Michael Phelps. The American.'

A tense silence falls in the living room. A horn sounds. Eight swimmers launch like arrows into the pool. An underwater camera shows Phelps' hips rolling, his long legs and flicking ankles churning the water back behind him. The swimmers break out on the surface in an explosion of white water. Phelps is almost a metre behind his rival Ian Crocker. It seems hopeless.

Phelps' enormous shoulders crane back, his bulk crashes down. Spray flies as he windmills into a somersault turn. He breaks the surface again, but he's still lagging. He'll never make it. Forty metres, thirty metres. At twenty-five metres to go, Phelps starts sprinting twice as fast. He gains on Crocker.

My eyes widen. Reach and crash, reach and crash. On, on. I catch my breath. It's so close. Three, two, one. Phelps and Crocker thwack the touch pad. It's Phelps. He's snatched gold from Crocker. Won by four hundredths of a second.

I stare spellbound at the screen. Dad stands and pumps his fist in the air. He spins round to face us.

'You see?'

On screen, Phelps rips off his goggles and gawps at the scoreboard. He brings both arms up in victory. I frown at the screen. I study his face, wonder if that feeling makes it all worth it. All that pain and sacrifice just for one instant of glory.

I never chose to be a swimmer. But from that moment on I'm hooked. My gut burns with ambition. I clench my fists. I no longer care what it takes. I'll follow Phelps to the top. To the Olympics. To gold. Or die trying.

2

Dad wants us to be the best swimmers. The very best. On Earth. Ever. He'll do anything to get us there. His expectations are astronomical, and we're expected to keep up. I start primary school a few weeks after Phelps' miracle win in Athens. The school is in Mazzeh district in western Damascus, on a square with an adjoining high school. I just have to work my way up through the buildings. From the bottom rung it looks like a long ladder. Dad sits me down one evening just after the start of term.

'Yusra, from tomorrow you're going to be a professional swimmer,' he says. 'You'll train every day for two hours from now on. You're going to join the Damascus youth team with your sister. Understand?'

I nod. I'm being told, not asked. My stomach writhes with excitement and dread. I see the rungs on the swimming ladder stretching up before me like the school buildings. I've made it onto the Damascus youth team. The next step is the Syrian national team, where I'll start swimming for my country in international competitions. From there, the Olympics will be in reach.

I fall into step with Sara's rigid routine. Dad has us both living like soldiers. School begins early and ends at lunchtime. But for us work isn't over. Dad waits for us every day at the school gates to take us to the pool. Some days after school I don't feel like swimming. But Dad silences protests with a single look. In the car, he bans music and all non-swimming related talk. He lectures us on technique and drills until we know all his speeches off by heart. Every day, Mum meets us at the pool and watches our training sessions from the spectator gallery.

One day, Dad and another coach are stretching Sara's shoulders before training. She kneels down while they pull her bent elbows back behind her head. We both hate that stretch. It can be painful, but it helps to get your shoulders supple and working. Dad tells us over and over again that we should stay very still. But this time, as Dad and the other coach pull back her elbows, Sara winces, jerks away and cries out in pain. She's in agony, so Mum and Dad take her to the doctors. They do an x-ray and find that she has broken her collarbone. Sara is taken out of training for several weeks, but Dad doesn't blink. One little accident won't stop his girls swimming. She's back in the water the moment she's healed. Dad doesn't go easy on her. He tells her to work harder than ever to make up for lost time.

That summer, I attend my first swimming training camp. Sara and I don't have to travel far. All the best young swimmers in Syria come to Damascus in the school holidays to train. We stay with the others in the athletes' hotel next to the Tishreen pool. Aged ten, Sara is already hanging out with the teenagers on the Syrian national team. I'm shy, so I stick with her. Gradually, the older kids coax me out of my shell. One of them, an older guy called Ehab, teases me and calls me 'little mouse'.

Swimming camp is also where I first meet Rami. He's from Aleppo but comes to Damascus often to train. He's sixteen, nine years older than me, but we become friends for life. At camp, I'm the youngest, so he's always nice to me. He's handsome, with an open, symmetrical face and dark hair and eyes. All the other girls are jealous of our friendship.

There aren't many older female swimmers in the camp. Many choose to give up swimming after they hit puberty. Some stop because they don't see a future career in swimming, or decide to stop when they go to university. Still more give up because this is the age Muslim women choose whether to observe *hijab*, wear modest clothing and a veil to cover their hair. *Hijab* is the word we use both for the veil itself and for modest Islamic clothing in general. No one in Syria is forced to wear *hijab* and lots of Muslim women choose not to, especially in the cities. It's completely acceptable as an observant Muslim to do either, as long as your clothing isn't too revealing. That's where swimming clashes with tradition. Wearing *hijab* gets complicated if you're training in a swimsuit. It's clear, as long as we swim, we won't wear *hijab*.

A lot of people don't understand about us swimming. They don't see the hard work and dedication it takes to swim. They just see the swimsuit. Neighbours and parents of kids at our school tell Mum they don't approve. Some say wearing a swimsuit past a certain age is inappropriate for a young girl. Mum ignores them. The summer I'm nine, Mum even decides to learn to swim herself. Because she wears *hijab* and covers her hair she can't learn at Tishreen, so she goes to another pool and does a summer course just for women. Dad encourages her and eventually trains her himself.

Dad seems unaware of the gossip. He lets nothing get in the way of us swimming. His training programme is paying off. Dad wants us to prove ourselves in both sprinting and long distance and we're getting fast in butterfly and freestyle. Sara has impressive muscles for a twelve-year-old girl. She's showing promise and is picked up by the coaches of the Syrian national team. Dad is overjoyed, but it means she's no longer his swimmer, only his daughter. I'm still both.

One day, not long after Sara starts with the national team, Dad takes my training group to visit them while they work out at the gym. We're too young for weight training, so Dad explains the exercises while we watch. We gather around a series of pull-down machines. Without warning, a girl from my training group grabs the bar of the machine nearest me and yanks it down. It's heavier than she thinks and she lets go. The bar flicks back and thwacks me just beneath the eye. I scream.

'What now, Yusra?' says Dad.

A thin trickle of blood runs down my cheek. My eyes well up with tears. Dad grabs my chin and lifts it to inspect the side of my face.

'It's nothing,' he says. 'Don't overdo it.'

Dad ushers our group back to the pool to get on with training. I stand next to the start block, snivelling from the shock. Training starts again. I've no choice. I get in. The wound burns in the chlorine.

I cling onto the edge of the pool. Eventually I'm saved by the father of one of the other kids in my group who tells Dad to take me to the doctor. Dad purses his lips. He's annoyed. He waves at me and I climb out of the water. After training he drives me to the emergency room. The doctors sew my upper cheek back together.

After that, I'm terrified of getting hurt. Not because of the pain but because training wouldn't have stopped. But there's nothing I can do to protect myself against some things. Like ear infections, for instance. It's agony, like someone is trying to inflate a balloon in my head. I get time off school, but not swimming. Dad doesn't trust doctors, especially if they take me out of the pool. One time the pain is worse than anything I've ever felt before. I howl as my mother pleads with the doctor. The physician shakes her head.

'It's a perforated eardrum,' she says. 'There's no way she can swim. Not for at least a week.'

I look at Mum. She raises her eyebrows and sighs.

'Will you tell Dad?' I say. 'I can't. I don't want to.'

I cry all the way to the pool. I'm petrified about what Dad will say when he hears. Dad is waiting.

'Well, what's the verdict?' he says.

Mum tells him. He's furious.

'What's she talking about? A whole week? I want a second opinion.'

We get back in the car and Mum takes me to a different doctor. This one tells her nothing is wrong, no perforated eardrum, no break from swimming. Dad is happy. I swim on in pain. Not long after that, Sara and I are waiting for the school bus one morning when I suddenly fall flat on my face. I'm out cold for thirty seconds. Dad sees me collapse from our balcony and rushes out of the house. He drives me to the doctors. They're baffled. Something to do with my ears. Or maybe my eyes. They send me to an optician who says I'm short-sighted. From that day on I wear glasses or contact lenses, but they don't prevent me suffering from intermittent fainting fits Around the same time, I develop red, itchy patches on my neck. The doctors say it's psoriasis. Dad is happy as long as it doesn't affect my swimming.

Dad may no longer be Sara's coach, but he keeps a keen eye on her. The Pan Arab Games are approaching, and he wants her to go to Cairo with the rest of the Syrian team. For the first time, the Games will include a modern pentathlon event. Dad hears the team hasn't yet found a female competitor for the mixed relay. The coaches ask Sara if she'd like to try out for the running, swimming, and shooting events.

Sara spends the summer in the Tishreen complex, running long distances and learning how to shoot a pistol at a target. I go along a couple of times to watch her. Once she lets me try with the gun. The weapon is heavy, cold, and unwieldy. I'm not sure I like it. Sara proves herself to the coaches, November comes around, and she travels to Cairo with the national team. She runs fast, shoots straight and storms down the pool. She and her relay team win a silver medal and help Syria come fifth on the medals table. When the team returns, Dad is beside himself with excitement.

'Maybe you'll get to meet the President!' he says to Sara.

The following week, the team coaches call a meeting. It's confirmed. President Bashar Al-Assad would like to meet all the medal winners. Sara is the youngest of them all. She gets the day off school and even manages to miss an exam, but is given full marks anyway. She comes back from the palace glowing.

'So, what happened?' says Mum.

'We waited in a long line to say hello to him,' says Sara, grinning. 'I couldn't believe he was real.'

'Did he say anything to you?' says Mum.

'He told me he's proud of me because I'm the youngest,' she says. 'And he said to keep going. He said keep winning and one day I'll meet him again. He was just a nice, normal man.'

Mum and Dad beam with pride. The meeting is a huge honour for our family. A group photo of Sara with the President is hung up at our school. Dad has a copy blown up and framed. He hangs it in pride of place on the living-room wall at home.

A few weeks later, Mum sits me and Sara down and tells us she's pregnant. I'm unsettled. I'll no longer be the youngest, the smallest, the cutest. I say nothing and smile. In March, the month I turn ten, Mum gives birth to a baby girl, a tiny angel with huge, sky-blue eyes. She calls her Shahed. Honey. We all melt. Once she arrives, I'm overjoyed to have a little sister.

If Dad is obsessed with our swimming times, Mum worries only about our academic grades. Sara and I are both good at English, so Mum hires us private tutors to encourage us. Dad introduces us to American pop music. We're big fans of Michael Jackson. We study his lyrics as if they were exam texts. We always have headphones on. On the way to school or to the pool, on the drive home from Grandma's house in Damascus to Daraya. Sometimes I ask Sara what an English word means and how to write it. Sara keeps a notebook where she writes her secrets in English so that Mum and Dad can't read them.

That summer, between training sessions, Sara and I sit down with Dad to watch the Beijing 2008 Olympics. Mum flits in and out, baby Shahed on her arm. This time, because of Phelps, swimming dominates the Games. I gawp, awestruck, as he snatches gold after gold, powering towards his record-breaking medal haul. The entire world goes wild for him. The Arabic press call him the New Olympic Legend. The Ultimate Olympian.

We're all waiting for the final of the men's 100m butterfly. The tension builds as Serbian swimmer Milorad Čavić says he's going to deny Phelps his seventh gold. The swimmers line up on the start blocks. Crocker is there too. The camera moves along the line. I study the neck, the arms. Wow, Phelps is a man mountain. In our living room, the air is electric. Dad insists on absolute silence.

Beep. They dart into the water. Čavić and Crocker are ahead as the swimmers surface. Crashing, pounding, propelling forwards. At the end of the first length Phelps is seventh. I hold my breath, wait for him to call on his full reserve of power. Thirty, twenty metres to go. Phelps takes Crocker, but Čavić is still in front. One, two, one, two. On, on.

Surely Phelps is leaving it too late? Come on. Flip the switch. Sprint. Fifteen metres to go and Phelps brings it all. He gains. He's exactly level with Čavić. They slam the touch pad together and I let out a squeal. No one can believe it. He's done it. Gold. By one hundredth of a second. Phelps shouts and crashes his huge arms down in the water.

Dad is on his feet.

'You see that?' he says. 'That's it, girls. That's an Olympian.'

Sara and I grin at each other.

'But how do we get there?' I say. 'How do we get to the Olympics?'

'Work,' says Dad and turns back to the screen. 'God willing, you'll get there one day. If your dream isn't the Olympics, you aren't a true athlete.'

For a while, Sara is the young star on the Syrian team. She's swimming strongly in both short butterfly races and long-distance freestyle. But the autumn after the Beijing Olympics, she begins to wobble. Her level yo-yos up and down and the team coaches begin to lose interest in her. It seems like she changes coach every week.

In Dad's training group, me and another girl, Carol, are the fastest. We're to be Dad's very own stars. All the national team swimmers, including Sara, are his competitors. He organizes a head-to-head between Sara and Carol. 100m butterfly.

Dad has us all gather to watch the race. Coaches, swimmers, and Sara's team mates. At the pool, Dad isn't Dad. He's coach. As Sara and Carol climb onto the start blocks, Sara isn't his daughter. She's his swimmer's competition. I stare, keep my mind numb. I've no idea who to root for.

Beep. They dive. Carol surfaces first. Sara whirls out after. At the fifty-metre turn, Sara's a full body-length behind. She powers on, but Carol sprints the last twenty-five metres and comes in a good five seconds ahead. Dad pumps the air in victory and grins over at the team coaches. His star won.

We drive home in awkward silence. Sara stares hard out of the window, headphones in. Once we set foot inside the house, Dad is Dad again. He rounds on Sara.

'What's wrong with you?' he shouts. 'You've let yourself slide. You lost all your speed.'

She glares at him. Her eyes flash fury.

'That's it, enough,' he says. 'No more going around to friends' houses after training. No more playing basketball. I'll have to fix you. I'll coach you from now on. You're coming back to me.'

Sara breaks down in tears. She jams her headphones on, gets up and leaves the room. I block it out. She'll cry, then she'll calm down.

After that, Sara joins me and Carol in training with Dad. One day, a few months later, Sara climbs out of the pool clutching her right shoulder.

'I can't carry on,' she says to Dad. 'I can't move my shoulder.'

Mum takes her to the doctor. Sara is given four weeks' rest and some muscle creams. Dad isn't happy. A month later Sara is back in the pool, but the break means her level is right down again. It's another two months before she battles back up to where she was.

Then, in spring, her other shoulder seizes up. The doctors look worried. They write her off for another month. Mum tries to help. Since learning to swim, she's been teaching water aerobics at a hot-springs spa an hour's drive south of Damascus, close to the city of Daraa. She's branched out into massage therapy and tries her new skills out on Sara's shoulders.

Before long, Sara's back at training. She fights harder than ever to regain her former speed. She doesn't confide in me, but I can see she's no longer enjoying swimming. She's distracted. She often disappears after training. In early summer, she starts wearing make-up. I suspect she's meeting guys. Dad's furious, but Sara doesn't care. Home life deteriorates into a series of set battles and showdowns.

'Look at your little sister,' shouts Dad. 'Why can't you be more like her?'

It never works. The more he shouts at her, the more she acts up. She shouts back at him, swears in his face. It works on me though. Seeing the fury Sara provokes, there's no way I'm going to step out of line. I give Dad no reason to get angry with me. I keep my head down, push hard in the pool, strive for those medals. I work hard in school to get the best grades. I'm so competitive that if another kid in class gets better grades than me, the psoriasis on my neck goes bright red and starts to itch. Sara thumps me and calls me a nerd.

That summer, Sara and I travel to Latakia, a city on the north-west coast of Syria, for a competition. Latakia is Syria's holiday destination. People go there to stroll up and down the long beach-front, sit out in the restaurants or ride the rollercoaster at the fairground. Sara and I are there for the sea. The competition is in open water, a five-kilometre swim from an island back to the shore-line.

Standing on the beach, the sea is calm and glinting in the sun-shine. We set off, all fifty of us. The competition is fierce, everyone battling to swim the most direct route back to the shore. Once we're out in open water, I feel a little uneasy. Swimming in the sea is different from swimming in a pool. The water is so mysterious and deep. There are no sides, no chance to rest. I'm worried about getting lost and I have to swim with my head up so I can see the buoys and boats set out to mark the route. I'm relieved when we arrive on the shore over an hour later.

Not long after the sea swim, both Sara's shoulders go at once. She can't even do one butterfly stroke. The doctors refer her to a physiotherapist for intense massages. She stops swimming for another month. By early the following year she's swimming again, but not at the same level as before. Sara doesn't talk to me much, even though we share a room. I worry about her, but at home, between the battles, we retreat into our own worlds. If we're miserable, we're miserable alone. Our lives are totally separate. We swim separately, learn separately, our friends are different.

Dad's attempts to change Sara's behaviour aren't working. She plays up in school, her grades suffer, the teachers mark her down as a troublemaker. She escapes and goes out after training, plays basketball, or hangs out at friends' houses. Many of her best friends are guys. The arguments at home get worse. The smallest trigger from Dad will set Sara off. We'll sit down to eat and he'll make some comment about her gaining weight. Or he'll start on about her grades. Or how she swam badly in training. Often, Sara just scrapes her chair back, stands up, and storms out.

'Oh, so now you're not going to eat?' Dad shouts after her.

'I don't feel like eating,' she calls over her shoulder.

I wince as the door to our room slams. I lower my eyes and shuffle food around my plate with my fork. Just obey and you'll be ok. I know Dad will be happy if I'm the best swimmer. And I'm getting good. My butterfly is fast and strong. That autumn, aged twelve, I make it onto the Syrian national team. The coaches say I'm ready for my first competitions abroad in Jordan and Egypt. It's a big step. I'm now a competitive swimmer, swimming for Syria, one rung further up the ladder towards my Olympic dream. As Sara falters and rebels, I'm Dad's prize swimmer.

PART TWO

The Spring

3

The men punch their fists into the air and chant into the camera. Flags burn and crowds scatter as smoke rises from buildings. It's March 2011. Libya is in flames. I look at Sara. She shrugs and changes the channel. Dad walks into the living room.

'Turn it back on,' he says.

Sara obeys. Dad sits down on the sofa. We watch the dramatic scenes unfold in strict silence. This is Dad's time. He has the TV every evening for exactly two hours. He watches the news, then gives us back the remote. In the past weeks, we've sat through revolutions in Tunisia and Egypt. Now Libya. I don't know why but Libya feels different, somehow closer to home.

'I think it's kind of cool,' says Sara quietly. 'Scary. But cool.'

Dad shoots her a look.

'Are you crazy?' he says. 'This will never happen here, understand? There's no way anything like this can happen in Syria.'

Syria is stable and sensible, he tells us. The people are calm and quiet. They won't make any problems. Everyone has a job, life is good, we're working, happy, getting on with our lives. Dad gestures at the protesters on the screen.

'Not like these people,' he says.

Libyan leader Muammar Gaddafi is now on screen. He's wearing a light-brown robe and a matching turban and is giving a speech on Libyan state TV, stirring his supporters to defeat the uprising in his country.

'I am calling on the millions from one end of the desert to the other,' says Gaddafi, waving his arms wildly. 'And we will march in our millions and purify Libya inch by inch, house by house, home by home, alley by alley, person by person, until the country is clean of dirt and impurities.'

Sara giggles. Dad shoots her another look.

'What?' says Sara. 'I'm not laughing at the situation. It's just, well, he's funny. Libyan dialect is funny.'

Dad shakes his head and turns back to the screen.

'It's time to work,' says Gaddafi. 'It's time to march! Time to triumph! No going back. To the front! Revolution! Revolution!'

Gaddafi bangs the lectern, raises his fist in the air, and walks off screen. Dad switches off the TV and walks out without another word. A few days later, Sara and I are standing on the street outside our house, waiting for the school bus. Sara says she had a dream that Gaddafi was killed. I tell her I don't want to know. The bus pulls up and we climb on board. All the other kids are staring at their phones and giggling.

'What's going on?' says Sara as we sit down.

A boy turns around from the seat in front.

'*Zenga, zenga,*' he grins.

'What?' I say.

The boy passes us his phone. A YouTube video is playing on the screen. Someone has remixed Gaddafi's televised speech and set it to a dance song. There's a scantily clad girl gyrating in the bottom corner. The dictator looks ridiculous. The whole bus giggles again as the song reaches the chorus. *Zenga, zenga,* Libyan dialect for *zinqa,* alley. At school, the song is everywhere. But the joke soon gets old. A week later, the school bus is silent. The other kids sit in pairs, talking in hushed whispers. My friend Lyne climbs on and sits down next to me. I smile at her. Her eyes widen. She leans in.

'Didn't you hear about Daraa?' she whispers.

'No,' I say.

I feel a sudden pang of anxiety. Mum works just half an hour's drive from Daraa. And the city itself isn't far from us in Damascus. Just a hundred kilometres or so.

'Some kids, some boys,' Lyne is saying. 'They wrote something on a wall. They got arrested.'

'What do you mean?' I say. 'What did they write?'

She looks around, bends her head towards my ear.

'*Ash-shab yurid isqat an-nizam,*' she whispers.

I gawp at her, stunned. *Ash-shab yurid isqat an-nizam.* The people want to topple the regime. But didn't Dad say an uprising could never happen here? I sit in silence, let Lyne's words sink in, grapple with what they mean. I lean in to whisper in her ear.

'That's what they said in Tunisia, right? And in Egypt?'

Lyne nods.

'And now in Libya,' she says.

I look out of the window at the traffic, the commuters on their way to work, the shops opening their shutters. So, people want things to change here too. Tunisia, Egypt, Libya, and now here? I'm filled with foreboding. Nothing good will come out of this. At school, the teachers say nothing about Daraa. Neither do Mum and Dad or the newsreaders on the state TV station. I get all my news from the school bus. A few days later, Lyne tells me there's been violence during protests in Daraa and that the protests have spread across Syria to other cities, Aleppo, Homs and Baniyas.

'They're even marching here in Damascus,' says Lyne.

My eyes widen. The tight-lipped silence continues at home. Dad still watches the news every night. He often switches to the foreign Arabic rolling-news channels, Al Jazeera and Al Arabiya. He watches without commenting. If he talks about the spreading protests at all, it's not with us. I understand. It's for our own good, to protect us. And anyway, what's he supposed to say to two teenage daughters? Ask them if they're happy with the situation? Mum is slightly more open. Her work at the hot springs outside Daraa provides another source of information. One day in late March, she comes home looking pale and shaken. I ask her what's wrong. She hesitates, not wanting to scare me.

'Today at the spa,' she says at last. 'I could hear explosions and shooting coming from the city. We tried closing the windows, but I could still hear it.'

I inspect my fingernails. My stomach squirms. I wish I hadn't asked.

'Over the past month there have been fewer customers,' says Mum. 'No one wants to come out to the spa anymore. It's getting too dangerous.'

I wish she would stop talking. I'm relieved when Dad walks

into the living room and Mum trails off mid-sentence. He sits down and switches on the TV. Shahed toddles in behind him and Mum scoops her up and takes her into the kitchen. We sit in grim silence. The newsreaders on state TV are still saying nothing about Daraa.

The next day, a classmate of mine, Eman, says she and her family are leaving Damascus. Her parents are from Daraa and they want to go back to see what's happening. It all happens very fast. We say goodbye and they leave the following week. I never hear from her again. I'm still not sure what became of her. It's the first of many similar disappearances. One day, not long after Eman leaves, Mum comes back earlier than usual from the spa. Sara and I are getting ready for training. Mum sits down, she's shaking.

'What is it?' says Dad.

'The noise today,' she says. 'They were firing all day long. It's been going on all week. Huge explosions, shaking the windows. Then, in the middle of the afternoon, the army came and evacuated us.'

Dad raises his eyebrows.

'You won't be going back then?' he says.

'No,' she says. 'I don't think so. I think the spa will close for a while.'

Mum eyes me and Sara, then looks furtively back at Dad.

'You know, my colleagues, they . . . they tell me the most horrible stories,' she says.

Sara gets up from the sofa, grabs my arm and drags me off into our room. I hear even less after Mum stops working near Daraa. She gets a new job as a masseuse at a newly opened sports stadium in Kafar Souseh, the district north of Daraya. I get my vague headlines from the school bus. Lyne tells me Daraa is under siege. She tells me when the protests swell in Homs, when they spread to central Damascus and Latakia. At the end of May, when the protests in Daraya get bigger, Lyne tells me they're about some kid called Hamza. Everyone I know stays away from both sides. We sit tight and wait it out.

It's no longer safe in Daraya. Every Friday after noon prayers the worshippers spill out of the mosques and onto the streets. Sometimes we hear a crackle of gunfire. We stop going out to eat on Friday nights. We sit in and watch state TV. The newsreaders blame the violence on terrorists. There's nothing to do but watch and wait, pray the unrest will stop soon.

And while I wait, I swim. Swimming is the best distraction. When I'm in the pool, nothing else seems to matter. I'm achieving my best times yet, breaking records and winning medals for the national team. The coaches say I can travel to other Arab countries, Jordan, Egypt, and Lebanon, to swim for Syria in international competitions. In July, Sara and I get up at three in the morning to watch the World Aquatics Championships in Shanghai. We watch Swedish swimmer Therese Alshammar win gold in the 50m free-style. To me it's like watching a favourite football team. I squeal and dance around the room. She's my new hero.

'Look at her,' says Sara. 'You could be like her.'

Mum comes into the living room, rubbing her eyes. She tells us to keep the noise down so we don't wake Shahed. I point at the screen. Alshammar is grinning and hugging the other swimmers in the lane.

'Mum, look!' I say. 'I could do that too.'

Mum yawns and smiles.

'I know, *habibti*,' she says.

'But how do we get to the World Championships if we're in Syria?' I say.

Mum sighs.

'Just keep it down, ok?' she says.

Watching Alshammar makes me impatient. Mum doesn't understand. I need to swim, I need to pursue a career. But with all that's going on in Syria, the violence, the protests, that's looking less and less likely. The future looks uncertain. My ladder to the Olympics is getting hazy.

That summer, swimmers from all over Syria arrive as usual in Damascus for training camp. I move in with them into the athletes' hotel near Tishreen pool. Many of the kids I know are from Aleppo, such as Rami. I talk to him about what's going on there.

Rami looks worried, but he tells me the situation there is like Damascus. There are some protests, but the violence isn't like in Daraa. A few days after I get home from training camp I find Dad watching Al Jazeera in the living room. He doesn't look up as I walk in. I sit down next to him and watch. On the screen, men are waving their arms and shooting automatic weapons into the air.

'What happened now?' I say.

'Tripoli fell,' he says. 'They've toppled Gaddafi.'

I stare at the screen as Dad watches on in stony silence.

Soon enough, the unrest spreads to our doorstep. Big protests erupt in Al Moadamyeh, the district to the west of where we live. The road we use to go to school, the pool and Grandma's, the way into the city, begins to feel tense. We stay in a lot, watch the TV. One morning in October on the school bus, Lyne tells us news of Gaddafi's gruesome death. I stare out of the window and wish everything would pause, rewind, and go back to normal.

I try to shut out what is happening, focus on swimming, school, everyday life. But normal life is starting to become impossible. In December, forty people are killed in suicide bombings in Kafar Souseh, the district where Mum works. The victims are ordinary people who just happen to be on the street, going about their lives. It's a shock. It's the first time we feel a general sense of danger, that we could be killed just being in the wrong place at the wrong time. Our parents, like many others, make us stay indoors after seven in the evening. We come home, close the blinds and switch on the TV.

Early in the new year there's another swimming training camp. Numbers are down. A lot of the older guys have disappeared. I can't find my friend Rami. I ask around. The other swimmers tell me he has gone to Turkey to stay with his brother. They say he plans to be back soon, but before long I see on Facebook he's started training with the Galatasaray swimming club in Istanbul. It looks like he'll be away longer than we thought.

The uprising is getting more serious by the day. In January, piles of sandbags appear all over Damascus. Armed soldiers stand behind them and keep watch, stopping every car that passes. They check IDs, ask people where they've come from and where they're going. Often, they search cars. It can take up to half an hour to get through. There are a lot of checkpoints along the main road from Daraya to Damascus. We start taking a back way through the olive orchards to the south and out west into the countryside. But whichever way we go, we often hit spontaneous, 'flying' checkpoints. One night in early spring, Mum picks us up from training. Sara and I sit in the back of the car either side of Shahed. Mum tries the main road, but we hit a stream of traffic heading the other way. Mum sighs.

'They've closed the road,' she says.

She turns around and takes a side street that will take us another way back into Daraya. The street is unusually dark and deserted. All the shops have closed early. There are no people and no other cars in sight. Mum drives slowly forwards. Ahead, on the right-hand side of the street, a pile of sandbags. A soldier walks slowly, calmly out from behind the checkpoint. He's carrying an assault rifle. Mum stops the car and winds down the window.

'ID,' says the soldier.

Mum fumbles and produces her white plastic ID card from her wallet. The soldier takes it and peers back at us in the back seat.

'Your daughters?' he says.

Mum nods, keeps her eyes on the road ahead.

'Where are you going?' the soldier says.

'Home,' says Mum. 'We live on the road between Daraya and Al Moadamyeh.'

'And where have you been?' he says.

'I've just come from work. My daughters have been swimming.'

The soldier peers into the back seat again. He walks around to the back of the car and opens the trunk. He opens the door next to me and flashes a searchlight down at our feet. Then he walks back to the driver window and tells Mum to get out of the car. My stomach drops. I'm terrified. Mum climbs out. Sara and I crane our necks through the window to see what's going on. The soldier searches her and lets us go. Mum climbs back into the car, breathing hard. We drive in silence the rest of the way home.

The next morning, we're on the school bus. We pass another pile of sandbags on the main road to Mazzeh. The soldiers flag the bus driver down and we pull up on the side of the highway. A gasp goes up from the kids at the front of the bus as four soldiers appear at the top of the aisle. The man in front is brandishing an assault rifle in the air. They march through the bus, searching our school bags, the luggage racks, checking under every seat. When they reach me and Sara, we stare ahead, careful not to make eye contact. They move on. I hear one of the younger girls behind me whimper. At last, they file off the bus and the engine starts again.

'What do they think we're going to hide in a bus of fifty kids?' mutters Sara as we pull away.

After that, Mum has us leave spare clothes at Grandma's in case something happens and we can't get home. Sometimes, on our way back from training, we hear gunfire coming from Daraya and turn back towards the city. Other times, soldiers turn us back at the checkpoints. Fridays are worse than ever. Every time someone is killed in Daraya, there's a funeral which turns into an even bigger protest. We stay inside or go to Grandma's for the weekend. Some nights I'm woken up by gunfire outside in the street. Dad worries about blasts and stray bullets, so he moves a large wooden closet up against the window in our room. By early summer, Daraya is emptying out. There are fewer people on the streets and on the school bus. It's eerie.

I'm confused about what's happening. The TV tells us nothing. Mum and Dad get their information from friends, relatives, and neighbours. But they don't talk to us. My Facebook newsfeed is full of jokes, gossip, heartaches, normal teenage stuff. One Saturday night towards the end of May, Sara, Shahed and I are sleeping in our room.

'*Allahu Akbar*,' shouts a male voice in the street below.

A burst of gunfire. Too close. My eyes flick open.

'*Allahu Akbar*,' a whole chorus of voices. '*Allahu Akbar*.'

I look over to Sara's bed. She's lying facing the wall, her back to me.

'Sara?' I say.

She doesn't move.

'Stay where you are,' she says, still facing the wall.

There's silence outside. I wait, frozen in terror. In the distance, screeching whistling noises are followed by deep, booming crashes. Light spills into the room as Dad flings open the bedroom door.

'Come on,' he shouts. 'Get up. Get away from the window.'

I pull off the sheet and jump out of bed. Sara does the same and we run together out into the corridor.

'There's no glass in our room,' says Dad. 'Go in there.'

Sara, Dad, and I climb into the massive bed with Mum and Shahed. I bring the sheet up to my face and try to blot out the terrifying noises outside. None of us gets much sleep.

The next day, life goes on as if nothing happened. As always, I focus on swimming. I'm training hard and have reached the level where I can compete internationally. The next opportunity to do so is coming up in July. I'm on the start list for the Children of Asia Games in Yakutsk in eastern Russia. I'm very excited. I feel ready to take on the world. The whole national team is going. Sara is still struggling with her injury and hasn't made the team.

One Friday in early July, a few days before I'm due to leave for Russia, we're on our way home from visiting Grandma in the city. Dad takes the back road to avoid the checkpoints, but we find soldiers waiting even on the country roads.

'They've tightened security,' Dad mutters from the driver's seat as we wait to pass through.

We wind through the olive orchards to the south. The streets are deserted. As we approach the turning to our road, a man appears out of a building, waving his arms and shouting. Dad ignores him, and swings left onto the long straight road we live on. Mum gasps from the passenger seat. Dad stops the car and turns off the engine. I crane my neck to see. Three brown tanks are squatting in a line on the road ahead. Dad waits. Nothing happens for a full minute. Then the tank on the left rolls slowly off into a side street in a cloud of black exhaust. The tank on the right does the same on the other side.

'They're going to let us pass,' says Dad.

We wait for the middle tank to move. Instead, the turret rotates to face us.

'My God,' says Mum and grabs Dad's arm.

At the same moment, a soldier appears from a side street. He fires his assault rifle into the air. The sound ricochets off the buildings. He shouts at us, waves his free arm.

'Get back, get out of here!' he yells.

Dad hesitates. The soldier takes aim at the car. Dad slams into reverse. The car lurches backwards as bullets spray the pavement in front. Mum screams. Dad jerks the steering wheel to the right; the tyres screech and we skid round to face the other direction. Dad spins the wheel and throws the stick back into gear. We jolt forwards and speed back around the corner into the side street. Dad breaks sharply and parks up. Mum's breathing hard.

'Dad?' I say.

Shahed starts to cry.

'What's going on?' says Sara.

There's a knock at the car window. I squeal. A man is staring into the car. Dad winds down the window.

'*Alhamdulillah*,' says the man. 'You're safe.'

The man peers into the back seat. We stare back at him, trembling.

'*Ya Allah*,' he says. 'And you're here with your beautiful family too. Did you see the tanks?'

'Of course,' says Dad. 'What's going on? We need to get home.'

Gunfire echoes through the blocks a few streets away.

'You've got to get inside,' says the man. 'Come to my home.'

Dad opens the driver door and turns back to face us.

'Come on,' he says. 'Let's go, let's go.'

I scramble out of the car, terrified. This stranger could be anyone. As we cross the road we hear an explosion. The tank is firing on our street. We don't have a choice. We pile in through the stranger's door and upstairs into a large apartment. The man gestures at a large sofa and tells us to sit down. Shahed climbs onto the sofa next to me. I put my arm around her and she snuggles into my shoulder. The stranger is pacing up and down, avoiding the windows.

'What were you doing out there on the street?' he says.

'Going home,' says Dad. 'We live at the end of the road. We were in the city visiting relatives.'

'You should have stayed there,' says the stranger. 'Didn't anyone tell you what was happening?'

'No,' says Dad. 'We haven't seen any news. What is happening?'

'Fighting,' says the man. 'The rebels attacked a checkpoint in Kafar Souseh near the foreign ministry. The army fought back and stopped a protest at the mosque there. Now they're attacking us down here.'

'What do you mean?' says Dad.

The tank fires again in the street. Faint thumping sounds echo in the distance.

'They're firing on us,' he says. 'On the rebels, I mean. From the mountain.'

Dad watches him warily.

'How do you know all this?'

The man smiles.

'I'm the mayor of Daraya,' he says.

More gunfire crackles outside a few blocks away. The mayor steps up to the corner of the window and twitches back the blind. The rebel army want to use Daraya as a base from which to invade Damascus, he tells us. The government is trying to flush all of the armed men out of the district. The fighting could go on all night. We sit tight and wait. After an hour or so, the streets grow quieter, the gunfire further away. Mum looks at Dad.

'We should leave now, go back to my mother's,' she says.

Dad frowns. Shahed's sleeping peacefully against my shoulder. I'm glad she's too young to understand what's happening. Sara is staring at the floor. She looks up.

'Let's go back to Grandma's,' she says. 'Please?'

Dad looks at me and then at Shahed.

'No,' he says. 'It's quiet now. Those tanks are gone. We'll go home.'

The mayor tweaks his blinds again. The streets are silent. Mum wakes Shahed gently and picks her up. The little girl puts her arms around Mum's neck and rests her head against her shoulder. Sara and I get to our feet. Dad turns to the mayor, puts his hand on his chest, and thanks him.

'*Allah yusallmak*,' says the mayor. 'God be with you.'

We creep out of the door and cross the road to the car. Nothing is moving on the street. The thumps and crashes of artillery fire are further off, in the distance, north towards Kafar Souseh. We climb into the car and close the doors as quietly as we can. Dad starts the engine and edges slowly back towards our road. He takes a left. I crane my neck from the back seat to see through the windscreen. No tanks, no cars, no soldiers. But the road is unrecognizable. The street is a tangle of twisted cables, broken wooden poles and fragments of trees. Electricity pylons lie like scattered twigs across the road, wires hanging uselessly, sparking. All the shopfronts and windows have shattered, leaving a bed of broken glass along the sidewalk. Dad swerves the car slowly between the debris until he can go no further and stops. A soldier appears, pointing his assault rifle into the air.

'Are you crazy?' shouts the soldier, his voice echoing down the devastated street.

He jogs over to the car. Mum grips Dad's arm.

'What are you doing here?' the soldier says to Dad. He glances at the back seat. 'You're with your family? You have to get out of here!'

'Go back!' says Mum. 'I want to go to my mother's. Now, Ezzat. Go!'

Dad doesn't move.

'I'm not leaving my house,' he says.

'Then get us out of here at least,' says Mum, her voice choked with panicked tears.

Mum cries out as Dad slams the gearstick back into reverse and stomps his foot down on the accelerator. He jerks the wheel and the car whirls around. We screech back down the side road past the mayor's house and out into the orchards. Mum is crying hard now.

Sara is pale and gripping tightly onto the handrail above her head. Between us, Shahed stares quietly ahead. I grab her around the shoulders to steady her as we twist through the deserted streets. Dad stops the car in Kafar Souseh. All is quiet. Faint rumbles in the distance suggest the fighting has moved on elsewhere. Dad leaves us and sets off alone on foot back towards Daraya.

Mum's shoulders are shaking as she gets into the driver's seat and fumbles with the car keys. We sit in the back seat, too shell-shocked to speak. Mum drives slowly, carefully back into the dark city to Grandma's house. The old woman meets us at the door, folds each of us in turn into her arms. We lie down exhausted on the sofas in the living room. I fall asleep to the sound of my mother weeping.

4

Violence is still raging near our house in Daraya when I leave for the Children of Asia games in Russia a few days later. I can't go home before I travel, so I only take a small bag of clothes with me. I'm not too worried. I'm sure everything will be back to normal by the time I get back.

I fly with the Syrian national team to Yakutsk. I'm glad to have the distraction of the pool, glad to have my team mates, who have become like a second family. I push away the nightmare vision of the three tanks squatting on our road and focus on the task at hand.

We're up against young athletes from Russia, Central Asia, the Far East, and some other Middle Eastern countries. I swim well and help our age group's relay team win two bronze medals in the 4 x 100m and 4 x 200m freestyle relays, beating one Kazakh and one Russian team. Two bronze medals. Just wait till Dad hears. He'll be so pleased. I call him from the athletes' hotel. I can't get through on his phone, so I try Mum. I tell her about the medals.

'Well done, *habibti*,' she says.

Her voice sounds flat and distracted.

'How are things there?' I ask. 'Are you back in Daraya yet?'

'No,' she says. 'We had a change of plan.'

Things got crowded at Grandma's, so Mum asked my aunt if they could stay in her empty house. My aunt's place is in Yarmouk Camp, a district of Damascus home to generations of displaced Palestinian refugees. Mum and Dad had hoped things would be quieter there, but after a few days protests erupted and descended into violence. One night, the fighting was so bad they couldn't get into my aunt's house. They had to go back to Grandma's.

'What?' I say when Mum has finished explaining. I'm alarmed and disturbed. Here I was in Russia, celebrating my medals, thinking everything was back to normal at home. 'Why didn't anyone tell me?'

'It's fine, Yusra, we didn't want to worry you,' says Mum. 'We'll go home when things calm down.'

Nothing is calm when I get back from Russia. Heavy artillery and tanks are on the streets in Daraya and all the southern districts of Damascus are out of bounds. Mum, Sara, Shahed and I spend the rest of the month camping out in my Grandma's living room. It's Ramadan, the Muslim holy month, in which we fast during daylight hours. Dad goes back and forth to our house in Daraya to keep an eye on it and protect it from looters. Most evenings, after dark, he comes to break the fast with us, then he runs the gauntlet of checkpoints back out of the city. Once he reaches the house he calls us to let us know he's safe.

At home, Dad hides the photo of Sara with President Assad. He's worried that if the rebel army finds it they will destroy our house, or worse. On the way back into Damascus every morning Dad shows our medals at the checkpoints, tells the soldiers his daughters swim for Syria. One night in early August, Dad doesn't call us to say he has arrived safely. We sit pale and worried in Grandma's living room. Sara tries calling him over and over, but he doesn't answer. She calls our uncle Hussam and tells him Dad is missing. He agrees to go to our house and check on him. It's late at night when Hussam calls Sara back. She hangs up and looks at us wide-eyed.

'Dad's alive,' she says. 'But he's been beaten up. Hussam has taken him back to his house. It's too dangerous at home.'

I gape at her.

'Won't we ever go back to the house then?' I say.

Mum and Sara stare at the floor. It's a question neither of them can answer.

The following day, my uncle Hussam picks us up from Grandma's and takes us to see Dad. He's in a bad way, lying on the sofa, clutching his back. He doesn't know who attacked him. A group of men grabbed him on his way back into the house and took him to a building somewhere in Daraya. They hung him upside down

by his feet and beat him. It was hours before they realized they had
the wrong guy and let him down. Then they dumped him on the
street and left him to crawl home. Hussam found him lying on
the floor just inside our house. I'm horrified.

'We'll have to find somewhere else to live,' says Dad, wincing
and shifting on the sofa. 'We can't stay in Daraya, it's not safe. We'll
go to Damascus.'

The room spins.

'But what about all our stuff?' I say.

Dad shakes his head.

'We got the most important papers out,' he says. 'We can't go
back there now.'

I never see our house again. It's the last time we enter an
opposition-held area. Later we hear rumours our building was
completely destroyed in the fighting, but we never know for sure.
We lose everything. All our old childhood photos and toys, the
clothes Mum made for us when we were tiny, the trinkets from
family holidays. A lifetime of memories buried in the rubble. The
only things I have left are the clothes I took to the competition in
Russia.

We move to Salhiyeh, a district near the old town in central
Damascus. Mum and Dad check us into a long-term hotel, a traditional Damascene house split up into several apartments. All the
other families in the house have fled fighting in Daraya or the other
Damascus suburbs. We have two huge rooms on the ground floor
with high ceilings and old doors and windows. In the hallway, a
long staircase with metal railings leads up to the apartments above.
The best thing about the new house is the location. We're right in
the old town and near to Grandma's place. The streets are comfortingly quiet and normal.

Despite the circumstances, I'm glad to be here in Damascus.
I'm proud of my city, one of the oldest capitals in the world. For
centuries, it's been famous across the Arab world as a centre of
culture and trade. The city has been the jewel of many empires,
from the Persians, the ancient Greeks and the Romans, to the
Islamic Umayyad dynasty, the Mongols, the Ottomans and the

French. But for me, as for so many others, Damascus will always be the city of jasmine. The green vines dotted with white, star-shaped flowers climb up every wall in the old town. They entwine above the narrow alleyways to form a heavenly scented canopy.

The calm beauty of the old town is a world away from the situation in Daraya. News reaches us that the fighting has grown much fiercer there since we left. We hear that hundreds of people have been killed, including many of our former neighbours. Many of them we simply never hear from again. We hear terrible stories, but there's nothing we can do. I'm relieved that we got out in time. It could have been us. But things happen so fast there's no time to reflect on it.

Like Daraya, Mazzeh is no longer safe so I have to move schools too. In September I start in the ninth grade at Dar Al-Salam school, close to our new apartment. No one at school talks about the war. The only difference is that people now seem to care about which religion you belong to. It never mattered until now that I was Sunni. Or that any other kid was Alawi or Christian. But since the violence began it seems to matter deeply. The kids get it from the older generations, their parents, and grandparents. Everyone is looking for someone to blame for what's happening.

One day in late September I get a call from Mira, a swimmer friend of mine in Jordan. She swims with an elite team there called the Orthodox Club. The club once visited Damascus for a friendly competition in which Sara and I won most of the medals. The coaches were impressed by us, Dad's swimming stars. Now Mira says the club is looking for a new coach and wants Dad to apply. I pass the message on. A few weeks later, Dad tells me he's got the job, he'll be moving to Jordan the following year. I'm happy for him. It's an amazing opportunity.

'It'll be great experience,' says Dad. 'And well, we could use the money. It looks like we'll be renting places in Damascus until this is all over.'

There's no talk of us going with him to Jordan. I wouldn't want to go anyway. I have my life. I love my city, my country. Things don't seem that bad in Syria. At least to me. At least not yet. But as

I digest the news I begin to feel uneasy. I'm excited for Dad but worried that he's leaving. He's my swimming mentor, my coach, the one who knows what's best for me.

One night, not long after Dad's announcement, I arrive late at the pool for training. Sara and the other swimmers are standing around outside. Many of them are in tears.

'What's wrong?' I say.

Sara turns to me. Her face is blank and pale.

'It's Ehab,' says Sara. 'He's dead.'

'Ehab?' I say. 'Don't be stupid, he was here in the summer.'

I think back to the last time I saw Ehab a few months earlier. It was just before I went to Russia. He was still teasing me about being small, still calling me 'little mouse'. Sara tells me Ehab's brother Mohammad was also killed. There are rumours, but nobody knows exactly what happened. I stumble away from the group, tears streaming down my cheeks. I'm shocked. I had been waiting for the situation to calm down. And now friends are dying. No one is in the mood for training. Some of the older guys drift away to go to the brothers' funeral. Sara and I go home. Back in our apartment, I struggle to understand why anyone would decide to fight. To kill and be killed.

Dad finds me crying on the sofa.

'I heard about Ehab,' he says, putting his hand on my shoulder. 'He's in a better place now.'

I look up, my face stained with tears. I catch my breath.

'He didn't deserve to die,' I say between sobs.

'No,' says Dad. 'He didn't. But you can't control everything that's happening in the world. People will die, and you have to be ready for that.'

Dad was right. People were going to die. A lot of people. Every night on the TV news a banner scrolls along the bottom of the screen announcing the daily death toll across the country. Usually the figure is around 150, but on bad days it can reach up to a thousand. A thousand lives snuffed out on a single day. Around me for a time, all anyone wants to talk about is politics. I watch families tear themselves apart because one brother is for and another brother against the regime. Hordes of young people disappear into one or other of the armies and never come back. I'm young, but I'm old enough to realize our country is descending into horror.

I'm devastated. I never asked for this, never wanted my country to fall apart. I'd do anything to turn back the clock. I keep hoping, praying, that the situation will calm down again, but the killing only gets worse. We hear stories about people from school dying in random airstrikes. Kids my age, killed by stray shrapnel in their beds as they slept. In the beginning, the fear eats me up inside, not knowing if I'll be next. And then, without me really noticing, the deaths become normal.

After Ehab's death, Sara starts skipping training. Then one day in mid-autumn, she stops coming to the pool altogether. There are no speeches, no goodbyes, she just stops. Dad is busy planning for his job in Jordan and says nothing.

'But why aren't you coming?' I say to her one night before training.

She looks up from her seat on the sofa.

'I just don't want to any more,' she says.

'But what do you mean?' I say.

Sara sighs and rolls her eyes.

'Look, it's my shoulders, ok?' she says. 'The injury makes me swim slower. All the younger kids are catching me up. I'm done.'

I gawp at her, try to imagine life without swimming. There'd be so much time. Not just day by day, but year by year. The rest of my life. I see the years stretching on into the future without competitions or training camps. Instead, marriage, home, kids. I shudder. Sara reads my thoughts.

'Don't worry about me,' she says and grins. 'I won't get bored.'

Sara uses her new freedom to explore the old city on our doorstep. I hardly see her. She spends her evenings trawling through the Souq al-Hamidiyah, an old market covered with a high, vaulted dome roof. The market is a haven of distractions and is always busy with shoppers browsing for clothes, jewellery, antiques, and trinkets. When she's not in the Souq, Sara hangs out in a cafe near my school, talking, singing, and dancing with her friends. Her closest

friends are a group of seven guys. Sara wears her hair up in a bun
and her wardrobe consists only of wide jeans and baggy jumpers. I
sometimes think you wouldn't be able to tell she's a girl sitting with
her male friends. Dad isn't at all happy. Sara and I share a room but
not much else. I swim, she socializes. We both do our best to ignore
the war. When we do talk, we speak in English so that Mum and
Dad can't understand.

'I'm jealous,' I say one night when we're getting ready for bed.

'What do you mean?' says Sara.

'I mean you don't care about what anyone thinks,' I say. 'You're
crazy, you never think about the consequences. I can't do that. I'm
always thinking what might happen.'

'Yeah, you're a safety pin,' she says and thumps my leg.

'I just mean maybe you should listen to Dad more,' I say. 'Then
he wouldn't freak out so much.'

'Nah, it's all stupid,' she says. 'They just say, you're a girl so you
should do some things and not others. They don't know anything.'

I shrug and climb into bed.

The lease on the apartment ends in late November. Dad tries to
renew it but the landlord refuses. Others are waiting and willing to
pay much more than us. Lots of people are moving into Damascus,
fleeing the fighting in the suburbs. There's good money to be made
from the housing crisis. Dad goes back to the estate agents. He
searches the city for an affordable apartment in a quiet, safe area.
The options are limited. Damascus is full. The estate agents are
sharks, they demand a ridiculous commission. But the landlords
are even worse. They know they can let any space in any condition
for high rates and that people will pay it.

At last, Dad settles on a dank, empty basement in Baramkeh, a
district in the south of the city centre. He signs a six-month con-
tract and sets about turning it from a neglected storage room into
an apartment. He redoes the plumbing and electricity, paints the
damp walls, and fills the rooms with brand-new furniture. He does
his best, but the first time I step inside the basement my heart
sinks. The only natural light comes from a set of doors that lead out
onto an inner courtyard. And it is winter, so they stay firmly shut.

I find Sara at the back of the apartment, scowling at a dark, creepy toilet full of spiders. I raise my eyebrows and follow her through the kitchen into a tiny alcove fitted with two single beds: our new bedroom. There's no door separating it from the kitchen, meaning our clothes smell constantly of cooking. When I arrive at the pool the next day, my coach sniffs the air and asks why I smell of fried aubergine. I blush deep red and walk off into the changing rooms.

One evening, a few days after we move in, there's an urgent knock on the door. Dad opens it and ushers in a group of uniformed guards. He tells me and Sara to take Shahed into our room. We get up off the sofa and traipse through into the kitchen. Mum comes in a little while later looking shaken. The guards are from the state security station next door, she says. They want to see our IDs. They want to know who we are, where we've moved from, and what we do. After that, the guards come by every other day, sometimes late at night. They sit for hours in the other room, talking with Dad.

The only good thing about living in the basement is that I can now walk to the pool. I'm gearing up for the next international competition. I'm on the start list for the Short Course World Championships in Istanbul. It's my biggest competition yet and I'm beside myself with excitement. It's a huge honour to swim for Syria in the World Championships. It's the next rung on the ladder towards the Olympics. I spend the next few weeks training hard. I'm focused, fast, and feeling confident. I fly to Turkey in early December with the national team. I do well in my races and set a new Syrian record for 400m freestyle.

My triumph is dampened when Dad moves to Jordan a few weeks later. I'm upset as we wave him off at the airport, but at the same time I can't help feeling a bit relieved. I'm sick of the constant arguments and tension with Sara. I know I wouldn't want to go to Jordan with him. Besides, all of us still believe the situation will calm down any day now. The violence will stop, and we can all get on with our lives.

I live for swimming. I have my sights set on the Asian Youth Games in China in the summer. I assume after my success in

Istanbul that the coaches will send me to start for Syria. For the next few weeks, I'm as focused as I've ever been. I'm preparing, training hard for the competition. I'm convinced this is my moment. One day in January, my team mate Nermeen comes to me after training. She's grinning wide.

'Guess what?' she says, 'They're sending me to China. To the Asian Games.'

I freeze.

'What?' I say.

I scowl as she scans my face.

'Oh, did you think…?'

I grab my bag, turn my back on her, and march off to find our coach.

'You're sending Nermeen to the Asian Games?' I say, fighting tears.

The coach frowns.

'Yes, Nermeen will go,' he says.

I stare at him. The rage builds in my throat.

'But I'm better than her,' I say. 'Do a test. I'll race her right now.'

The coach shakes his head.

'It's not your turn, Yusra,' he says. 'You went to Turkey.'

'What?' I shout. 'Since when was it about taking turns? The better swimmer has to go. Do a test.'

The coach folds his arms.

'She's going,' he says. 'End of discussion. You've had your go.'

I turn and storm out of the pool. Ten minutes later, I stomp down into the basement, my face wet with angry tears. Mum wants to know what's wrong, but I tell her to leave me alone. I can't talk now. I'm too upset. I throw myself onto my bed and sob. Nermeen can't go to China. She can't. I love her and she's a good swimmer, but I'm better. And Dad taught me that in swimming, you're on your own. It's not about anyone else's fight, it's about yours. It's tough and I don't want to hurt anybody, but this is sport. It's not about being nice, it's about winning. I have a goal and I have to reach it.

That's impossible if no one takes me seriously. I'm just a little girl to them. Without Dad, there's no one to fight my corner. He would have taken on the whole swimming federation to make sure I got a test. And now he's gone, it's pointless without him. I fall asleep exhausted and confused. I go to the pool the next day and train as normal. But something's missing. I feel empty. Every criticism from my coach makes me want to walk out, quit right there on the spot. I go through the motions, swim on like a zombie.

One night in late February, Sara meets me after training at the pool. Mum is due to pick us up in the car and take us to Grandma's. We're walking together along the road that runs alongside the stadium when a whistling screech rips through the air above us. Sara shoves my shoulder and sends me flying onto the concrete. I bring my arms over my head and brace as a mortar shell hits the road ahead. The ground shakes and torrents of glass rain down onto the pavement. I look up, breathing hard. The blast has blown out all the windows of the athletes' hotel. Sara grabs my arm and I stagger to my feet. We're both shaking. I can hardly breathe.

'Look!' shouts Sara and points to the end of the road.

Ahead, Mum's car is slamming into reverse and screeching into a three-point turn. More whistling above our heads, fainter this time.

'Run!' shouts Sara.

We sprint past the hotel, crunching over the broken glass. We reach the car, throw open the doors, and jump in.

'Wait . . . Mum,' I say between breaths. 'My friends are still at the pool.'

'I'm not waiting for anyone,' says Mum.

She stomps on the accelerator. Another screech tears through the sky above. I whip my head round as we speed off. Through the back window I watch the shell rip my world apart.

PART THREE

The Bomb

5

'I'm done with swimming,' I say.

My heart thumps in the stillness of the basement kitchen. Even if I leave now I'll be late for training. For the first time in my life I don't care. Mum looks up from the pan she's stirring.

'What?' she says. 'How can you say that? What do you mean you're done with swimming?'

'You saw them bomb the hotel,' I say. 'I could have died.'

Mum steps towards me, her forehead wrinkled with concern. She puts her hand on my shoulder.

'You're going to throw everything away?' she says. 'After all that work? All you've done?'

I shake my head. Those bombs at the hotel were too close. The blast had killed a man inside the building. Youssef Suleiman, a twenty-six-year-old striker with the Homs soccer team Al-Wathba. He'd been in his room on the first floor when the mortars hit the road outside. The windows blew out. Youssef was hit in the neck by a shard of glass and died later in hospital. He left behind a wife and a six-month-old baby. Photos in the press later showed the team sitting dazed and devastated in the hotel lobby. I had stayed in those rooms so many times. It could have been me, Sara, or any one of my swimming friends killed that day.

'I mean it,' I say to Mum. 'I'm never going back to that pool again.'

Mum's face hardens. She turns back to the spitting pan.

'You'll speak to your father first,' she says.

I step into the alcove, take a deep breath, and call Dad. I tell him I'm giving up swimming, that my coach won't let me compete in the Asian Games, that he's sending Nermeen instead. It's not fair. The coach doesn't care who's the better swimmer, he won't even do a test. And anyway, I say, there's no point in swimming. There's just no future for female swimmers in Syria.

'Slow down,' says Dad. 'Think it over. It will be very hard to go back to swimming later if you stop now.'

But I'm certain. There's no way I'm going back to the pool. I try a different tack. I tell Dad about the bomb at Tishreen hotel. It could have been me instead of that footballer. Should I risk my life to swim? There's a silence on the other end of the phone.

'Maybe I'll bring you here to Jordan,' says Dad.

'No,' I say. 'I don't want to leave. I have school, friends. This is my home. I love it.'

Dad sighs.

'Well, if that's the way you feel I can't force you to swim,' he says. 'It's your decision.'

I hang up and slump down on my bed. I put my headphones in and blot out the world for the whole two hours I should be in training. I don't go to the pool the next day or the day after that. I don't tell any of the coaches I'm quitting, or the other swimmers. I just disappear, like it's no big deal. The days stretch out, unfamiliar and long. I sit around the house after school. Lost.

Mum is worried about me. She tries to get me to reconsider. There are other things I can do with swimming, she says, like become a coach. I don't want that. I want to compete professionally. I want to aim for the Olympics. For gold. But without Dad to fight my corner that's impossible. Sara is on my side. She sees that unless I have someone to push me there will only be years of work with nothing at the end.

Eventually Mum gives up. She doesn't have the time or the energy. As well as being both Mum and Dad to three daughters, she's still working full-time as a masseuse and physical therapist at the club in Kafar Souseh. The area is tense, there's often fighting on the street. But Mum doesn't have a choice. We need the money. Dad sends us some of his salary from Jordan but it's not enough to keep up with inflation. The war is weakening the Syrian pound, making everything feel more expensive. Mum's wages can buy less week by week.

Sara gets a job to help out and bring in some extra money. She goes back to Tishreen pool and coaches the youngest kids. A few nights a week I drag myself along to the pool with Sara to swim, just for fun and to stay fit. I avoid running into any of the coaches. I still see some of the swimmers outside the pool. No one asks about my unexplained absence from training. They know what has happened. They have seen enough girls disappear from the pool without warning.

One day at the end of March, Sara, Shahed and I are sitting in the basement after school. Sara is about to go to Tishreen to work. She turns to me as she packs her stuff and asks if I'm coming to the pool. Before I can answer her, a whistling screech rips through the air above the house. We wince and brace for impact. A boom rocks the street outside. The walls shake. A few seconds later another shell hits. I look at Sara in terror. She holds up her hand. Gunfire crackles in the distance.

'Ok,' says Sara. 'We wait.'

Shahed curls up next to me on the sofa. I can feel her trembling, tensing up after every screech. Just five years old and she knows the sound of mortar fire, she can distinguish it from an airstrike or a tank battle. We listen to the crashing explosions. Some nearer, some further away. A whistle rips through the air above our heads. We brace. The shell hits the road outside our front door. The walls shake again and a small stream of plaster crumbles down from the ceiling. It's so close, I wonder if they're aiming for the hospital across the road from our apartment. Another shell hits. Too close. That hit the building next to us. Glass shatters and chunks of masonry clatter as they fall against the bolted basement doors.

'That's it,' says Sara. 'I'm calling Mum.'

Sara pulls out her phone.

'Mum, you have to come home. The walls are falling down outside. Stones are hitting the doors. We might get buried. We'll be stuck.'

She waits.

'No, we can't go out,' she says. 'They're firing at the street. What shall we do?'

Shahed begins to snivel. I put my arm around her.

'Ok, ok,' says Sara into the phone. 'Be careful. We'll see you soon. I love you too.'

She hangs up and looks at me.

'Mum's coming,' she says.

I breathe out a sigh of relief. Mum will know what to do. The attack continues. We wait in silence, huddled together on the sofa, flinching at every explosion. We've no choice. Leaving seems as dangerous as staying put. I think about Mum, travelling across the city under fire. What if something happens to her on the way? I push the thought away and squeeze Shahed tight. I look at Sara, she's staring at the floor, her head in her hands.

After half an hour, the mortars stop and are replaced with bursts of echoing gunfire. They sound close, on the street outside. I dig my fingernails into my palms, clench my toes, and pray silently that Mum is safe. *Ya Allah*, let her get through to us. At last the door opens and Mum stumbles down into the basement. Shahed jumps up, runs to her, and flings her arms around her waist. Mum looks from me to Sara. Her eyes are glazed and far away. Mum opens her mouth, but no words come out. She closes it again.

'Mum?' I say.

She picks her way slowly, carefully, to the sofa and sits. Shahed climbs onto her lap. Her mouth opens and closes again. She looks at us with sad, wide eyes and shakes her head. She's not hurt, but she can't speak. My heart aches with worry for her. We sit in silence, waiting for her to recover, listening to the booming echoes of far-off mortar fire. It's over an hour before she regains her voice.

'I had to run,' she stammers at last. 'Across the Baramkeh bridge. They were firing and...'

'Where did you leave the car?' says Sara.

'At Kafar Souseh,' says Mum. 'At the crossing.'

Mum swallows and takes a deep breath. Her eyes well up with tears.

'The army wouldn't let me drive any further,' she says. 'They told me I couldn't cross. But I said I have to get to my daughters, they're alone. The soldiers tried to stop me, but I got out of the car and walked. I had to show them papers to prove I lived here. The road was empty. There were soldiers watching me from behind the sandbags. I was so scared.'

Mum takes another deep breath. A tear rolls down her cheek. She swallows and wipes her eyes with the back of her hand. She says she couldn't tell who was firing at who, or from where. Someone had ordered her to stop and asked her where she was going. All she could do was point at the house.

'I was so scared I didn't know what I was saying,' says Mum and squeezes Shahed again. 'Then a good man, a soldier, told the others to stop firing and told me to run across the bridge. I ran as fast as I could. I just wanted to get to you. There were so many people outside the door. I thought... I thought something had happened to you.'

I stare at Mum as she steadies her breath. Slowly it dawns on me. She could have so easily been killed or hurt on her way over to us. I thank God she's safe. That we all are. The street outside is quiet now. Now and then we catch the sound of distant gunfire. Exhausted, we pick at some food and go to bed. I close my eyes and know it won't be long before we move again. In some ways it's a relief. Our days in the miserable basement must be numbered.

The TV news next morning blames the attack on terrorists. Several nearby targets were hit, Damascus University, a nearby school, and the offices of the state news agency. Three civilians were killed, including a female student. We know we'll have to move again, but it won't be easy to find a new place. Mum says she'll ask around to see if her friends know of an apartment free. Security tightens around our apartment after the attack. The state security guards appear again that evening. And the next, and the next. They want to know at all times if we are in or out. More checkpoints spring up in the streets outside. That Thursday, another mortar attack on the university kills fifteen students. Tensions are so high that Mum takes us to Grandma's for the weekend.

A friend of Mum's recommends an apartment in Muhajireen, within walking distance of Grandma's place. I grin when Mum tells us. Muhajireen is one of my favourite areas in Damascus. The name means migrants, after the Greek Muslims who moved to the area two hundred years ago. The district sprawls up one slope of Mount Qasioun, the mountain that rises over the city to the west of the

Presidential Palace. The area is affluent, pretty, and above all, quiet. The houses climb the hill in a numbered grid. At the top is the fifth avenue, where our new apartment stands. The rooms are beautiful and spacious with high ceilings and there's a large balcony with a view of the whole city.

Our lives are transformed instantly when we move in. The danger, the pressure, evaporates. It's like someone has opened a window. After four months in a basement with no natural light, God has given us a balcony. I spend our first night there standing out on it, transfixed, watching the first stars twinkle through a dusky sunset. The call to prayer echoes through the ancient streets. I sigh, I'm in paradise.

The apartment isn't cheap. Money is tighter than ever. Mum and Sara are working, and Dad is sending funds from Jordan, but our Syrian pounds aren't worth what they used to be. We're safe, but we don't know for how long. No one can say what will happen next, so Mum puts money aside for emergencies. With housing so scarce, rents are rising fast. Maybe next year we won't be able to afford to keep the flat, or move again, or even buy food. We have to be careful. We no longer go shopping for fun.

Most evenings I spend on the balcony. I write in my notebook, watch the stars move over the city. On Thursday nights, the first night of our weekend, there's always a lot going on in the street below. Sara and I stay up late and watch. Every week, around midnight, we see a beautiful girl going into the apartment opposite. She's about Sara's age, with huge dark eyes, long black hair, and dark skin. She's always wearing high heels, a dress, and outrageous make-up. We gawp at her, burning with envy.

'My God,' whispers Sara. 'Her parents must be so chilled. Do you think they let her go out like that?'

The girl puts her key in the door.

'They must do,' I whisper back. 'She isn't hiding.'

The girl hears us and looks up at the balcony. She frowns, turns back to the door, and steps inside.

'I know her,' whispers Sara. 'I've seen her around.'

Late the following Thursday night, I'm woken up by the sound of laughter. I get up. Another cackle. It's coming from the balcony. I open the door. Sara and the girl from the apartment opposite are sitting at the table, painting their nails a violent shade of pink. The girl looks up and smiles at me. I frown sleepily and look at Sara.

'What are you doing?' I say.

'Painting our nails,' says Sara and giggles. She points at the girl. 'This is Leen.'

I watch them in silence for a minute, then shrug and go back to bed. From that day on, Leen and Sara are inseparable. The next Thursday evening, Sara announces she's going out with Leen from over the road. I expect an argument, but Mum just says she wants her back by midnight. I'm surprised. Dad would never have allowed this. Later, when Sara gets back, she's undergone a complete transformation. Gone is her normal look, hair in a bun, wide jeans and a hoodie. Instead, she wears a borrowed dress and strappy shoes. Her fingernails are the same bright red as her lipstick, and her eyes are lined with thick black kohl. She's straightened her long dark hair.

'Wow,' I say. 'You look...'

'You should come out with us next week,' says Sara, grinning. 'Leen can teach you a whole lot.'

The next Thursday, Sara and I go over the road to Leen's early. Leen has the contents of an entire cosmetics factory in her room and she's dying to show us how to use it. We spend hours listening to music, perfecting our outfits and make-up. Around eight, a friend of Leen's picks us up in her car. The four of us drive around the city all night, dressed to the nines, windows down, music blasting. It's the most fun I've ever had.

Thursday night becomes a ritual. We get ready at Leen's to save Mum having a heart attack. We never wear the same outfits twice. We drive around or hang out in the cafes in an elegant district called Malki, drinking coffee, or parading up and down. Every week the streets there are packed with kids, gossiping, flirting, consumed with their latest crush or teenage drama. My cousins are there, my friends from school, even some of the swimmers from the pool. Now and then, when one of them has a birthday, they book out a whole restaurant and we dance all night. Sara and I are the happiest we've ever been. The kids around us weren't in Daraya. They weren't even down the road in Baramkeh. Their world has never been split apart by mortar shells or tanks. We pretend none of it ever happened. No one asks about our story or if we lost our home. They just talk about where we should go out tonight.

Beyond our bubble, the war rages on. One Sunday in early May I'm staying overnight at Grandma's. It's late, I'm sitting on the bed, listening to the usual deep explosions rumbling in the distance. Without warning, I'm knocked sideways by an invisible force. The whole house shakes. A few seconds later a crack echoes out, followed by the loudest blast I've ever heard.

'Woah, what was that?' I say out loud. I grip onto the bedsheet and wonder if I'm getting sick, or about to have one of my fainting fits. The door opens and Mum comes into the room.

'You felt that too?' says Mum.

'Sure,' I say. 'I thought it was just me.'

'No,' she says. 'Look at the sky.'

I stand and walk to the window. I draw up the blinds and peer out at the night sky. Above Mount Qasioun the horizon is a smear of crimson light, as bright as a sunset. Clouds of red dust and sparks fly up to meet the stars. It's as if the mountain is on fire.

Mum and I walk into the living room. Grandma and my uncle Adnan are already gathered around the TV. The state news agency is saying the explosion was a foreign airstrike on the weapons facility in Jamraya, on the other side of the mountain. I stare at the screen as it shows amateur footage of the explosion. Orange flames flicker on a dark hillside. Then a colossal ball of fire mushrooms into the night. It fades, leaving a downpour of sparks and ash in its wake. It's the biggest explosion I've ever seen. Bigger than the ones in American movies.

Grandma gasps.

'God protect us,' she says.

The weapons factory attack is so big, the destruction so terrifying, it puts everything else into perspective. It makes even the mortar shells seem like a minor problem.

One day, I'm walking down the hill from our apartment to Malki when I hear a shell hit the road behind me. The ground shakes and I duck into the doorway of a nearby pharmacy. I peer out back up the road as windows shatter and glass rains onto the sidewalk. Two minutes earlier and I'd have been killed. I barely even register the danger. I wait five minutes and then carry on walking, meet my friends as if nothing had happened. When I get back home I tell Mum about the shell. She flips out.

'What?' she shouts. 'Are you crazy? You didn't come back?'

I shrug.

'Nothing happened, Mum. I just wanted to see my friends.'

Mum sighs. There's not much she can do to protect us from that kind of random attack. She's very busy working, cooking, looking after the house and Shahed. Sometimes she stops us going out, but without Dad there she struggles to keep us in check. She does her best, she wants to know where we are, who we're with. But things are falling apart so badly everywhere that it's hard for her to keep a sense of order in our lives. Meanwhile, Sara and I are the closest we've ever been. We're happier not discussing the future, or wondering what happens if we lose the apartment. If I get scared, I deal with things in my own way. I prefer to withdraw, escape, forget. Sara and I both have key exams in the summer. Sara will finish high school and I've got the ninth-grade tests. We're both struggling to take the exams seriously. Some days we don't bother going to school. Mum tries to get us to study, but it's difficult to focus on our futures with everything that's going on.

'Shouldn't you be studying?' says Mum as I head towards the door.

'I am studying,' I say, grinning, pulling on my shoes.

'Well, at least take your sister out with you,' she says.

Shahed looks up expectantly.

'Ok, come on then,' I say.

I take Shahed out into town to buy her ice cream. One of our favourite places to go is Bakdash in the old town. The store is over a hundred years old and famous across the Arab world for its Booza ice cream. Booza isn't like other ice creams. It's made from mastic, a resin which makes the ice cream kind of stretchy and

58 BUTTERFLY

chewy. It melts slowly and gets stringy, like melted mozzarella. Part of the fun in Bakdash is watching them make it. Shahed watches spellbound as the chefs pour milk and mastic paste into deep, open-topped freezers. They churn and spread it around the cold metal, then pound it with long wooden mallets until it comes together into a frozen dough. Booza is served in small metal bowls, sprinkled with chopped pistachio nuts. Shahed grins up at me while she eats. Everyone spoils her. We feel bad for her, growing up during a war, without her Dad, moving from house to house.

We all focus on getting by. There isn't space for much else. That summer, I don't do as well as I should in my exams. None of it seems to matter. We're escaping in our bubble. In the autumn, I start studying at a business school. Three years left until I graduate high school. I think vaguely about going to university, but that seems a long way off yet, anything could happen. Sara has just graduated and enrols at Damascus University to study law, but she doesn't go to lectures. She feels this isn't the time for studying and so she works full-time as a coach and a lifeguard instead to support the family. Life is tough, so we get our fun whenever we can. By winter, we're so used to dressing up and going out that we let our guard down with Mum. Sometimes Leen comes to ours to get ready, instead of us going to hers. One Thursday, Mum comes home early and catches me, Leen, and Sara going out for a big birthday party. I'm wearing very high heels. Mum's eyes widen.

'Where are you going in those?' she says. 'How are you going to even walk down the hill?'

'Mum, it's fine,' I say, tottering towards the door.

'And what have you done to your face?' she says. 'What if someone sees you looking like that? What will they think of us?'

I pout.

'Relax. It's not like I'm wearing hotpants or a short skirt.'

'I should think not,' says Mum. 'You know better than that. Your body is all you have.'

'Don't worry, Mervat,' says Leen, gently. 'We'll look after her.'

Mum smiles at Leen.

'I know, *habibti*, I know.'

Her face hardens as she turns back to me.

'Well, it's up to you, of course,' she says. 'You're the one who has to get into paradise, not me.'

I roll my eyes and we totter out of the door. But Sara and I are careful not to overdo it. Neither of us wants Mum to have problems with her friends because of what we're wearing. Not everyone is as relaxed as she is. Now that I'm no longer swimming and approaching sixteen, Mum occasionally raises the *hijab* issue. She asks gently whether I've thought about putting on the veil. I shrug. Sara isn't covering her hair and wearing *hijab*. I don't feel any pressure to do so. For us, it's not a requirement to be a good Muslim. I think vaguely that one day, when I get married maybe, I'll put on the veil. Mum makes it clear that she's never going to force us to do anything. It's entirely our choice.

One evening in spring, Sara and I are sitting on the balcony watching the sky grow dark. Below, the city lights twinkle enticingly. I sigh and think of all of the people out there in the city. Working, living, loving, trying to find normality in a place where bombs fall from the sky. Mum comes out to join us. Her face is drawn and pale.

'I have some news,' she says.

We both sit up.

'What?' says Sara. 'Not the apartment?'

Mum puts a hand on Sara's arm.

'I'm afraid so,' she says. 'The owner wants to give it to her sister's family.'

My gut plummets. I gasp. The apartment is our bubble, our safety, our escape from the death and destruction. My mind races. Where will we go if we can't stay here?

'No,' I say. 'There has to be something we can do. Can't we offer her more money?'

Mum shakes her head sadly.

'I've already tried everything,' she says. 'It's no good. The owner wants us out by April. We'll have to find somewhere else. I'm so sorry.'

Panic fills my chest as my world crumbles for the fourth time in three years. The noose is tightening.

6

Sara and I stare out of the window at the spring rain. Our new apartment is only a twenty-minute walk from where we were before, but the move has drained all the fun out of life. We're further from our friends and nearer to the fighting. Suddenly we feel the cold. Sara sighs and says for the third time that day she wants to leave Syria. All her friends are getting out, leaving for Lebanon, Turkey, or even Europe. I get anxious whenever I hear Sara talking this way. It feels like defeat to admit the fighting isn't going to stop soon, that a future without war is only possible if we leave. Mum walks into the room. Shahed is clinging to her skirt just like I used to.

'I don't like this apartment,' I say. 'I miss our balcony.'

'I know, *habibti*,' says Mum. 'I liked the other place too. But there's nothing we can do about it.'

Mum pushes Shahed gently forwards. The little girl looks up at us with her big, blue eyes.

'Take your sister with you when you go out,' says Mum.

Sara and I wander out into the rain, Shahed trotting along beside us. In Malki, we run into some old swimming friends. They tell us about another swimmer who has been killed in a bomb attack somewhere in the north. We sit around, listless. The war, the deaths, the mortars. It's all become so normal. I think back to the shock of leaving Daraya. It seems like it happened to a different girl, another Yusra. Now, if I hear shelling, I hold my breath for five seconds and then get on with whatever I'm doing. I only notice it when the guns stop firing. When the jets stop flying overhead.

By the summer, all anyone can talk about in the cafes in Malki is the latest disappearances among our friends. I sit with my school friends Hadeel and Alaa, making lists of people who've left. Some of them we never see again. Others pop up a few weeks later in

Germany, Belgium, Sweden, France. The details are always vague. It's never quite clear how they get there.

In early autumn, one of Sara's best friends, Hala, manages to get to Germany on a student visa. She writes to Sara telling her she's in Hanover. Hala says Germany is a good place to study. Sara is fascinated by the idea. Hanover. Germany. A good place to study. A good place for a future.

'I'm leaving,' says Sara one night at dinner.

I roll my eyes. She's been talking about nothing else for months. She shoots me a look.

'What?' she says. 'Really. I'm going to Germany.'

'What does your Dad say?' says Mum.

'All my friends are leaving,' says Sara. 'Mum, I have to go.'

I look down at my plate and wonder what would happen if Sara really did leave and go to Europe. Would I go with her? Would I want to? I'm not at all sure. Leaving Syria seems like a very big step.

'Your father is the one who can afford to send you,' Mum is saying to Sara. 'You know it's up to him.'

Sara sighs. She has already spoken to Dad about leaving, but he tells her to wait and see what happens. She can't go without his approval. He's the one who will pay for the journey. The idea is put on hold. Sara goes back to dreaming of Hanover and scheming her escape.

One Thursday night in early October, I meet swimming friends from the national team out in Malki. They're excited, fresh from the World Cup in Dubai, where they won a bronze medal in the 200m freestyle relay. As we talk, one of my old team mates shows me a photo of the medal ceremony. I gaze at the smiling, proud faces, the shining medals around their necks. My eyes well up with tears. For the first time, I see what I threw away. The loss hits me like a punch to the gut. All the passion, all the determination, all the ambition rushes back at once. I get to my feet. There's no time to lose. I have to get back into the pool. A shudder of excitement runs down my spine. I hurry home to tell Mum and Sara my decision. I want to start training again. Mum sighs.

'But it's dangerous at the pool,' she says.

'It's not as bad as it was,' I say. 'I'm willing to risk it. I can't sit around here my whole life. I want to do something.'

'What's the point?' says Sara. 'You're too old now anyway. It's not worth it. There's no future in it.'

I scowl at my sister and give Mum a pleading look. She shrugs and says I should speak to Dad. I call him up the next day and tell him I'm going back to training. I'm hoping he, of all people, will be behind me. He is less supportive than I'd hoped.

'If you want to swim, I understand that,' says Dad. 'But don't expect any help from me. You left alone, you can go back alone.'

I hang up. I'm not disappointed, I'm more determined than ever. I'll go back, I'll swim, I'll get good, and I'll be back on top. With or without my family behind me. This time, no one will be forcing me. It'll be entirely my choice. I'll choose to swim.

Some of the coaches raise their eyebrows when I turn up at training the following week. But no one says anything. I'm just back. The break of almost a year has taken a huge toll on my speed. All the cute little girls in the group are faster than me. I accept it as a challenge. I stop going out with friends. Every night, I train for two hours after school. After that, I go to the gym for another hour. On the way home from every session, I remind myself what swimming means. I can sacrifice all the teenage fun now. There'll be plenty of time for that when I'm thirty, when I'm done with my swimming career. Some nights I come home blue in the face from training so hard. I eat and go straight to sleep. Mum looks worried and tells me not to overdo it. But there's no way I'm giving up now. I have to get back up to the level I was at before I stopped. Sara is no help either.

That March, I turn seventeen. Sara books an entire restaurant for my birthday. Maybe she's trying to persuade me to stop swimming and enjoy life again, or maybe she feels bad for not supporting me. Either way, we have an incredible time. Leen comes over to our house with her box of tricks and we dress up like film stars for the occasion, just like old times. Mum frowns as I totter out into the road in the highest heels I've ever worn. I wave at her cheerfully and set off down the hill. Men stare at us all the way to the restaurant. One guy looks like he's about to fall over as we walk past. We laugh and dance and celebrate. The war has never seemed so far away. I didn't know it then, but it was to be one of our last big nights out in Damascus.

Life goes on. Training, school, training. I try to keep my head down, get through my last two years of school, but the war is always there to disrupt and distract me. Some nights, electricity outages plunge whole swathes of the city into long hours of darkness. In places, power is rationed to just four to six hours a day. Some Damascenes get around the blackouts using big car batteries, or, if they can afford to run it, a diesel generator. We adjust until the outages, too, become a part of daily life.

Death is random and ever present. It falls from the sky in the street, in midday traffic, without warning, then we dust ourselves off and carry on. In the spring, the attacks in Baramkeh around the Tishreen stadium start up again. The area is full of targets. The university, the state news agency, hospitals, schools, the stadium itself. Mum is beside herself with worry. A few nights every week, she calls me on my way to the pool. The conversation is always the same.

'Come back home,' she says.

'Why?' I say. 'I'm going to swim.'

'Just shut up and come back,' she says. 'Right now.'

I hurry home to find Mum waiting for me with news of more mortar or rocket attacks. I know she wants to protect me, but deep down we both know I'm no longer safe anywhere in the city. I could just as easily be killed in the pool as outside on the street or at home in my bed. We know a lot of people who die at home. A fire, a bomb, or just a stray bit of shrapnel.

Often I hear the mortars falling around Tishreen once I'm already training. One evening I'm in the pool, pushing myself as hard as I can. My face is burning against the cool water. I battle the urge to stop and rest. Another length, another whirl and scoop, just a few more metres. I reach out and grab the end of the pool, rest for a few seconds. My shoulders jerk up towards my ears in alarm as a splitting crash thunders around the pool. There's a

moment of silence. Then the swimmers spring into action, scream-
ing and shouting as they splash over each other to reach the sides.

'Out! Everybody out,' shouts the coach, urgently waving his
arms towards the exit.

There's no time to register what's happening. My mind is blank
as I haul myself out of the water. Crowds of swimmers push past
me, shivering with shock and panic as they hurry towards the
doors. I reach the exit and turn back. I look up to the ceiling and
spot a ragged hole in the roof showing a tiny speck of open sky. I
look down at the water below. There, shimmering on the bottom
of the pool, is a metre-long, thin, green object with a conical bulb
thinning down to a point at one end. It's an unexploded RPG. A
rocket-propelled grenade. I stare at the bomb, unable to tear my
eyes away. Somehow, it had ploughed through the roof and landed
in the water without exploding. A few metres in either direction
and it would have hit the tiles, killing everyone within a ten-metre
radius. It takes a few seconds to sink in. I'm lucky to be alive.
Again.

I turn and rush down the corridor to catch up with the other
swimmers. We file down into the underground gym as more explosions resound around the streets outside. We wait. The coach paces,
looking worried. The attack sounds muffled from down here. I tell
myself we're safe. My hands trembling, I text Mum and tell her
what happened. She's distraught. She waits until the attack has
stopped and then comes to pick me up from the stadium.

'Please, Yusra, it's too dangerous,' says Mum as we wind back
home through the now-quiet streets. 'Just stop swimming. You'll
be much safer away from the pool.'

I shake my head. There's no way I'm giving up swimming.
There's only one way I can carry on training. I'll have to go somewhere bombs don't drop into the pool.

'I'm not stopping,' I say. 'Swimming is my life. I'll have to go to
Europe.'

Mum sighs and stares out of the window for a few minutes.
Then she grips the steering wheel tighter and sits up, as if she's
made a decision.

'I'll speak to your father again,' she says.

One by one, friends and neighbours drift away. Groups of siblings, whole friendship groups, families disappear. The majority
leave for Lebanon or Turkey and then overstay their tourist visas.
Some of them end up in Europe. Most of the boys my age are either
planning to leave or have already gone. Once guys hit eighteen,
they're eligible for compulsory military service in the army. Only
students and men without any brothers are exempt. In normal
times, it's just a fact of Syrian life. But now there's no doubt: going
into the army means kill or be killed.

Sara now has a fixed plan in her head. She dreams of travelling
to Hanover to find her friend Hala. She'll study there, start a new
life, work for a new future. Dad is still hesitating. Some days, he
says the journey isn't safe. Other times, he says he'll arrange for us
to come to him in Jordan. Now and then, he says we can go to
Europe. But the money doesn't materialize. The plan is on hold.

One night in early summer, Sara and I are on our way to Leen's.
She tells me another group of her friends is leaving the following
week. Each time a group leaves, they tell her to come with them,
say they'll look after her on the way. It's tempting for her, but it's
clear, without Dad's support, she's going nowhere.

'All my friends are messing with my brain, telling me to come
with them,' says Sara. 'I mean, well, you don't want to go anyway,
so...'

I look at her, stunned.

'What are you talking about?' I say. 'Of course I want to go. If
we go to Europe I can keep swimming. All the swimmers are leaving. To Sweden, Russia, Germany.'

Sara frowns.

'You'd go too?'

I'm surprised myself by my answer. Yes, I would go. To get away
from the death falling from the sky. To have a future again. A place
where I can swim in peace, or simply a place where someone like
me can keep swimming. I don't see the point of sitting around,
cleaning, cooking, and raising children. I'm a swimmer. I'm going
to show them. And I can only do that if I leave Syria.

'Ok,' says Sara. 'So you can help me persuade Dad. He'll be happier if we go together.'

My mind works quickly. Convincing Dad is the toughest part. Not being here in Damascus, Dad doesn't know how many kids are leaving. We need to make him understand how bad things have got. The best way is to find someone he trusts who is leaving and persuade him to let us tag along with them. I'm shocked at how determined I suddenly am. Leaving Damascus, leaving Syria, leaving my home. How did it get this far? The whole four years of the war flit before my eyes. The tanks, the bombs, the mortars, the gunfire. I'd stay if it stopped tomorrow. If only it would all stop.

One thing I know. If I'm leaving, I'm going to prove myself in swimming first. I have to show them all it isn't a waste of time. My friends at the pool are thinning out as the swimmers melt away. We rarely say goodbye. I just see on Facebook that they're in Turkey, or France, or Germany. One day in mid-June, just before the start of Ramadan, I get a message from a swimmer friend, Rose. She tells me she's in Turkey. She got out with her cousin, leaving her mother behind in Damascus. I'm stunned. Rose's mother dotes on her. She's her only daughter, she's all she has. Rose is only fifteen years old. There's no way her mother would send her to Turkey unless she felt the situation was truly desperate. Maybe if I tell Dad about Rose he'll understand what's going on here. I call Dad and tell him Rose's mum sent her away to Turkey. There's a silence on the other end of the phone.

'Rose?' he says at last. 'Really? Her mother let her go alone?'

'Yes,' I say. 'With her cousin.'

'Why didn't she tell us?' he says. 'You could have gone with her.'

'What?' I say. 'You would have let me go with Rose?'

'Yes,' he says. 'Tell me if you hear of anyone else going. Someone I know and trust. I'll send you with them.'

My heart is beating hard.

'Sara too?' I say, struggling to keep the wild excitement out of my voice.

'Yes,' he says. 'If she wants to go.'

I hang up and take a deep breath. My chest fills with a sense of endless possibility and adventure. I've no idea what the journey entails. All I've heard is vague tales of boats and borders. I don't think about it. I envisage swimming in Germany. Without bombs. With a future.

Dad begins to research our options. He calls Rose's mother to find out more about the journey. Mum and Dad discuss it. There's a shift, they both decide leaving is the best thing for both of us. They talk to us about the legal situation in Europe. I'm still under eighteen, so if I go ahead alone I can apply to the authorities for Mum and Shahed to join me. Legally, safely, on a plane. Mum and Dad agree Sara and I should go together. And it should be soon. I have to arrive in Germany before I turn eighteen next March if we're going to apply for family unification. All we have to do now is find someone Dad trusts.

It's Ramadan, the Muslim holy month. Sara is working hard, saving up for Eid, the three-day festival marking the end of Ramadan when it's traditional for older kids to give their younger siblings gifts of money. Sara's day is full, she works two coaching jobs and a lifeguarding shift. Every evening during Ramadan she works in a clothes shop. After dusk the streets are always bustling, full of people meeting to break their fast. One night in mid-July, just before Eid, Sara comes home later than usual from work. She rushes into our room and does a little dance.

'I've done it!' she says.

'Done what?' I say.

'Found us our way out,' she says. 'Nabih.'

Nabih is our second cousin. His father is our Dad's cousin. He's around my age. When we were kids, we used to see him sometimes at family gatherings in Damascus. His school isn't far away, we often run into each other in Malki. He has a short beard, dark eyes, and wears his hair gelled up at the front. He's a typical crazy teenage boy.

'Nabih?' I say. 'Our cousin Nabih?'

'Yeah,' says Sara. 'I met him on the street tonight. He said he's going to Germany, I think together with one of his uncles. He has to leave soon because he's about to turn eighteen. He doesn't want to fight. We're family, we could all go together. I've already written to Dad to tell him.'

A charge of excitement shoots to my gut. I get up and throw my arms around Sara. That's it. She's done it. Going with family is perfect. There's no way Dad can say no. A few days of discussions follow. Dad speaks to Nabih's father and then calls me to confirm it. He'll let us go. It doesn't seem real. Mum sits us down the same evening. Her face is sad and thoughtful.

'Your father has asked me if I want to go with you to Europe,' says Mum.

Sara scowls and shakes her head.

'No way,' she says. 'What about Shahed? She's only seven. What about the sea?'

'But I don't like the idea of being apart from you,' says Mum. 'And Shahed will miss you both so much. I'll miss you too, of course.'

I'm torn. I don't want to be away from Mum either, but I hate the idea of Shahed on a flimsy boat. It's too dangerous. She's not a swimmer.

'It's ok,' I say. 'We'll apply for you to join us as soon as we get to Germany.'

Mum sits in silence for a minute, fighting tears.

'Don't,' I say. 'It won't be long and we'll all be together again.'

Mum takes a deep breath and takes hold of my hand across the table.

'Ok,' says Mum. 'The main thing is you get out. We'll wait and come later.'

Things move very fast. Dad calls Nabih's uncle, Majed, who will also go with us. Someone needs to get our cousin Nabih out of Syria, and Majed is young enough and willing. I've met him once or twice at family gatherings. He is a serious, slightly nervy guy in his late twenties with short dark hair and sensitive features.

Majed has the plan. He's found a website full of advice for the journey, posted by others already on the road. It isn't cheap, but the safest and most reliable way out of Syria right now is to fly. At this point Syrians don't need visas for Turkey. With enough money, we can just book ourselves onto flights to Istanbul. There's no law against getting on a one-way flight. We won't be doing anything illegal by leaving Syria. The dangerous part of the trip will begin in Turkey, when we contact smugglers to get a boat to one of the Greek islands. Once we reach Greece, we'll be in Europe. Then we cover the 2,500 kilometres to Germany by bus, car, or train. I'm ready to walk there, if that's what it takes.

I go with Majed and Nabih to the travel agents. Dad puts up the money and we book flights to Istanbul via Beirut for the following Wednesday, 12 August. It's real. It's happening. Dad calls us to discuss the plan. He says he'll transfer cash via Western Union for us to pick up in stages along the way.

'When you get the money you'll hide it,' says Dad on the phone. 'You'll have to be very careful with it. Don't let anyone know you have it. Don't show it to anyone.'

There's no time to think about what's happening. We spend every evening of that last week out with friends, saying goodbye. The goodbyes are final. We all assume we'll never see each other again, or at least not for many years. An end to the war seems unthinkable. Anything could happen to me on the way. Or to them, left behind in Damascus. We sit and try not to cry, but the tears are never far away. I always get up and leave abruptly. The worst goodbye is with my closest friends, Hadeel, Alaa and the others. They give me a framed photo of our friendship group. On it, they write their memories of our best times together. I leave it at home. Maybe I can come back and collect it one day. Grandma comes to the apartment to say goodbye, along with a steady stream of cousins, aunts, and uncles.

Mum buys us warm clothes, bags, and boots for the road. We buy a large backpack each and a smaller bag for valuables. We download a tracking app for our phones that sends out a GPS location even when the phone is off. That way, Mum and Dad can see where we are at all times. We set up a group on WhatsApp for our closest relatives, so they can stay in touch easily. Sara and I turn our apartment upside down deciding what to take. We have so little space. Sara puts all of her antiques and jewellery into a big box and gives it to a friend to look after. We take only some clothes, our phones, and our passports.

On the morning of our flight, Mum gets a phone call from Majed saying our flight has been delayed by three hours. My heart sinks. I'm dreading the goodbye, and this will just drag it out. I'm impatient to get going. Everyone is nervous. None of us wants to miss the plane. Majed and Nabih are going to the airport early just to double-check. I tell Mum I want to go with them, she can bring Sara later.

Majed and Nabih arrive in a taxi to pick me up. The taxi is bigger than I expected, a minivan rather than a car. And it's full of people. In the back with Majed and Nabih sits a man I've never seen before. Another stranger is in the passenger seat. I sling my backpack into the trunk and scramble into the van. The man in the back is in his early forties and has a mischievous face that reminds me of Dad.

'I'm Muhannad,' he says. 'I'm an old friend of your father's. We grew up in the same neighbourhood. I'm coming with you to Turkey.'

I smile. He even talks a bit like Dad. We fall silent as the taxi winds through the old town. I stare out of the window at the baking Damascus streets. At the ancient mosques and the shops and the cafes and the beeping traffic. I drink in the things I've seen a million times, try to capture them and lock them away. We pass places I know. Places I worked, places I laughed, places I won and lost. We pass the pool. All those hours of sweat, humiliation, triumph. The houses thin out and we hit the airport road. I look back. Mount Qasioun looms, glowering over the city blocks. I'm first out of the taxi when we arrive at the airport. I watch the others wipe tears from their cheeks as they step down after me. I'm shocked. I've never seen grown men cry.

Inside the terminal, I ask Nabih about the second stranger in our group. Nabih tells me the man is his aunt's husband, Ahmad. He wants out too.

'I didn't realize so many were coming with us,' I say.

Nabih shrugs.

'Everyone's leaving,' he says.

It's another three hours before the others arrive. I'm bored, in limbo, but happy not to be dwelling on the goodbyes at home. None of it seems real. At last, Sara, Mum, and Shahed walk into the terminal. Mum walks up to me, arms outstretched, blinking back tears.

'Goodbye, *habibti*,' she says and holds me tight for a full minute.

I turn to Shahed. She stares up at me with wide, curious eyes.

'When are you coming back?' she says.

I draw her into a hug and kiss the top of her head.

'No, *habibti*,' I say gently. 'We're not coming back this time.'

I let her go. At last Shahed understands what's happening. This isn't like when we go away for swimming competitions. This is different. She breaks down.

'No,' she says and clings to Sara's waist. The tears are streaming down her cheeks.

'Please don't go,' she says. 'Don't go.'

Her little body shakes with sobs.

'Don't... go,' she stammers. My heart breaks for her. Sara pushes Shahed gently away, bends down, and takes her by the shoulders.

'Listen to me,' says Sara. Shahed wipes the tears from her cheeks and gazes at Sara.

'Very soon, we'll be together again,' says Sara. 'We'll bring you to join us. You, me, Mum, and Yusra. In a different country. Just wait a few days, a few weeks maybe.'

Sara hugs the little girl. Then, without another word, she walks off towards security. Mum looks at me, her face is pale, her eyes wide and wet with tears. I squeeze her again and step away. Sara's promise to Shahed rings in my ears. Whenever it is I see her again, I pray my little sister won't remember we began our journey with a lie.

PART FOUR

The Sea

7

The humiliation starts as soon as we leave Syrian airspace. As we wait in Beirut for our transfer to Istanbul, there is nowhere to eat or sit down. We sit on the floor while the Lebanese give us dirty looks. They look at us like we have no money, no clothes, no home. They make us feel like the scum of the Arab world. The insults step up a notch on the two-hour flight from Beirut to Istanbul. As we begin our descent, a Lebanese flight attendant comes on the intercom.

'Please note,' she says, 'that any passengers attempting to take life jackets from the plane will be caught and prosecuted. The security staff will be checking your belongings as you leave the aircraft.'

The words take a moment to sink in. I look at Sara. Her eyes are wide with shock. We are both too stunned to speak. Too humiliated to be angry.

In Istanbul, at least, we have friends. I contact my swimming friend Rami, who has been living here with his brother since the start of the conflict in Syria. Rami agrees to meet me while I'm here, but he can't help us out with the next part of our journey. For that, Ahmad knows a guy through his work as a tour guide, a Syrian living in the city. Ahmad tells his friend we are coming and together they arrange a place for us to stay while we work out our next move. The man meets us at the airport and takes us to the apartment in his car. Then he leaves us to sleep. The next morning the friend comes back. We gather in the apartment for a conference.

The friend tells us we have two options. We can cross to Europe by sea or we can walk. Walking is the less expensive way. We would pay a smuggler to drive us north to the Turkish–Bulgarian border. From there, we'd continue on foot, trekking for about two days until we reach Bulgaria. But the border isn't safe. The Bulgarians are building a giant fence to match the barrier along the Greek border further south. We would have to walk around that, through the mountains. The Bulgarian police patrol the paths day and night. People say they beat anyone they catch: women, children, invalids. They are rumoured to break arms, even legs, and then leave people out in the forest to crawl back to civilization. If you're lucky, the stories go, they might only steal your phone, money, or passport. I stare in horror at the friend as he speaks. That doesn't sound good.

Our second way is to go by sea on a smuggler boat that will take us from the Turkish coast to one of the Greek islands. First we'd contact a smuggler here in Istanbul to see us all the way through to Greece. They would put us on a bus from Istanbul to the coastline, somewhere near Izmir. There, we would wait our turn to take the boat. Going by sea is more expensive. Fifteen hundred dollars each.

Our group is split. Ahmad isn't happy about spending all that money to cross the water. Besides, like many Syrians, he fears drowning in the sea. The others, Majed, Nabih and Muhannad, don't seem too thrilled about the idea either. Only Sara and I can really swim. The others can maybe tread water for a few minutes, but they wouldn't stand a chance without life jackets. And even then, we've heard stories about fake jackets stuffed with packaging that dragged people down when they got wet. We've heard all the stories. Everyone is terrified of the sea.

'You won't drown with us there,' says Sara.

I shoot her a look.

'I'm serious,' she says. 'We're swimmers, I'm a lifeguard. We're not going to leave you to die.'

Nabih is sitting in a corner, staring at his phone. He glances up now at Majed.

'We're girls,' says Sara. 'We can't go sneaking around in the mountains, being hunted by police, and waiting to get our legs broken. We can swim, let's go by sea.'

She looks at me. I run through the worst-case scenarios in my head. The sea is not a swimming pool. Even swimmers die there. What if you get injured, knocked unconscious somehow? A fight, an attack, an accident, anything could happen. But there doesn't seem to be much choice. Walking sounds horrific. And we can swim. I decide to put my trust in God. And in Sara.

Nabih and Majed nod at Sara. Muhannad shrugs. At last, Ahmad sighs and gives in.

'Alright,' says Ahmad, not sounding at all convinced. 'We'll take the boat. The swimmers will save us, of course.'

The friend gets up from the sofa. He says he'll contact the smugglers on our behalf and have them call us to arrange the next part of the journey. We're to give the money to a middleman at an office here in Istanbul. When we arrive in Greece, the middleman will call us and check we are ok. If we've made it to Europe safely, the man will release the money to the smugglers.

Majed takes charge of the money. He tells Dad about our plan and arranges for him to transfer our share. Majed goes out to a Western Union branch to collect the cash. Back at the apartment, he reaches into his money belt and pulls out a wad of US dollars. He spreads it out on the table and begins separating it into piles. My eyes widen. I've never seen so much money in my life. Majed bundles the cash away again into his belt and says he'll look after it for us until it is time to hand over to the middleman. Then he hands us each a five hundred euro note and two hundred Turkish lira.

'Spending money,' says Majed, his expression deadly serious. 'Keep it safe.'

I stare down at the notes. It's the most money I've ever held in my hand. Sara snorts with laughter and waves the pink euro note in Majed's face.

'Wait,' says Sara. 'Doesn't this mean it's party time?'

Nabih and I giggle. Majed frowns, but says nothing.

Sara and I spend the following day exploring Istanbul's old town. I like the city, the markets crammed with antiques, the crowds, the skyline studded with domes and minarets. It reminds me of home. We wander into Aksaray, a neighbourhood nick-named 'Little Syria' by the locals because so many of us have settled there since the war began.

We hear people speaking Arabic with Syrian accents on the

street. Above the shopfronts, our familiar script announces Syrian restaurants and kebab houses from Damascus, Aleppo, and Homs. We walk past bakeries selling stacks of sticky pastries flecked with mint-green pistachio, and grocery shops stocked with mounds of za'atar spice blend, jars of mate tea and cardamom coffee. The walls and lampposts are plastered with posters in Arabic advertising apartments to let.

It's easy to see why so many Syrians have ended up in Turkey. For one, it's the easiest escape route. At this point, the long land border between Turkey and Syria is still open and Syrians don't need a visa to cross it. By the time I pass through, there are already two million Syrians living in Turkey. Some live in temporary camps along the border, but the majority have set up new lives in the cities. They might be safe from the violence at home, but life is tough. Turkey only grants Syrians temporary protection and they aren't allowed to work. Those who work illegally can often be exploited and underpaid.

A lot of Syrians in Turkey fled early in the conflict and thought they'd only be gone a few weeks. Four years later, many of them are now thinking hard about their futures. They may be running out of money, any savings they had now gone. Nobody wants to rely on charity forever. Especially the younger Syrians dream of studying, earning, starting families. They look to a brighter future in Europe. If they can afford it, they risk the sea crossing.

Later that evening, Sara and I meet Rami at a shisha cafe, where customers smoke flavoured tobacco through a water pipe. It's been four years since I last saw him. He looks much older, a bit out of shape. He sits across the table from me, the shisha coals glowing red and black on the foil between us.

'So, you're swimming?' I say.

'I'm training with Galatasaray,' he says, blowing on the coals and sending a shower of red sparks into the air. 'But they won't let me swim in competitions. It's the rules here. You have to be Turkish.'

Rami picks up the shisha pipe, unwraps a new plastic tip, and fits it on the end. He takes several deep, bubbling draws and exhales a thin cloud of white smoke.

'Then what are you doing here, Rami?' I ask. 'I mean, how long are you going to live here like this?'

He frowns and scans my face.

'I mean it,' I say. 'There's no future for you here. Come to Europe with us.'

'No,' he says.

Rami sucks on the pipe, the water bubbles deeper this time, and he exhales the smoke in a thicker, larger cloud.

'It's ok here,' he says. 'I can speak Turkish now, I have friends, my brother is supporting me. I can swim.'

I frown at him.

'Somewhere to train, yes,' I say. 'But what about your dream? How long are you just going to train without competing? Where will that take you?'

He looks down at the table, listening hard.

'And anyway, you're better than this,' I press on. 'You can go really far if they'd let you. And they'll let you in Europe.'

Rami shifts in his seat and passes me the pipe. I suck in, the coals glow, the water bubbles. I blow the smoke over in Sara's face. She looks up from swiping through photos on her phone.

'Come to Europe with us,' I say again. 'We'll do it together. We can swim, we'll train hard, we'll get really good again. We can go all the way.'

'I'll think about it,' says Rami, and downs the rest of his juice. 'You go. Tell me what it's like when you get there. Maybe I'll change my mind.'

That same afternoon, Majed speaks with the smuggler on the phone. A bus is leaving Istanbul for the coast in two days' time. We have twenty-four hours to decide whether to take it. As we talk it over, Ahmad announces abruptly he is leaving for the Bulgarian border. He is too afraid of going to sea on a rubber dinghy and says he would rather try his luck walking through the mountains. He's gone by the time we wake up the next morning. We never see him again. Much later, when we get to Germany, we hear Ahmad was turned back at the Bulgarian border and ended up back in Syria.

At the time we don't discuss it. We've made up our minds.

Majed calls the smuggler to say five of us want seats on the bus to Izmir and places on a boat to Greece. The man on the phone says we should meet him the following evening in a square in the city centre. He says we need to bring our own life jackets. That's a rule. No life jacket, no bus, no boat, no Europe.

We get up early the following day. Majed says there's a place in the Malta market in Aksaray that sells life jackets. Sara and I wait outside on the cobblestone street while the men go in and get them. Nabih comes out first, grinning and carrying an oversized plastic bag. He opens it to show me. Inside are two bulky, dark green objects. I'm surprised to see they aren't orange like the ones in the photos.

'They're made for soldiers,' explains Nabih.

'Does that mean they're less likely to be fakes?' I say.

Nabih shrugs. Muhannad comes out of the shop next. His face lights up as he spots someone behind us and spreads his arms in greeting. I look back to see a man with dark-blonde hair wearing thin-rimmed glasses. The man embraces Muhannad warmly and they wander off, deep in conversation.

'Who's that?' I ask Majed.

'He's a friend of Muhannad's from Damascus,' says Majed, fussing with two more massive plastic bags. 'I think he's been here in Istanbul a while but now he wants out. He's coming with us to Greece.'

I shrug and ask no more questions. We never know much about the man, not even his real name. We giggle, christen him Blondie behind his back. The four of us wander through the crowds, discussing what else we might need for the crossing. Muhannad and Blondie follow at a distance.

'What about those for the phones?' says Nabih, pointing at a packet of resealable freezer bags lying on display among a variety of household items. 'To keep them safe from the water?'

Majed picks them up and inspects the packaging. The bags look big and sturdy. We'll be able to fit more than just our phones in there. Maybe even our passports and the money too. He buys us one each. Sara grabs my arm and drags me off towards a small shop selling phones and accessories. She wants to buy local SIM cards, so we can send photos and messages to Mum. As Sara scans the deals and haggles with the shopkeeper I wonder what Mum is doing, whether she is thinking about us too. I promise myself I'll write to her as soon as we get back to the apartment.

Back in our room, Sara and I repack our stuff. Majed gives us each one of the sealable plastic bags and tells us to put our valuables inside. He says we should keep our own bag safe at all times in case we get separated. Sara closes the door to our room and we put the bags in the safest place we can think of: inside our bras.

The sun is hitting the tops of the buildings when we arrive in the square that evening. We can tell we are in the right place from all the people. They stand and sit around in groups on the pavement, chatting. Mostly they are talking Arabic, I hear a lot of Syrian accents. We're on time, but nothing is happening, so we sit down on the pavement with the rest to wait. Everyone seems relaxed. I'm surprised to see there are no police.

The crowd grows denser as the sun sinks and the wispy clouds above glow first orange, then red. Families of parents, children, and grandparents huddle on the concrete in the gathering dusk. Young men loiter in twos and threes nearby, chain-smoking cigarettes. I check my phone. It's already past nine. Two hours late and still no sign of the smugglers. I scan the crowd again. The light is disappearing fast. My gaze lands on a group of three women. They've covered their hair with *hijabs* and they wear *abayas*, floor-length fitted jackets. One of them is holding a tiny baby wrapped in a shawl. They sit on the pavement a few metres away, whispering together and looking over at us.

I nudge Sara.

'Yeah, I know,' she says, grinning. 'Poor ladies. They're like, are you girls coming with *us*?'

Just then, a broad-shouldered man barges his way through the throng. He wears jeans and a black t-shirt and has a bushy, jet-black beard. A pair of designer sunglasses balances on his forehead. He stops in front of us, his feet planted wide apart.

He claps his hands.

'Ok, *yalla*,' he says. 'Let's go.'

The chattering around us quietens down to a murmur.

'*Yalla*,' he says again. A hush falls as everyone turns to look at him. 'Your bus will be here in a minute. First I want to see everyone's life jackets.'

The man speaks in Arabic, but his accent sounds weird. Kurdish maybe, probably from northern Iraq. Sara grins at me and points her thumb towards the boss man as we get to our feet.

'He's a big strong man, eh?' she whispers. 'Ooh, look at those muscles. Big Man.'

I snigger. The smile hardens on Sara's face. I look up. Big Man is watching me. I lower my eyes and stare at the floor.

'What's so funny?' he says.

'Nothing,' says Sara. 'Is laughing against the rules or something?'

Big Man turns from me to stare at Sara, taking in her messy bun, hoodie, tracksuit bottoms, and trainers. Two younger men appear out of the crowd. One is tall, with long, black hair tied back in a ponytail. The other is shorter, with wavy, brown hair that falls to his shoulders. He has lighter skin than the other two and is very thin. Neither looks like they've slept in a bed or eaten a proper meal in days.

'They're here,' says the smaller one.

He points over his shoulder with his thumb. Behind him, a fleet of six battered-looking coaches are lumbering through the square. They park up one by one alongside the crowd.

'And this little guy looks just like Mowgli from *The Jungle Book*,' mutters Sara in my ear.

I snort, try to suppress another laugh.

'Oh hi,' says Mowgli, looking at us for the first time.

He speaks with the same accent as Big Man.

'Oh hi,' Sara mimics him.

'Psst,' I say in a low whisper. 'Stop it.'

'Whaaat?' she says loudly.

'Shh!' I say. 'Stop acting like you don't care. Look at everyone else, they're scared of them.'

'I'm not scared,' says Sara, making no effort to keep her voice down.

The smugglers are too busy to worry about us. The man with the ponytail strides over to the coach doors. The crowd is growing restless. Some people are already pushing forwards, ready to grab the best seats. Big Man and Ponytail herd us onto the coach. Inside it's dark, hot, and smells musty like old carpet. The windows are all closed, the curtains drawn firmly shut across them. We squeeze our bags into the luggage racks above our seats. The engine starts, and everyone rushes to sit down. Big Man appears at the top of the aisle.

'Ok everyone, phones off,' he says over the chugging engine. 'From now on, no calls, no messages, no internet, no GPS. I'll come and check they're all off. And keep the curtains closed.'

Sara and I turn our phones off. I think of the tracker app on my phone. It sends out a signal even when the phone is off. I'm comforted that Mum and Dad will be able to check where we are. They can even watch us moving on a map. A hush falls again as the coach sets off in darkness. Our cousins Majed and Nabih sit in front of us. The others in our group, Muhannad and Blondie, are across the aisle. Most of the passengers fall asleep quickly. I sit in silence, wondering what they've been through, what horrors have forced them on this desperate route across the sea.

Before long, a young woman behind us begins chatting in a loud whisper to her neighbour. I overhear her say she is Lebanese-Syrian. She says she had been living in Beirut before she set off for Europe. Her neighbour, an older woman wearing a *hijab* headscarf, says she is from Iraq and is travelling with her two kids to meet her husband in Germany.

I crane my neck to look across the aisle behind me. A small boy and an older girl are asleep in the seats opposite. The younger woman sees me looking back at them. She has short, cropped hair and wears western-style clothing. She smiles and introduces herself, says her name is Coco. I wish I wasn't so shy. There's a pause while I try to think of something to say.

'Do you think we'll stop somewhere along the way?' I say at last.

'No,' Coco whispers through the gap between the seats. 'I heard someone else ask one of the smugglers. They say no stops, for toilet, water, eating, whatever. We go straight there.'

'Oh, right,' I say. 'Thanks very much.'

The conversation seems to be over, so I turn back in my seat and slump down, pulling the hood of my sweater down over my face. I sleep for several hours until the coach comes to a sudden stop and the engine cuts out. The change in pace wakes me up. The other passengers stir, stretch, and murmur to each other. A baby wails somewhere near the front.

Sara is fast asleep, her head lolling against my shoulder. Nabih is awake in the seat in front. He twitches the curtain back and looks out. I do the same. Maybe we've arrived. There's no way of telling. For the first time I realize how little control we have over what's going on. Orange lights flash outside the window. There's a beeping noise as a giant truck loaded with a shipping container reverses slowly past our side of the bus. When it's clear, the bus starts up, drives forwards, and draws alongside another identical truck in front. Then it reverses back into the gap left by the first truck. I look to my left. Across the aisle, Muhannad has also drawn back his curtain. I watch as the original truck draws level with the left side of the coach. We are surrounded. Hidden.

'Woah, hey, close the curtains,' shouts Big Man from the top of the aisle.

I let the curtain fall back across the window and slump back in my seat, trying to work out what I've just seen. I listen to a series of deep, metallic clanking noises. Then the sound of more vehicles reversing and parking up around the coach. A shuddering vibration springs up beneath us, then the low rumble of a much bigger engine. A little while later comes a faint rolling sensation.

Could we be on a ferry? No one said anything about getting on a boat. I look at Sara. She's still fast asleep. I reach over the top of the seat in front and tap Nabih on the shoulder. His face appears over the headrest.

'What's happening?' I mouth.

Nabih shrugs. Down the aisle, Big Man is standing, staring straight at us. Nabih sits back down. Twenty minutes later, the ferry engine slows to a low rumble. Then more beeping and reversing noises. Our driver fires up the engine and drives slowly off the boat. I'm too wired to sleep. About an hour later, the coach stops again. I sneak a look outside. Pine trees. This must be it.

Big Man appears again at the top of the aisle and tells us we'll be walking from here. We're to collect our own boats from the luggage hold underneath the bus and follow the smugglers.

'No talking, no smoking, no lights, no loud noises,' says Big Man. 'Stay close and don't wander off.'

Sara rubs her eyes, stretches her arms above her head, and stands up in the aisle. She passes me my bag down from the overhead luggage rack.

'He says we're going on the boat straight away?' says Sara. 'We should change our shoes then. Put our flip-flops on. Don't want to be wearing heavy boots in the boat, right?'

We swap our walking boots for flip-flops and file off the coach with the others. I step down onto a snaking mountain road. More people are spilling out of the other coaches parked up in front and behind us. It seems we're all going to the same place. Majed tells me to wait while he and the others join the crowd around the hold luggage hatch. I look up. The sky is bright with hundreds of stars, far more than I've ever seen in Damascus. A steep slope rises from the road to my left. On the other side, the land drops down sharply into a thick forest. Between the pines, on the horizon, a faint smudge of orange. Dawn is coming.

The woman with the tiny baby I'd seen in the square stands nearby. She scans the people as they walk past in twos and threes. Each pair carries a large, rectangular cardboard box between them. The woman's face relaxes. A man with a heart-shaped face appears out of the crowd. He puts the box on the ground, then carefully lifts the baby out of the woman's arms. The baby looks even tinier close up, not more than a few months old. It stirs and waves its little arms, its round, pale face still screwed up in sleep. Then the baby opens its eyes. They are huge and pale blue and shine like twin moons. I look up. Big Man is watching too.

'Take it easy on the way down,' Big Man says quietly to the man with the baby.

The man looks at him in surprise. Big Man clears his throat, rolls back his wide shoulders, and strides off to where Mowgli is guiding a steady stream of people down into the forest.

8

'We could swim it,' says Sara.

'Don't be stupid,' I say.

We're standing on a rocky outcrop in the baking midday sun. Far below, the Aegean Sea sparkles menacingly. The sun throws a blinding band of liquid gold on the water. Beyond, the hazy shapes of green and brown hills rise out of the sea. The island. Greece. Europe. Tantalizingly close.

'Well, I could swim it,' says Sara. 'I mean, if I got flippers.'

'What's that?' says the smallest smuggler, Mowgli, back from taking a pee in the forest. 'You can swim to the island?'

My chest tightens with panic.

'No,' I say quickly. 'She's joking.'

Sara turns to face him.

'What if we could?' says Sara. 'There'd be fewer people on the boat. Would you let us go for free?'

'You're crazy,' says Mowgli. He turns away and slouches off towards the shade of the pines.

The heat is unbearable. We follow him down the steep slope, winding between the trees towards the camp. In the pines above our heads, the cicadas chirp like buzz saws. We walk in single file. I pick my way carefully between the rocks and scratchy shrubs. I stare down at my scratched bare feet. It's only been a week since I kissed Mum goodbye in Damascus. I wonder what she'd say if she knew we were sleeping rough in the forest without food, at the mercy of gangsters.

We enter the clearing, where hundreds of people are sitting waiting for their boats. We've been waiting here all day for the smugglers to tell us it is time to leave. Mowgli leads us to where the other two smugglers, Big Man and Ponytail, are lounging in the shade of a pine tree. With them are three men and a little boy of about six. The boy is arranging the pine cones, piling them on top of each other and letting them tumble down onto his outstretched legs.

'These two reckon they can swim it,' says Mowgli. 'They say they're swimmers.'

Big Man looks up and raises his eyebrows. He looks sceptical. I'm not surprised. It's ten kilometres across to Greece from here. I doubt whether he's worried about our safety. It's more a matter of bravado. He doesn't like the idea that someone can cross to Europe from here without his help. I also have my doubts.

'Ten kilometres is a long way to swim,' says the older of the three men, placing a hand protectively on the little boy's head. Deep worry lines are etched into the man's face. He looks at Big Man. The smuggler eyes us and chuckles.

'Ok, so here's the deal,' says Big Man. 'How about I send a boat with you and you can swim alongside it. If you really swim the whole way you won't have to pay.'

All eyes are on Sara.

'Alright,' she says. 'But if we do it, our whole group goes for free. On the boat, I mean. There's four more of us.'

The smile freezes on Big Man's face. He stares at her, weighing up whether she's serious. He shrugs.

'We can do that,' he says at last.

My stomach tightens. I grip Sara's arm. We're really going to swim it? Without a wetsuit? In our clothes? Ten kilometres is a long way with no flippers. Sara must be mad. She reads my thoughts.

'You'll have to get us swimming stuff,' she says.

Big Man laughs and waves his hand. I breathe a sigh of relief. The subject is closed for now.

The two younger men sitting on the floor are staring at us. They have the same eyes. The older one has a round, friendly face, a full beard and moustache. The younger man is handsome, with thick eyebrows. He smiles at me, showing off a set of perfectly straight, white teeth.

'I'm Ayham,' he says and holds his right hand to his chest. 'This is my brother Bassem.'

'Yusra,' I say. 'My sister Sara.'

'I swear I know you,' says Ayham. 'Aren't you from Damascus?'

'Well, I don't know you,' I say, alarmed.

We're a long way from the cafes back in Malki. I put my hand on Sara's arm.

'Let's go find the others,' I say.

We weave our way through the crowds sitting in small groups in the clearing. This part of the forest belongs to Big Man, but his is just one of hundreds of smuggler gangs working this stretch of the Turkish Aegean coast. The smugglers are doing good business. Between them, they send thousands of people to Greece on small rubber boats every day. It is in everybody's interests to keep the peace between the gangs. A few hundred metres down the coast from us is another camp run by Afghan smugglers. The Afghans coordinate with Big Man and take it in turns to send boats out, waiting until the sea is calm and the Turkish coastguard is out of sight. The smugglers don't have to worry too much about the police. The authorities sometimes make arrests, but there are just too many good hiding places along this coast for them to shut the smugglers down for long.

We reach the other side of our camp and find Nabih and Majed lying at the edge of a large shelter rigged up with blankets between the trees. It's high enough so that I can stand up underneath it. I flop down onto the ground next to Nabih. I'm starving. I've only had two Snickers bars since we left Istanbul. I ask Majed if we have anything else to eat. He frowns and shakes his head. The two young men, Ayham and Bassem, follow us over. They sit down under the shelter and strike up a conversation with a man in his mid-twenties with a dark beard and thick eyebrows. With him are two women both wearing *hijabs*.

The man with the thick eyebrows says his name is Ahmad, he's Syrian, from Latakia. I smile and picture the palms and the high-rise hotels along the seafront there. Ahmad points at the rest of his group and says he's travelling with his two sisters and some friends. The women smile shyly and lower their eyes. Ahmad points to a boy about my age and says he is his friend, Bashar.

We sit around, chatting with the guys to pass the time. The smugglers assure us we'll be going any minute. But the hours wear on and no boats leave. I try to ignore the rumbling in my stomach. Even if there was more chocolate left, I'm not sure I could face another melted Snickers bar. Chocolate was a short-term solution. The idea was to make you feel full without making you need the toilet. There really wasn't anywhere we could have gone. I frown at the half-empty water bottle at my feet. We've nearly finished our water supply.

Nabih reads my thoughts and stands up.

'Isn't there a shop or something round here?' says Nabih. 'We could charge the phone too. I'll go and ask the big guy.'

He wanders off to ask the smugglers. A moment later he's back. Big Man has told him there's a shop back up the hill and along the road. Nabih takes Majed's phone and says he'll be right back. I wonder for a moment whether we should go with him. I look at Sara. She's picking her nails with Majed's penknife.

'Eww, Sara, you know what you look like?' I say.

'What?' she says.

'A smuggler's wife,' I say.

'Shut up!' she says and thumps me on the arm.

I look up but Nabih has already disappeared off up into the forest.

The trees are throwing long evening shadows along the ground by the time he returns, red-faced and sweating and carrying three full plastic bags. He sinks down next to us under the shelter. I fall on one of bags. I fish out six tired-looking sandwiches wrapped in plastic, and several packets of sesame sticks. The other bags are full of bottles of water.

Nabih looks exhausted. It was over an hour's walk to the shop and when he got there he found it was only a gas station. The good news is he has managed to charge Majed's phone. Nabih takes it out of his pocket and hands it over to Majed.

'Don't wave it about like that,' says Majed. He points over to where Big Man and Mowgli are sitting at the edge of the shelter, chatting to the brothers, Ayham and Bassem. 'They might see.'

Majed hides the phone in the crook of his arm. He writes to Mum and Dad and tells them we're ok and that we haven't left Turkey yet. I unwrap my sandwich and sniff it. Between the soggy bread is a slab of salty white cheese and some squashed slices of tomato. It isn't great, but I'll take anything over another melted chocolate bar.

I'm chewing my first mouthful when I look up and see the little Iraqi girl from the bus. She's standing about a foot away, her big brown eyes fixed on the sandwich in my hand. She's about nine years old, with a pretty, open face and dark skin. She wears a light blue *abaya* jacket and matching *hijab* headscarf. She puts her head on one side and shyly twists her fingers together in front of her belly.

I smile and hold the sandwich out to her. The girl spins round and gallops the few steps back to her mother, who is sitting further back under the shelter, a little boy lying with his head in her lap. The woman looks over at me and smiles. The girl is still staring at my sandwich. I smile and hand her one of the packet of sesame sticks. She takes it and her face breaks into a nervous grin.

'I hope she wasn't bothering you,' says the woman.

'No, it's fine,' I say. 'I'm Yusra.'

'I'm Umm Muqtada,' says the woman. She points at the girl and the boy lying at her feet. 'My daughter and my son.'

Umm Muqtada strokes the boy's thick black hair back from his forehead. His eyes are glazed and faraway. He looks unwell. I point at him.

'Is he ok?'

'He's sick,' says Umm Muqtada. 'He needs to see a special doctor. He can get better treatment in Europe. His father, my husband, and my youngest son are in Germany.'

Umm Muqtada gestures around the clearing at Coco, the Lebanese-Syrian girl from the bus, and a group of men sitting nearby. She says they are all travelling together in a group to Budapest to meet her husband's brother Ali, a smuggler who will take them the rest of the way to Germany.

Everyone says Hungary will be the worst part of the journey, after the sea crossing. The borders are heavily patrolled, we might

need to pay a smuggler to help us get across. And many Hungarians
are afraid of Muslims. We'll have to be careful.

I hear a gurgling noise coming from the middle of the shelter.
I look over. It's the baby. The man with the heart-shaped face is
sitting with his young wife, who doesn't look much older than me.
Between them lies an improvised cot made from an inflatable
rubber ring covered in a shawl. I can just see two chubby pale legs
and little feet waving in the air above the rim. The young mother
is bending over the ring, cooing softly to the child. I pop the rest
of my sandwich in my mouth and get up, still chewing, to take a
closer look.

'How old is she?' I say, standing over the rubber ring.

'Four and a half months,' says the man.

He studies me carefully. Beside him and his wife sit the two
women who were staring at us in the square in Istanbul. One of
them is older, in her mid-sixties, the other is same age as the baby's
mother, about eighteen. With them is another man I recognize
vaguely from the coach. I realize for the first time that they're all
part of one big family.

'She's lovely,' I say, turning back towards the baby.

All the women are looking at me now and my cheeks start
burning. There's an awkward pause. I've got to say something else.
I introduce myself. The man with the heart-shaped face puts his
hand on his chest and says his name is Zaher. He points in turn
to his companions and introduces them. His wife, his sister, his
mother, and his brother.

'And the little one?' I say.

'Her name is Kamar,' says Zaher.

Kamar, moon. I look down at her again. She's wriggling her legs
and feet and gazing up at me with those wide, pale eyes. Kamar, it
suits her. Around her neck is a small red string with a plastic wallet
attached.

'What's that?' I ask, pointing.

'It's just information about who she is,' says Zaher. 'And names
and numbers of people to call if they find her.'

He pauses.

'You know, in case something happens.'

I battle against the sudden vision of this baby as another statistic, another unidentified body washed up on a strange shore.

'Nothing will happen if we're on your boat,' I say. It's out before I know what I'm saying. 'My sister and I are swimmers.'

The women exchange glances and look over to where Sara is sitting laughing with Bashar. She's drawing circles in the dirt with a long twig. I give up my charm offensive and stroll back towards the others.

The brothers, Ayham and Bassem, come and sit with us as the sun sinks quickly beyond the trees that border the clearing. They're with another man with a diamond tattoo on his wrist who says his name is Abdullah.

'So you're the famous swimmers,' says Abdullah.

I catch his eye and blush.

'That's us,' says Sara. 'We could beat any one of you in a race.'

Abdullah laughs.

'Not on land,' he says.

'Try it,' says Sara.

My cheeks turn red again and I look away. A couple are sitting under a tree in the middle distance. I stare at them through the twilight. They're holding hands and kissing on the lips. I'm shocked. Bashar follows my gaze.

'My brother,' he says. Then, seeing my expression: 'And his wife.'

'Sorry, it's just...' I say.

He laughs.

'I know,' says Bashar. 'They're always like that. They've only been married a few weeks.'

'Romeo and Juliet,' chuckles Sara. 'Quite the honeymoon.'

The smugglers, Mowgli and Ponytail, catch the end of the conversation as they melt out of the half-light to join our group.

'Are you married?' says Ponytail, sitting down next to me.

'No,' I say firmly, my face darkening again. 'I'm a swimmer.'

The group under the shelter begins to settle down for the night. I'm relieved when Zaher's mother takes charge. She beckons to us to come and join the other women in the middle of the shelter.

'Yes, Mama,' says Sara, laughing.

I'm not laughing. As the last light fades I'm glad Mama is there. She might disapprove of us, but she's got a lot of sense. Standing up, I peek outside the shelter into the grainy night. Together with the Afghan camp there must be at least a thousand strangers out here on this stretch of coast. I join Mama and the other women bedding down in a heap. In the centre, Kamar lies in her rubber ring next to her mother. Umm Muqtada lies down nearby with her two children. The men form an outer ring around us.

Mama hands me a sleeping bag. The Lebanese girl Coco grabs the other end, so we agree to share. Before I get in, Sara, Majed, and the others hand me their plastic bags of valuables. I shove them deep down into the bottom of the fabric next to my feet. Sara stays up with Bashar and some of the others at the edge of the shelter, their hands cupped over the ends of their cigarettes to hide the light. I hear Sara laugh as I wriggle and try to get comfortable on the hard ground.

I sleep badly, the ground is rough and uneven with stones and branches. We sleep in a jumbled pile of limbs. We've pitched our camp on a slight slope and I keep slipping down it whenever I drift off. The first light of morning is in the eastern sky when the helicopters come. I wake to the noise of what sounds like a giant insect buzzing overhead. My heart beats hard, but somehow after the random shelling I saw in Syria, the danger seems dampened and far away. I'm curious more than anything else.

I clamber out of the sleeping bag, trying not to wake Coco. I duck out from underneath the shelter and see a sweeping shaft of white light beaming down through the trees. The shelter roof is flapping in the wind. The helicopter is directly above us. A distorted voice blast outs a message in Turkish through a loudspeaker. Sara appears, rubbing her face and shielding her eyes against the blinding search beam. The wind flattens our hair as we stand just beyond the shelter, frozen to the spot and gazing helplessly at the sky. The loudspeakers erupt again, this time in Arabic.

'Come out, we know you're there.'

I look at Sara and wonder whether we should run. She stares, spellbound, her eyes fixed on the searchlight sweeping the forest canopy above us. Big Man comes jogging over. He looks relaxed, but he's carrying a small handgun.

'What's happening?' says Sara.

'Nothing, nothing,' says Big Man. 'Just ignore them. We run this place. Sit down and wait. They'll go soon.'

He's right. Thirty seconds later, the wind begins to drop, and the helicopter rises and pulls away inland. The buzzing sound quietens. Sara and I wait in silence until it disappears altogether. I stretch and yawn and wander back to my makeshift bed. I climb back into the sleeping bag. Coco stirs, rolls over, and resumes her deep, regular breathing. I stare at the blanket roof of the shelter, wide awake, mind racing, until daylight creeps into the camp.

Zaher, Mama, and the rest of the family rise quietly at dawn and go out of the shelter to pray. I get up, but there isn't much to do. I lounge around the camp most of the morning, trying not to fantasize about Burger King. I chat with the guys to distract myself from the rumbling in my stomach. The sun is overhead and Zaher's family are praying a second time when Ponytail ducks into the shelter and says the smugglers have a boat ready. We have to decide between us who will go first. Zaher rises from his prayer and raises his hand. I look from Mama to baby Kamar. They can't stay out here with no food or shelter forever. It makes sense that Zaher and his family should go first.

Umm Muqtada, the Iraqi woman with the two young kids, raises her hand next. I look at her little boy. His face is pale and solemn. He looks like he needs urgent help. I wish I could click my fingers and get him straight to the doctors in Germany. Ponytail nods at the two families and looks around for more volunteers for the first boat. I scan the clearing. There is no sign of the rest of our group, of our cousins Nabih and Majed, or the other men, Muhannad and Blondie. The brothers, Bassem and Ayham, are looking restless and staring at me and Sara. I shrug at them. We can't go without the others.

Coco gets to her feet to volunteer. Abdullah, the guy with the tattoo, stands, followed by Bashar and three other men. That makes fifteen. Ponytail ducks out of the shelter, beckoning to the volunteers to follow him. A few minutes of chaos follows as the group grabs a few possessions and decides what to abandon in the forest. Each of them leaves a pile of clothes underneath the trees and takes only a small plastic bag of valuables. I watch Zaher's wife wrap baby Kamar in a shawl and clutch her to her shoulder. The family are gone before we can say goodbye. I mutter a quiet prayer for the baby.

Sara jumps up.

'Come on,' she says. 'Let's watch them go.'

The cicada chorus is deafening as Sara and I climb up through the steep forest to the rocky outcrop, where we can have a clear view of the sea. Covered in sweat, we arrive just in time to see a grey dinghy packed with tiny figures appear from beneath the treeline below. A small smudge of white smoke rises from the back as the engine splutters into gear. The water is as still as a mirror. We watch in silence as the boat glides out to sea under the unforgiving midday sun. I screw up my eyes against the white light and wipe the sweat from my forehead.

Sara breaks the silence.

'If something happens when we get out there, you know what to do, don't you?'

I don't answer.

'Yusra? You know what to do, right?'

I watch the dinghy carve out a wake in the glassy water as it chugs towards Europe. I think of Kamar's big moon eyes, the ID tag around her neck.

'What do you mean?' I say.

Sara turns and grips both my shoulders, spins me around to face her.

'If the boat sinks out there, you swim,' she says. 'You hear me? You forget everyone else and just swim. You and me, we'll swim, ok? We'll be alright.'

I squint to see her face against the blinding light. She's serious.

'Yusra, you hear me?'

I nod and turn away, ducking into the shade of the trees.

9

'Bad news,' says Mowgli, crouching down in front of what's left of our group under the shelter. 'Your boat is broken.'

My heart sinks. So we won't be making the crossing tonight either. That means another night out in this forest. We'll have to wait until the smugglers find a replacement boat. No one can say how long that will take. Maybe tomorrow, maybe the day after that. My stomach rumbles in protest. We've been out here for two days already.

'But we're starving,' says Muhannad. 'You can't keep us here forever. There are women and kids out here. Either you take us tomorrow or we'll go back to Istanbul. You won't get a cent out of us.'

There are murmurs of agreement from the stragglers under the shelter. An Iraqi woman I've not seen before joins the group as we talk. She's carrying a baby and her two young children, a girl and a boy, trail behind her. The group stops murmuring as Big Man ducks under the blanket.

'You'll go tomorrow,' says Big Man firmly. 'We'll get a boat and you'll all go tomorrow.'

I look around. Several more boats have set out that afternoon and the camp has emptied out. But there are still more than twenty of us left. He can't mean we're all going on the same boat. Big Man waves his hand and walks off. Mowgli shoots a look at me and Sara, then turns and disappears off into the pine forest. Half an hour later he's back, carrying a long, canvas bag.

'A palace for the princesses,' says Mowgli grinning, slinging the tent onto the ground in front of my feet. 'For you, *habibti*.'

The boy and the older man I saw sitting with Big Man on the first day stroll over to inspect the tent. The boy's father, who says his name is Idris, helps us pitch it just outside the shelter. His son,

Mustafa, watches us with big, serious eyes. That night I lie next to Sara in the tent, staring at the canvas roof. My mind wanders back to Damascus, to the bustle of the old town. I picture Mum and Shahed buying groceries in the market. I drift off to sleep wishing I was with them.

I rise as soon as it gets light the next morning. I wander around the camp, my stomach growling. I walk up alone to the rocky out-crop. I want to see the sea. The morning haze lifts to reveal the green and brown hills of the island. It looks closer than ever. It's as if I could reach out and touch it.

I get back to the camp just in time to see Big Man stumble in clutching his arm. He's bleeding. Ayham hands him a t-shirt to use as a bandage. Big Man says there's been a fight with the Afghan smugglers down on the shore. It was probably them who slashed our boat. The other gang is angry, they say Big Man's gang broke the rules by sending too many boats off at once.

Mowgli jogs into the camp and beckons urgently to his boss. Big Man hands the bloodstained shirt back to Ayham and follows Mowgli off down the path towards the shore. At noon, the three smugglers, Big Man, Mowgli and Ponytail, return. They are red-faced and sweating in the baking heat.

'Yalla,' says Big Man, standing legs wide apart and clapping his hands like he did back in the square in Istanbul. 'Time to go. All of you come with me, right now. Get your life jackets on. And get on with it. We don't have long.'

Fear and excitement shoot through my empty stomach. This is it. I scramble to my feet and start back towards our tent to collect our things. Sara is already climbing out of the zip door, carrying both our bags. She ducks back in and throws out the bag with the life jackets.

'Leave everything behind,' Mowgli calls after me. 'No room for bags.'

Sara shrugs, leaves the bags where they are and turns to follow Mowgli. We take a left out of the camp down a steep stony path towards the shore. I have only what I'm wearing and the bag of valuables. I pull on my khaki life jacket and look down at my boots.

No time to change into my flip-flops. I skid down behind Sara and Mowgli onto a small stretch of stony beach hidden from view on both sides by high rocks.

One by one, the group spills off the path onto the beach. Idris appears with his son Mustafa on his shoulders. Then comes the Iraqi woman carrying her baby, the girl and the boy holding hands and following close behind. Then comes a Somali woman I've not seen before. Then the brothers, Bassem and Ayham, followed by two Afghans, two Iraqi guys, and five Sudanese men I don't know. The rest of our group, Muhannad, Nabih, Blondie and Majed, bring up the rear. I count them as they come. Twenty-four including me and Sara.

Big Man is not around, but Ponytail is waiting for us, trousers rolled up and standing knee-deep in the green shallows. He stoops and holds onto a grey inflatable dinghy bobbing behind him on the water. Up close, the boat is absurdly small. It's about four metres long. It looks like a toy for tourists. The sides are formed from a thick inflatable tube which meets at a point at the bow. A thin rope runs along the top. There are no seats in the middle, only a flat bottom section. A knee-high plastic barrier forms the back of the boat. Mounted on it is a small, white outboard motor, the kind with a pull cord. There's no time to wonder how we'll all fit in.

'Come on, come on,' urges Ponytail, waving his free arm. 'Get in.'

Mowgli shoves Ayham in the small of his back and sends him stumbling towards the dinghy. The movement kickstarts a scrum as everyone tries to get on at once. Mowgli ushers us, the other women, and the kids towards the front of the boat, batting one of the Sudanese guys out of the way. Sara lifts the little girl in as the Iraqi mother struggles with her baby.

The boat lurches violently. Ponytail tries to steady it. I perch on the bow at the point where the two sides of the inflated tube meet and try to make myself as small as possible. The boat is impossibly full. It sits so low that the water is close to brimming over the edge. If I push down on the inflated tube it would spill in and flood us.

'Everyone stay as still as you can,' says Muhannad, sitting

hunched at the back. Ponytail and Mowgli push the boat out until the water comes up to their shoulders. Mowgli hauls himself on board, pushing one side down. Seawater sloshes onto the floor.

'Watch it,' says Muhannad as the boat rocks, the pointed bow sinks behind me, and water seeps into the seat of my jeans.

I look at the children. Something's wrong. The boat can't take all of us. Mowgli plants his feet in the tiny spaces between the jumble of limbs at the back of the boat. He pulls the engine cord. Nothing happens. On the third go, it splutters and catches, sending up a small cloud of white smoke. We set off slowly from the shore. Seconds later, the buzz of a much larger engine erupts behind us. Over my shoulder, I watch a white speedboat zoom into view.

'Whoa!' shouts Mowgli, cutting off the engine. 'Ok, all of you, out, now!'

Out at sea, the speedboat slows its engine and pulls around in a circle to face us. There's a red stripe up the bow and black writing down one side. The Turkish coastguard. The boat is waiting, blocking our path, stopping us leaving. Ponytail shouts something from the shallows and splashes out towards us. I climb off the bow and help the others drag in the boat. Most of the passengers are still on board. Further back, a loudspeaker sounds from the speedboat.

'My babies, they can't swim,' calls the Iraqi woman from the dinghy. Sara reaches into the boat, grabs the woman's daughter, and plonks her down on dry land. The woman's son lets out a wail as Sara wades back through the water to grab him.

On the next step, my right leg jerks back behind me. I pull it, but it won't move. My boot is stuck between two big rocks on the seabed. The men are spilling out of the front of the boat now, pushing past me, shoving me hard from both sides in their rush to get on shore.

'Hey, watch out,' I shout. 'I'm stuck. Help!'

No one hears me above the panic. My foot doesn't budge. Someone shoves my shoulders from behind and I topple over forwards. I put both hands out and hit rock, grazing my palms on the bed of sharp stones. Salt rushes up my nose as my head and shoulders dunk under into the water. I feel a twinge of pain in my foot as it twists in its trap. I straighten up, gasping for air.

Mowgli and Ponytail are pulling the boat out of the water. Beyond them, the others are already disappearing into the forest. I look up to see Sara carrying the girl on her back and dragging the wailing boy by the hand. She ducks into the pines.

'Hey, wait!' I shout between huffs.

My breath comes in short rasps. I pull on my foot with both hands. It's stuck fast. Sara doesn't look back.

'Sara! Wait for me.'

The smugglers are the last to scramble up the stony slope, carrying the boat between them. In seconds, the little cove is clear. I'm alone. Behind me, in the open water, the coastguard boat revs the engine. Sobbing in panic, I reach down into the water and scrabble with the laces of my right boot. I release the knot and hold the shoe down with both hands, jerking my foot up sharply. It hardly budges.

'Come on, come on, please,' I moan, grabbing the back of the boot heel and tugging my foot.

It's loose. It slides out into the water. I'm free. Panting and sobbing, I abandon my right boot and splash on shore, hobbling back up the sharp scree in my soaked sock. I clamber up into the forest and hop along the path to the camp. Sara is waiting for me at the edge of the clearing. I stumble into the camp, breathing hard and crying. I slump to the floor, hug my knees to my chest, and rest my forehead on my forearms. I'm hyperventilating.

'Yusra?' Sara kneels in front of me. 'What's going on, what's wrong?'

I'm too panicked to answer. Not far off I hear the Iraqi woman shouting at the others.

'You'd all leave my kids to drown,' she screams. 'We're not getting back on that boat. You're all murderers. Don't touch me.'

I block it out and focus on my breath. By the time I can speak again, the woman and her kids are gone. I don't blame her. Tensions are high. Everyone is on edge, losing patience. We all want to leave the camp. But now we've seen the boat, heard the engine fail, felt how low it sat in the water.

The afternoon air is thick with foreboding. Majed is pacing restlessly. He's impatient to leave. Either we get on the boat or we go back to Istanbul. It's clear we can't stay here another night. Big Man is back, striding around the clearing, looking agitated. He says we can go once the coastguard has gone.

I take my useless boot off and toss it into the bushes. My clothes dry off quickly in the afternoon heat. Sara lays out some of our clothes on the floor and I lie down on top of them. The wind picks up and rustles soothingly through the tops of the pines, calming my shaken stomach. I doze off.

'Ok, let's go! Let's go!' shouts Big Man.

I open my eyes and sit bolt upright. Big Man is jogging back into the clearing, shouting at us to put on our life jackets. Standing above me, Majed is looking pale. He moves slowly and deliberately as he pulls his phone out of his plastic bag and types something into it, turns it off and puts it away. He puts one arm through his life jacket and looks down at me. I look around, dazed.

'What time is it?' I say.

'About six. Come on, Yusra, get up,' he says, passing the tapes around his waist. 'I just told your parents we're on our way.'

I pull on my flip-flops and my life jacket. This time the smugglers can't get us to hurry. We traipse back down to the shore in silence. The wind is blowing hard now, loosening strands of my hair out of its bun and whipping them around my face. I think about Mum and Dad and Shahed. I wonder where they are, who they're with and what they're doing. I wonder if I'll ever see them again.

We reach the end of the trees where the path drops down to the beach. The sight of the ocean stops me dead. In the cove, the green water is chopping heavily and crashing onto the stones. Beyond is the darker open sea, flecked with white rows of churning teeth.

Ponytail is standing as before, waist-deep in the water. But now he braces himself every few seconds against a new wave, the swell battering the little boat behind him. The wind rips back my hair and flattens my jeans against my legs. There's a crush as we climb on board and the boat pitches precariously.

Ponytail and Mowgli pull the boat further out to where the waves are no longer breaking. It sits higher without the weight of the woman and her children. Mowgli hauls himself on board. He pulls the engine cord four or five times until it shudders and catches. The bow rises and we bump out of the cove.

Mowgli beckons to one of the Afghans sitting near him at the back. They huddle together over the engine for about a minute. Then, without a word, Mowgli swings his legs overboard and launches himself off the back of the boat. He sets off through the waves in a sloppy front crawl back towards the shore. I watch him, open-mouthed. No one said anything about one of us having to drive the boat. I tap Sara on the shoulder and she turns her head. I point to where Mowgli had been standing a few seconds before.

'He's not coming with us?' I shout above the engine.

She shrugs and shakes her head.

The waves loom bigger and darker beyond the shelter of the cove. They march towards us, glinting metallic in the sun. The dinghy hits the first one head on, rides up over the crest and crashes down into the trough. I'm drenched from behind by a wall of cold salt water. It sloshes over me onto floor of the boat and runs down the dinghy floor as we rise again on the next wave. We plunge down into the trough once more and water washes over the bow, hitting me in the back.

I wipe the hair from my forehead and take off my glasses to save them being knocked off. I can see without them, but the details get a bit soft. I hadn't counted on this. We're on a boat and I'm soaked. The Afghan misjudges the next wave and it hits the boat side on, sending us lurching over to the right as the crest sweeps under us. That's when the first prayers begin.

'*Ya Allah*!' calls Idris. 'There is no God but Allah.'

I repeat his prayer, mouthing the words under my breath as we ride down another wave. White water splashes up in the trough and hits my back and my arm. The wind rips and I shudder with cold.

'Glory be to Allah most great worthy of praise,' says Muhannad.

The others join in, repeating the prayer over and over as we rise again towards another crest. The passengers chant the words in one voice over the spluttering engine, mouthing the familiar phrases as the Afghan takes the waves one at a time. Mustafa gazes around, still smiling happily as the adults pray for their lives.

'*Astagh-Ferulah*,' I say, looking at him. 'Allah forgive me. Oh God, please help us.'

Fifteen minutes out into the open water, the engine chokes and gives up. We slow, and the bow of the boat drops down in the water. The prayers stop, and nobody speaks. All eyes are on the Afghan. He's pulling on the cord. We strain our ears, the boat spins, rises and falls, but the engine lies quiet.

A large wave rises from behind and the boat rides up it backwards. Nabih grabs the rope around the side of the boat. I do the same. We ride over the crest and crash down into the trough, spinning as a load of white water washes over the Afghan's back. A deep pool sloshes around my feet on the dinghy floor. The panic rises as the prayers begin again, louder than ever.

'Throw everything you can over the side,' says Muhannad, standing up and steadying himself on the tube.

We dump bags and shoes into the sea. We scoop up water in our hands and bail it out over the side. It's no good. More water washes in every time we plunge into a trough. We spin around and hit waves side on. They threaten to capsize us. Without the engine, we seem certain to sink. I stare in horror at the white, fizzing foam below. The others wouldn't survive if the boat emptied us out into these waves.

'We have to do something,' says Muhannad above the prayers.

He looks around the boat wildly. Then his face hardens. He's made up his mind.

'There is no might nor power except in Allah,' he says.

Muhannad bends down to grab the rope that runs around side of the boat. He swings one leg over the tube and straddles it, then he leans forwards and lifts his other leg over into the water. Still clinging onto the rope, he lowers his torso down until he's chest deep in the rolling waves. His eyes are wide, his face pale. I stare at him in admiration. This man can't swim. I look down at the water behind me. The boat has lifted slightly without his weight.

Sara struggles to her feet. She hands her plastic bag with the valuables to the Somali woman and turns to peer down into the water.

'We belong to Allah and to Him we shall return,' says Sara. She grabs the rope on the other side of the boat from Muhannad, straddles the tube and disappears down into the water. I watch her, open-mouthed.

The boat seems to be sitting even higher with Sara now in the water. Muhannad's idea is working, but still the boat needs more lift. I watch the Afghan pull on the engine cord and listen to the desperate prayers.

My heart is beating hard. I'm a swimmer. I'm not going to sit here crying like a baby. I've got to help. I'd never forgive myself if anything happened to these people. I look around at everyone's faces. Mustafa is still grinning at me like it's all a brilliant game. Nabih is pale and shivering. Majed looks like he's going to be sick. The Somali woman is watching me carefully.

I stand and dump my glasses in Majed's lap. I grip the rope and look over the side at the swell. Fear grips me for a second and I hesitate. I've never been in water like that before. I bend over the side and look down at Sara. She's treading water, staring up at the rising wave. She turns towards me.

'Don't you dare, Yusra!' she shouts. 'Stay on the boat.'

I frown and shake my head.

'You hear me?' Sara shouts. 'I mean it! Sit your ass back down.'

I grab the rope, swing my legs over the tube and slip down between the waves.

10

Sara's voice rises above the desperate prayers.

'Yusra! What the hell are you doing?'

I ignore her. The swell rises and falls. The shoulders of my life jacket stick up awkwardly around my ears. Now I'm in, the water is warmer than I imagined. At least near the surface. I wrap the rope tightly around one of my wrists and grip it in my fingers.

'Yusra!' she yells again. 'Get back on the boat.'

'No!' I shout. 'I can swim too. Why shouldn't I be in the water?'

'But without your glasses?' says Sara. 'You could get dizzy and faint. You know you can't control it. And then what? You'd let go of the rope and...'

I cut her off.

'If it's so dangerous, why are you in the water?' I shout. 'Stop freaking out. I'm a swimmer, I can do it.'

I stare at Sara, defiant. I'm going nowhere. The Afghan is pulling on the starter cord. Every few pulls produces a splutter, but the motor doesn't catch. This is a bad dream. It's just a nightmare. Nightmares have to end. I grip the rope more tightly.

Between the waves I glimpse the island: hazy green hills dotted with patches of grey rock. It's so close, but we could easily die within its sight. Half an hour away maybe. Just hold on for half an hour. Stay alive. Keep your nerve. Sara's with you. The others can't swim. We can save them.

The fragile boat rises and falls, drifts and spins. The Afghan pulls the cord. The engine doesn't even splutter now. One of the Sudanese passengers joins Muhannad in the water. It's working. Without us, the boat is higher in the water. But without the engine the rudder is no match for the whirling waves. Each one spins the dinghy round like a toy in a bathtub.

Another surge rises, the dark water looms above. We spin around full circle, back to face the way we've come. If the next wave hits at the wrong angle, it could easily capsize us.

'Turn it around,' shouts Muhannad.

We stop treading water and start kicking, pushing the bow to the left, to face the island. The boat hits the wave head on and rides up and over it, crashing down into the trough behind.

The pool is not the sea. In the pool, the water is limited, tame, and knowable. There are sides, there's a bottom. Swimming in these conditions it's like I have no muscle memory, like I've never swum before in my life.

We kick, push, and pull, but it's no good. We're swimmers, but in these waves, it just isn't possible for us to move the boat by swimming alone. Without the engine, we can't make any progress.

I focus on what we can do. We can stay in the water, make the boat lighter, lift it higher above the waves. We can support the boat from the outside, spin it round to face the swell head on, prevent it from capsizing. And we can make sure the boat is facing the right way, towards the island. We can ride the waves, ensure they are washing us in the right direction. Sara and I kick, scoop, and drag but it's no use. However hard we try we can't budge the boat. If our efforts move us towards the island at all, it's a matter of metres.

Ayham and Bassem are sitting on the tube directly above us. They both look down over the side, gazing at us in admiration.

'Hey, Ayham,' calls Sara after about twenty minutes. 'Can you do something about my jogging pants?' says Sara. 'They keep falling down.'

'I've got a knife,' says Ayham. 'We'll cut them off at the bottom. Pass me your leg.'

Sara spins around to face the open sea and lifts her right leg up out of the water towards him. Her trousers sag around her thighs, exposing her underwear. Despite everything, Bassem and I can't help but giggle. She's laughing too. I reach out with my free hand and hoist up the waistband to save her more embarrassment.

Ayham grabs her leg below the knee with both hands and hauls it up until her calf is resting on his thigh. Up on the boat the others are craning their necks to see. Behind Ayham, the two Iraqis and one of the Sudanese men are standing, knives out, ready to help.

'Woah,' says Ayham. 'Careful. Watch out for the boat. And there's a leg in there don't forget.'

He shoos them away and begins sawing at the soaked material, cutting it off in a rough circle just above her knee. Sara swaps legs and he does the other one. The two sides are uneven and ragged, but the trousers are lighter, and the elastic holds around Sara's waist.

'Better?' he asks.

'Better,' says Sara and resumes her earlier position.

Ayham stares into his phone. He has signal. Bassem digs in his pocket and hands him a scrap of paper. Ayham bashes in the Greek coastguard number and presses the phone to one ear. He waits. The prayers on the boat have stopped. Everyone's listening.

'We're drowning,' he shouts in English into the phone. 'Twenty persons. Women and children too. A tiny kid. The engine is broken. The boat is sinking.'

There's a pause while Ayham listens to the response.

'No, you don't understand,' he says. 'We can't go back; the motor is broken. We're dying. Please, you have to save us.'

He takes the phone away from his ear and stares at the screen in disbelief. Ayham frantically bashes more numbers into his phone. He can't get through to anyone else.

'The Greeks just said to go back,' he says. 'I can't reach the Turkish coastguard.'

No one on the boat has a number for Big Man, Mowgli, or Ponytail, so Ayham calls the middleman smuggler contact back in Istanbul. The man says there's nothing he can do. At last, Ayham tries his parents.

'Dad?' says. 'Don't panic. I need your help. We're in the sea and our boat is broken. Can you post on that Facebook group for boats in distress? I'll send you the pin of our location.'

I think of Mum and fight back the tears. What will she do if she sees the post on Facebook? Will she think we've died? Or will she expect us to swim, to save the others?

'We love you too,' Ayham is saying. 'I have to go now, to save the battery.'

Ayham hangs up and puts his phone away. No one speaks as the waves batter the boat. The Afghan pulls the cord, but the engine lies dead. The passengers are weak with hunger and fear. They begin to pray again, chanting in one voice.

I battle the waves. At the top of each swell, a choppy peak of seawater thwacks my head against the boat. Salt water shoots into my eyes, nose, and mouth. At the bottom of each trough, my jeans suck and pull me down, the life jacket pushes up around my ears and the scratchy material rubs raw against my neck.

Muhannad calls from the other side of the boat that he's had enough. It's someone else's turn to get in the sea. Idris bends over the side and helps Muhannad and the Sudanese man out of the water. The boat rocks dangerously as they flop down onto the floor. Muhannad stands and looks around. He points at Nabih and Majed.

'Your turn to go in the water,' he says.

Majed stands and looks queasily over board.

'But I can't swim,' he says.

'No time for arguments,' says Muhannad. 'I can't swim either. Just hold onto the rope.'

'I can't see anything without my glasses,' says Majed. 'I'll die.'

'Yes, I suppose that's the situation,' says Muhannad. 'Probably that's the worst that could happen. But then it would all be over, eh? Nothing more to worry about.'

Majed folds his arms, shakes his head. The boat sits low in the water with the extra weight. Each wave spins it around ninety degrees. The bow hits the next big wave head on and rides over the crest. It hits the trough and a bucketload of water sloshes onto the floor. The panicked passengers bail it out with their hands.

'We're facing the wrong way,' shouts Sara. We kick and steer the bow around, aiming the boat back towards the island.

Nabih stands, looks over the side and takes a deep breath. He straddles the tube and disappears down into the water. Majed stands and looks like he's going to be sick. He purses his lips and climbs in next to Nabih. After ten minutes they want to get out and Blondie hauls them up. Muhannad looks around the desperate passengers for another volunteer. Ayham and Bassem look at each other. Bassem stands.

'I'll go,' he says. 'I'm heavier.'

Bassem climbs into the swell between me and Sara. He grips the rope tight with both hands, his face pale, his eyes wide.

'Just hold on,' Sara tells him. 'You'll be ok.'

He forces a laugh.

'If you can do it, I can,' he says and blows her a kiss.

Holding the rope, I shimmy around to the other side to balance the boat. Idris slips into the waves next to me. Mustafa's face appears above us in the gap where his father had been sitting. He looks at me with big, serious eyes. He points at me, then at his father, then at the hunched row of adults praying on the boat. They ignore him.

Mustafa looks back at us and claps his hands together with a shout. His face breaks into a smile. I stick my tongue out at him and catch a slosh of salty water in my mouth. I screw up my face in disgust. Mustafa claps his hands again and chuckles. I cross my eyes and blow out my cheeks. He points again and screams in delight.

The Afghan is pulling on the cord. I look again at the island and fight a rising well of despair. It looks further away than ever. The engine is dead. We're drifting. There's little more to do than hold on and wait. When the waves spin us round, the four of us guide the dinghy back on course for the island.

The prayers grow louder. The dinghy rides down another towering wave and spins ninety degrees to the right. A jet of water splashes up and sloshes forwards into the boat. We kick and guide it around to hit the next wave head on. The rope is cutting red friction burns into my palms. I wrap it again diagonally around my wrists. I look at my fingertips. They're wrinkled and pale.

The sun is hanging lower in the sky, inching down towards the island. It's slanting into my eyeline, blinding me. I guess we've been on the water about an hour and a half. An hour and a half to cross ten kilometres of water. We might be arriving about now if the engine hadn't died. A shrill, high-pitched blast sounds out from the boat above. Mustafa has found the dinghy's standard-issue distress whistle and is blowing it, hard. Idris calls to him from the water next to me.

'Cut it out, Mustafa,' his voice is weak and exhausted.

Muhannad bends sideways towards the boy, his hand outstretched.

'Give it to me,' he says.

'No,' says Mustafa.

The boy shrieks with laughter and clasps the whistle with both hands, pulling it into his stomach. Muhannad stands and grabs Mustafa by the shoulders, but he twists out of the grip. The older man shrugs and sits down. Mustafa grins and blows triumphantly on the whistle. Everyone winces from the piercing noise, but no one has the strength to stop his fun. He's not registering the danger. Let him play.

A collective shout goes up from the boat. The Afghan is agitated, shouting in Farsi and pointing to something behind me. I turn my head and see another dinghy, sliding through the surf about thirty metres away.

'Help, wait, over here!' I join the shouts and free one of my wrists from the rope. I lift my arm in a wide, arching wave.

The dinghy is dark grey, like ours, but far longer. About forty figures in bright-orange life jackets huddle on top of the inflatable tubing, facing inwards. Despite the cargo, the long boat is riding high, dipping and rising in the swell, bracing confidently against the onslaught of the waves. A proud, foaming white wake crashes from its bow.

We shout louder. Mustafa laughs and blasts on the whistle. Two of the huddled figures nearest us turn their heads and point towards our boat, shouting something to the driver. They don't change course. The boat ploughs headlong into the waves. After a few agonizing moments, it disappears altogether. We're alone again. Just us, the setting sun and, between the waves, the maddening view of the island.

I wrap the rope more tightly around my wrists. I'm stunned.

They had room for us. How could they leave us to drown? The shock deepens to anger, a warm rage fills my belly. The sun is sinking faster now down to meet the island's peaks. The island looks as far away as ever. As near as ever.

I screw my eyes shut. We're swimmers, we'll save them. We can keep the boat on course, keep it from capsizing or sinking. The wind whips and the cold sets in again, working into my feet, my calves, and my thigh muscles. I can feel my legs beginning to seize up. I wish the waves would stop for a minute.

My mind races. Maybe the current will take us. Maybe the waves will wash us up on shore. Maybe the engine will come back on. Maybe we can swim it after all. What was it that Sara said before? Forget everyone else and just swim. It could be a way out. We could swim. It's like our secret weapon. I could shimmy round the boat and get Sara. We could set off into the waves together. Leave the others to their fate. It's not my fault they can't swim. But how could I live on after that?

Mustafa is staring again from the boat. I suck my cheeks in to make a fish face and cross my eyes. He giggles. One of the Sudanese guys turns in his seat above and smiles down at me.

'You're so brave,' he says.

I force a grin.

'Let's just get there,' I say.

I look away at the water. The rolling waves are glinting dark purple, the white crests creamy yellow in the last rays of the sun. I struggle. Just leave me alone, I think. This is no time for talking. The man's voice echoes in my head. So brave.

I hear Bassem and Sara laughing from the other side of the boat. She's not going anywhere. Next to me, Idris grips the rope in grim silence. I wish I had Bassem to distract me. Another huge wave comes barrelling up ahead. We're probably safer holding on here, I tell myself as we spin the boat back to face the island. I doubt even strong swimmers can survive alone out there. And besides, we're the swimmers. We said we'd save them.

The last slither of red sun slips down behind the island. The top slopes of the hills are deep pink. Above them, the sky is brownish yellow and fades gradually up into pastel blue. A faint semi-circle moon appears in the sky.

My eyes are stinging and swollen from the salt. I screw them shut and focus. Scenes play out against the red of my closed eyelids. Dad throws me into the water. The tank takes aim on our road in Daraya. The bomb rips through the roof and sploshes into the pool. We huddle in the basement, listening to the masonry falling around outside.

If I drown now, it was all for nothing. No time to live, no time to win. I'm in my bed in Damascus. I form the words in my head. I'm not here. This isn't happening. We rise on another big wave and I open my eyes. Overhead, the brightest stars prick through the deeper blue of the night. The light is fading fast and the swell is blue-black and higher than ever. I close my eyes again, fight to shut it all out.

What if there's a fish, says a voice in my head. A bolt of fear shoots to my gut. A huge fish in the darkness below, a swimming mouth, all muscle and giant teeth. I picture my legs from below, dangling helplessly in the swell. Prey. A meal. I open my eyes. Push the voice away. Look, there's Mustafa, up on the boat, he's still smiling. The dark waves march on. I strain my eyes, try to see through the surface of the inky water. It glimmers in the last light like emulsion paint.

Before long the voice is back. This place is a cemetery, it says. Think of all those people, just like you, who drowned right here. Young people, old people, mothers and their babies, thousands of lives snuffed out in the waves. There are probably remains of bodies on the seabed below you. Never buried, never taken home to their loved ones. Never even identified. Just another statistic forgotten by the world.

I tell the voice to shut up. But it is clearly enjoying itself. Hour after hour they suffered like this, the voice goes on, battled to survive on the sea. For nothing. The water took all their strength, and then it took them. All those horrible deaths. And nobody listening to their cries for help. I bet it hurts when you drown, says the voice, full of malice. Why don't you just give up now and get it over with?

Just let it be over, I shout at the voice in my head. Either we drown or we arrive. Something has to happen. I shudder. My muscles ache from the gnawing cold, my stomach clenches from the sea water I've swallowed. Tears blur my vision. I fight them back. Another five minutes and the engine will come on. Another five minutes of pain. Just survive, stay alive another five minutes. Let your body take over. Trust it. Shut down your mind and let it work.

I let my mind drift and it stays quiet. Minutes pass. I cling onto the rope, turn the boat, tread water, survive. Then at once I'm hit by the absurdity of the situation. I almost laugh out loud. Maybe the voice can explain. What are we doing here, I ask it, taking on the raging sea in a flimsy toy? How did it get this far? When did our lives get so cheap? Is this really the only way out, the only escape from the bombs?

The voice is ready with an answer. That's the gamble, it says. Or would you rather wait until the bomb drops on your home, the roof collapses in on your bed while you sleep? That's the choice you took. That's the deal, those are your options, get out or die trying. My eyes still screwed shut, I open my mouth and lift my voice to join the prayers.

'Save us, God,' I say out loud. 'Give me strength. Give me courage. Make the waves stop, kill the wind, lift up the boat on the water. *Ya Allah*. Let this be over.'

I open my eyes and look up to the darkening sky. There, soaring and bobbing on the thermals at the bow of the boat, is a small white gull with black-tipped wings. It stays level with us and hangs on the air as if it wants to show us the way. Look, I tell the voice. God is with us. He hears our prayers.

'I can't any more,' comes Bassem's voice from the other side of the boat. 'Bring me up.'

Ayham bends over and hauls his brother out of the sea. Bassem is stiff, his limbs rigid. Ayham lays him out on the floor of the boat like a dead man. He lies there shivering, unable to speak or move. Idris lifts his arm weakly, signalling he has also had enough. Muhannad hauls him out. I realise my legs have seized up completely. After three hours at sea, it's only the rope and the life jacket that are keeping my head above water.

'I want to get out,' I say.

'And me,' comes Sara's voice from the other side of the boat. 'Someone else's turn.'

Muhannad reaches down from the boat. I grab his hands and he pulls me up onto the boat. I slump on the floor, shaking with exhaustion, my teeth chattering from the cold. Ayham pulls Sara in. She drops to the floor next to me. We clamber to sit on the tube. The waves batter and spin the boat around once more. Water sloshes in as we ride the waves.

Next to me on the bow, Nabih is shaking violently, his eyes vacant, his face deathly pale. His breathing is shallow and raspy. I try to catch his eye but he's no longer registering what's going on. Majed is beside him, his skin sickly yellow, his eyes glazed over. He stares grimly at his feet. The Afghan renews his efforts. He pulls on the cord. It splutters.

'Where are my glasses?' I say to Majed.

No response. I reach out and wave my hand in front of his face. He points down at the water behind him. He's thrown them overboard.

'What?' I shout. 'Majed! I need them to see. I asked you to look after them.'

Majed stares through me, not registering what I'm saying. He's concentrating on the spluttering engine. The Afghan pulls the cord again and the motor coughs alive. I draw breath as a roar erupts from the engine. The bow lifts out of the water and starts forwards, churning white spray out behind it. The low foaming wake crashes and fizzes out into the deep blue.

'*Alhamdulillah*,' breathes Muhannad. 'Praise God.'

Hope, joy, and relief electrify the exhausted passengers. More stars appear against the blue overhead. A thin smudge of orange still hugs the horizon above the hills to the right where the sun went. A blurry row of white lights dances on the shoreline below, marking where the black sea ends and the black island begins. Is it nearer than before? The engine is running well now, but no one has the energy to celebrate. And anyway, we've learned not to trust it.

'We'll get there faster if somebody gets back in the water,' says Muhannad, looking around the drained faces.

Nobody speaks. Everyone looks at Sara, shivering next to me on the tube. Their stares take in her strong shoulders, her powerful legs. Some of them look at me, too. My teeth chatter, my shoulders shake uncontrollably. Their eyes flit back to Sara.

Wasn't she the big swimmer, their eyes seemed to say, boasting about how she could swim to Greece? Sara looks from face to face, drinking in their pleading looks. I look around the boat. It's not fair. Surely someone else will step up. The silence lasts, the stares intensify. Their eyes bore into Sara, willing her, daring her, to finish what she started.

At last, Sara sighs and stands again. Her face is drawn and desperate, her eyes red and almost swollen shut from the salt. I say nothing, but I'm filled with pity, gratitude, and pride. My brave sister. Shivering, she grabs the rope and climbs once more into the black water.

Ayham turns around to face her and kneels on the floor, leaning head and shoulders over the tube towards her.

'Grab my hands,' he says. She reaches up with one hand, holding onto the rope with the other.

'My shoulders,' she moans over the noise of the engine. 'Stretch them.'

Sara lets go of the rope and catches Ayham's other hand. He holds her out of the water while she hangs limply, the water running by her chest, her head flopping forwards onto the side of the boat. Nobody speaks. At last, we're making progress. We raise our eyes towards the island, looming larger, darker now against the navy sky.

After about twenty minutes Sara lifts her head.

'Please,' she begs. 'Please. I'm so cold. Let me back on.'

Ayham hauls her onto the boat. She sinks onto the floor in front of me and leans her back against my legs. I can hear her teeth chattering. She hugs her knees to her chest and lets her head fall between them.

The wind drops, and the waves die down as we approach land. The engine chugs and the boat rides easily through the dropping swell. Through the grainy night a long smudge of straight, grey beach looms ahead.

'We're close,' says Muhannad. 'Mind the rocks.'

Sara lifts her head and hauls herself up to sit next to me on the tube. She unfastens her life jacket and drops it on the floor in front of her. Then she straddles the tube and slides back into the inky water. I watch, open-mouthed, as Sara treads water, holding the rope and pulling a kind of half-breaststroke with the other arm. Passing the rope through her hands, she shimmies along the bow, kicking off the submerged rocks when she finds them and guiding the boat on shore.

She dunks underwater to check the depth. A few seconds later she surfaces again. I watch her, waiting for a sign. She sinks under again and surfaces faster this time, grinning.

'That's it,' says Sara. 'That's land.'

11

I jump down into the knee-high water. The other passengers spill out of the boat behind me. Mustafa climbs onto Idris's back, flinging his arms around his father's neck. The Afghan is the last to get out. He leaves the motor running and the boat smashes into the boulders at the end of the beach. The group lets out a sigh of spite and relief. Justice for the boat that almost killed us. The prayers of thanks ring in my ears as I wade on shore.

'Thank God,' I mutter under my breath, too exhausted to feel anything but numb relief. 'Thank God. Thank God.'

Fist-sized stones cut into my bare feet and I remember my flip-flops. I'd last seen them in the boat. I hobble over to where the dinghy lies in a rock pool. The bow is partly crushed and jammed between two boulders. I can just make out a pair of men's black trainers in the water sloshing around inside. Nothing else. There's no sign of my flip-flops. Or my glasses. I rip off my life jacket and check. Yes, my passport is still in the plastic wallet in my bra.

Several of the men advance on the boat, their faces screwed up in anger. Each of them carries a knife in one hand. They fall on the boat, ripping into the tube in few fast, furious movements. It spews out the air in a sigh of protest. Deflated it looks so small, nothing but a grey rag. I turn my back on it.

Sara is standing a little way off, motionless, hands on hips, gazing down the long straight beach towards the lights. The Somali woman runs to her, pulls her into a tight bear hug. Then the woman comes to me, arms outstretched, tears streaming down her face. In her arms I feel nothing, only cold, exhaustion, and a terrible thirst.

'You're my hero,' she says into my ear and kisses my red, swollen cheek.

It hits me. We survived. My arms and legs feel like dead weights. I bend double. I take a few deep breaths and let the euphoria wash over me. We made it. It's over. The joy lasts only a few seconds. My mind races quickly onto the next set of urgent problems. I need water, food, sleep.

Our cousins Nabih and Majed are already traipsing down the scrabbly beach, stumbling over rocks and shreds of spiky, dry driftwood in the dark. The other passengers are unfastening and discarding their life jackets onto the stones. Many have their phones out, the lights from the screens fan out along the beach like glow-worms.

The beach is narrow, the group walks in single file. An old stone wall rises to the left, covered in scratchy coastal vines. Majed talks into his phone at the head of the procession. He stops and waits by a low stone building. Sara reaches him first and he gives her the handset.

Sara passes me the phone when I draw level. It's Dad. I don't feel much like talking. Dad's words sound a long way away, like he's calling to me through a fog. I stare at a rusting iron gate in the stone wall and try and focus on his voice. I picture Mum's face as he talks. I wonder whether she knows we're alive.

I pass the phone back to Majed and glance at the time on the screen. It reads 9:38. We're still on Turkish time. Three and a half hours since we set off into the waves. It felt like ten. Thirst grips me again and I set off, following the others down the beach towards the lights.

I reach a collection of wooden tables covered with chequered blue plastic. A cobbled pathway leads to a low restaurant building. Either side, bare bulbs are strung up between the fruit trees. Business looks slow, the tables are deserted. I stand at the end of the path and peer in.

An older man sits at one of the tables. He wears a blue and white chequered shirt that matches the table cloths. He's leaning back, his right arm hooked over the back of his chair, a lit cigarette in his hand. He watches me in silence. To his right, sits a younger man in a navy t-shirt. The man is leaning forwards with his legs apart, his hands clasped between his thighs. He's watching me too.

A large, blonde Labrador looks up from under the table. I take a step forwards on the path. The dog jumps to its feet and barks, ears back, tail thrashing, shifting between its two front legs and staring me down. I hesitate.

'I just want to buy a bottle of water,' I call over to the men in English.

The older one mutters something but doesn't move. The dog barks frantically.

'Hello?' I try again. 'Water? Juice? Cola? I have money.'

At last, the younger man stands and grabs the dog by its collar.

'No,' he calls and flicks his hand as if he's shooing away a stray cat. 'No water.'

I turn back towards the beach feeling like I've been punched in the stomach. The hurt turns to anger. The men must have had a perfect view of our landing. They could see my wet clothes, hear the shakiness in my voice. What human refuses to sell water to a girl who just washed up in front of their restaurant?

Sara raises her eyebrows as I stagger back towards the group. She knows not to ask.

'Let's get out of here,' I say.

Idris is watching us from further down the beach. He's carrying Mustafa on one arm. The little boy giggles and struggles when he sees me. Idris puts him down and he gallops over the stones and wraps his arms around my waist. I put one arm around his shoulder and we slip and slide together across the gravelly beach.

I follow the group off the beach and onto a dirt road lined with a row of buildings that look like private homes. Mustafa's teeth are chattering, he's shivering violently. I start off down a little track to the first house, the boy still clinging to my waist. As we get nearer, I see a blonde girl about my age watching us from behind a gate. I stop. Mustafa tries to hide behind me.

'Hi,' I say in English.

'*Yassas*,' she says.

She looks at my soaked jeans and my bare feet and then at the little boy shivering by my side. I take a deep breath.

'Do you have anything dry for the kid to wear?' I say.

'Sure,' she says. 'Wait here.'

She disappears inside the house. Moments later she's back, carrying a pair of scuffed lace-up trainers and a large navy-blue pullover. My heart sings. The girl hands the shoes to me and holds up the pullover in both hands. I smile and put my right hand on my chest.

'Thank you,' I say, putting the shoes on the floor and taking the pullover.

I turn to Mustafa.

'Arms up,' I say.

I pull it over his head. It's thick and dry, but much too big for him. The sleeves hang over his hands, so I roll them up over his wrists. I bend down and pull the shoes onto my feet. They're too big, but I tie the laces tight and they stay on. I straighten up and give the girl two thumbs-up.

'Wait one second,' she says and jogs back up the steps into the house.

She returns seconds later with two glasses of water. I smile gratefully and drain the glass. Mustafa does the same. I look back through the trees along the dark road. Idris is loitering at the end of the track waiting for Mustafa. I smile at the girl again. We head off to find the others. The boy runs ahead into his father's arms.

'Nice pullover,' says Idris, mussing the boy's hair.

We follow the rest of the group down the road, Mustafa between us. I notice Idris isn't wearing shoes.

'Hey, Mustafa,' I say.

The boy looks up.

'Did you enjoy the trip?' I say.

He frowns.

'On the boat,' I say. 'Did you have fun? You want to do it again?'

'No,' he says firmly and shakes his head.

'Why not?' I say, laughing.

'Daddy was in the water,' he says.

I grimace and push away the vision of the marching waves. After a few hundred metres, the dirt road meets concrete, makes a hairpin bend to the left and begins to rise inland. Sara is waiting for us at the corner. She's wearing the black shoes I saw floating in the boat.

They're several sizes too big for her and she squelches with every step.

We trudge on, past the last of the small farms. On our right, clusters of pines cling to a sheer rocky slope. The light breeze dies, the wash from the sea grows quieter and the cicadas louder as we start to climb. The black landscape rises sharply ahead. Far above, only the stars mark the line where the hill ends and the night begins. There's no electric light in sight.

Sara breaks the silence.

'What happened to his mum?' she says.

Idris looks up. His face hardens.

'His mother and her whole family were killed,' says Idris. 'In one airstrike.'

I catch my breath.

'I'm sorry,' says Sara.

'It's just us now,' he goes on quickly. 'If I were alone I would have stayed in Iraq. I had a good job, I was making good money. But he needs a future.'

We walk on in silence and find the others waiting for us at a fork in the road. One path snakes back down the hill to our right, the other turns sharply to the left and heads on up the mountain. Majed and Ayham are looking at their phones. They are both running out of battery. We look around. Still no lights in sight. I look back down the road we've just walked up. A little further down, I can just make out two dark-skinned men approaching. Each carries an orange life jacket. As they pass us Muhannad asks them where they are going. They shrug and say something in a language we don't understand. They turn left and walk off up the mountain.

'Left it is then,' says Muhannad and starts off up the road.

I sigh and follow. The others are laughing with relief. The brothers Ayham and Bassem are giggling to each other, joking about Sara's ragged trousers.

'Good job, Ayham,' says Bassem. 'When we get to Germany you can start a new life as a tailor. Here comes Sara in this summer's hottest fashion: distressed sea shorts.'

As we climb on, my mind empties and grows blank. I don't

think about the sea. I'm so exhausted, I don't even notice how thirsty I am. I just want to sleep. I concentrate on my breath and keeping up the same pace. Steady, deliberate steps. We trudge on, up the winding road under the stars. After an hour or so I hear a faint murmur of voices. Turning another corner, I look up to see a cluster of lights on the hill above. A village.

We wind on up the road, round the next corner, and see the source of the noise. A large, flattened niche in the side of the road. A bus stop. Tonight, it's a makeshift campsite. Hundreds of people are lying or sitting in small groups on the concrete. As we pass, a few of them stare and point at Sara's massacred jogging bottoms. She ignores them. I spot the two Farsi men we followed up the hill. They lie side by side on the edge of the road, their heads resting on the life jackets.

We walk on. We're all starving and desperate for somewhere to sit, rest, and eat. The road forks and we turn right, following a line of people squatting along a tall stone wall. The people thin out as the road bends and cuts into the mountain. On our right, the land drops steeply down to the coast where we landed, on our left a village clings to the rising slope.

At last, we find what we've been looking for. A crowded terrace on our right, bordered with vine-covered trellises. On the other side of the road stands a humble, one-storey building. Above the door: 'Η Ρεματιά. Bar. Taverna.'

We file onto the terrace. We're too tired to register the stares of the Greek families finishing their meals in the warm night. All twenty of us settle around a few long, low tables in the corner furthest from the entrance. I sit on a bench overlooking the shadowy valley. Above, the stars, below the darker blue of the sea.

A middle-aged woman with springy, brown hair comes over to take our order. She smiles at us. Sara orders water and fries and follows the woman inside to find a plug to charge our phones. I get up too, cross the road, and climb some steps to find the toilet, a stone hut on top of the building's flat roof. I turn on the bare light-bulb, sending long-legged insects and mosquitos flitting around the white walls. I peer into the mirror.

Both of my shoulders are raw from the life jacket. A long red scratch runs from the corner of my left eyebrow down to my cheek and a purple bruise is already rising above my left temple. My whole neck is swollen red from the salt. I feel dizzy and miss my glasses. I lean on the sink and close my eyes. The waves roll behind my eyelids. Nausea rises, I open my eyes and steady myself, drawing deep breaths.

Back at the table there are several big bottles of water. I grab one and down half of it in one go. The woman brings bowls of bread, olives, and fried potatoes. We eat in silence, like machines. Everyone is too tired to talk. The woman comes back to collect our plates. She looks at me, then at Sara. Then she sees Mustafa and smiles again.

'Are you refugees?' she says.

That word. It's strange to finally hear it spoken out loud.

'We just came on a boat,' says Sara.

'Do you have somewhere to sleep?' the woman asks.

Sara shakes her head.

'Follow the road down the hill,' says the woman. 'There's a small church. It's open. You can all sleep inside.'

Sara looks surprised.

'But we're Muslims,' she says.

The woman raises her eyebrows and puts her hand on Sara's forearm.

'You think I care about that?' she says. She sounds almost offended. 'No one will bother you.'

The woman tells us we should go to the bus stop around the corner the next morning. Some volunteers are running a bus from there. It leaves every morning at seven and will take us where we need to go. Sara thanks her and holds out two yellow fifty-euro notes. The woman's eyes widen. She takes one of the notes and disappears inside.

'What's your name?' Sara asks the woman when she comes back with the change.

'Nicki,' says the woman. 'And yours?'

'Sara,' she says, then points at me. 'My little sister, Yusra. Thank you for your help, Nicki.'

We drag ourselves to our feet and slog another ten minutes down the road. At last, we reach a tiny white chapel on a raised platform nestled into the mountainside. The building isn't much bigger than a stable. An iron cross stands at either end of the sloping tiled roof. The church door is set facing away from the road. I try it, it swings open. The Somali woman looks around nervously. She has covered her hair and is wearing *hijab,* she can't sleep in a room with men who aren't her relatives.

Muhannad takes charge. He tells me, Sara, Mustafa, and the Somali woman to sleep inside. He says the men will sleep on the long stone table and benches set into the paving stones to the left of the door. It's freezing, and all of us are still damp from the sea. I feel bad for the others, but there's no other way.

'Whose shoes are these, anyway?' says Sara, undoing the black trainers.

'Mine,' says Idris. He walks over and takes her hand in his, lifts it up and brushes it against his cheek. 'You can keep them after what you did.'

'Don't be silly,' says Sara. 'We're all family now.'

I push the wooden door and step inside the tiny church. The only light comes from three lit candles stuck into the sand on top of a black metal stand in one corner. The candles throw flickering shadows on the bare stone walls. I stare at the gold and brown pictures mounted on them. One shows a mother carrying a baby. Another shows three flat-faced men with circles round their heads.

Mustafa curls up on an old, patterned carpet against the far wall. The Somali woman takes off her headscarf to use as a pillow. I lie down next to Sara, back-to-back for warmth. I can feel her shivering.

I close my eyes and the waves march behind my eyelids. They rise over and over, and I feel the swell lifting me and sucking me down. I'm still in the sea. I lie flat on my back and open my eyes to stop the rolling sensation. I close them again and see strings of blurry white lights dancing on the shoreline. Then Mustafa's face breaks into a toothy grin.

PART FIVE

The Trap

12

My eyes flick open. My muscles twinge as I shift onto my side. The little boy, Mustafa, is sitting nearby, on the church floor, looking at me. I stand and steady myself on the whitewashed wall. We made it across the barrier, across the sea. We're in Europe. And we're alive.

The wooden door creaks as I push it open. I step out and screw my eyes up against the light. The sun has already risen. We have a bus to catch. Majed stands nearby, studying his phone. He says we're outside a village called Sikaminea. He pronounces the word syllable by syllable, reading carefully from the screen. I peer over his shoulder at the map. We're on the northern shore of an island called Lesbos. It's a full day's walk south from here to Mytilene, the island's capital city. All new arrivals need to go there to register with the authorities and buy a ferry ticket for the onward journey to mainland Greece.

We aren't the only new arrivals. For years, islanders have watched a steady trickle of Syrians and others landing here on smuggler boats from Turkey. But this summer is different. No one had been expecting so many of us. In August 2015 alone, the month we arrive, more than eighty thousand newcomers arrive by sea to these islands. Greek authorities are struggling to cope and are relying heavily on the support of volunteers. Lesbos isn't a wealthy community, but the locals are generous. Fishermen take their boats out to sea on spontaneous rescue missions. Others donate food, medicines, and clothes, and even open their homes to those seeking shelter.

I cup my hands into the old fountain opposite the church door. I splash the cool water on my swollen face and raw neck and turn back to the others. Bassem and his brother Ayham have woken up and are getting ready to leave. Sara steps out of the church and I stifle a laugh.

'My God,' I say. 'What happened to you?'

Her face is red and covered in scratches and blue bruises. Her hair has come out of its bun and sticks up in wiry strands around her head. The ragged remains of her trousers are streaked white with dried salt.

'Shut up,' says Sara sleepily. 'You should see what you look like.'

Majed leads the group back along the road, past the restaurant we stopped at the night before, towards the car park to find the bus. We turn the corner and stop dead in our tracks. It's chaos. A scrum of people is pushing and shoving, fighting their way desperately onto a tiny minivan. It's the only volunteer-run transport leaving from this village today and everyone wants to be on it. I scan the crowd. A blonde woman in a high-vis jacket stands at the bus door. She seems to be in charge. Sara marches over, tells the woman we want to go to Mytilene and asks if we can get on the bus.

'Don't you have a stamp?' says the blonde woman and points at the back of Sara's hand.

Sara shakes her head. The woman points at the crowd. The others have been waiting here for days to get on a bus, she says. The ink stamp on their hands marks their place in the queue. I sigh in despair. We're all exhausted, in need of a shower and a bed. None of us are in a state to walk the forty-five kilometres to Mytilene. We might not make it by nightfall. That would mean another night out in the open. I shudder at the thought. The woman takes pity on us and tells us to walk further inland, to a town called Man-tamados. Another bus will there leave at midday. There have been fewer arrivals there and we'll have a better chance of getting on board.

Majed finds the town on the map. It's a three-hour walk away. My heart sinks and my stomach growls. I'm achy, starving, and still covered in salt from the sea. But I don't have a choice. We have to keep moving. We follow Majed up along the winding mountain road. Terraces of olive groves cling to the rocky slope to our right. To our left, a dry valley plunges down to the sparkling sea. The sight of it makes me feel sick. I avoid looking at it and focus instead on the baking concrete beneath my feet. The sun is high by the time we turn a corner and spot a cluster of red rooftops in the valley below. A dusky-pink church spire rises between the buildings.

'That's it,' says Majed, consulting his phone. 'Mant-a-ma-dos.'

The road plunges downhill and winds steeply back up through the town. We trudge up the hill until we reach a bus stop. A crowd of waiting Syrians and Afghans tells us we're in the right place. We settle down next to them in the sun to wait for the bus. From among the rooftops the church bell chimes half past eleven. After a few minutes, Sara struggles to her feet and says she's going to look for some new trousers. She reaches out her hand to pull me up. I follow her up a side road and into a small, dark clothes shop. A woman looks up from the back as we walk in.

'*Yassas*,' says the woman and smiles.

Sara smiles back and points to the ragged material round her thigh. The woman raises her eyebrows, turns, and walks to the back of the shop. The shopkeeper picks Sara out some black sweatpants and hands them over. Sara thanks her and gives the woman a large, pink euro note. The woman's eyes grow wide as she looks at it. It's a small fortune.

'Five hundred,' says the woman and points at the number in the top corner. 'Five hundred euros.'

'Sorry,' says Sara. 'It's too much?'

The woman sighs, tells us to wait, takes the note from Sara and disappears out of the shop. A few minutes later she returns with a wad of yellow notes and begins counting them slowly out onto the table. Just then our cousin Nabih appears behind us at the shop door.

'It's here,' he says.

Sara grabs the notes and her new trousers, and we sprint out of the shop. Back at the bus stop we find an ancient navy minibus waiting, engine chugging. The others are crowding around the door. At the head of the crush stands a male volunteer.

'Families first,' he shouts.

The volunteer points at Mustafa.

'Where's this kid's mum?'

Sara doesn't miss a beat. She raises her hand.

'That's me,' she says.

She points at me and the others.

'This is my sister. And these are my cousins.'

The volunteer stamps the back of our hands with ink as we climb on board. Who cares if we aren't really all blood relations? We feel like family after what we've been through. I rest my head on the minibus window and stare out as we wind south across the island, rising and dipping with the coastal road. An hour later, the minibus drops us in a large car park outside the port in the city of Mytilene. I gaze around. Hundreds of people are camping on the concrete. Many of them are waiting to register with the authorities. Others have already registered and are waiting to buy a ferry ticket to the mainland. A disorderly queue leads into the crumbling port authority building where registrations are taking place. We settle down to wait on the tarmac. It's several hours before we get inside the building. A man in a uniform takes our photo, then he asks in English where we are from and where we are going. Sara translates for the others.

'Germany,' Sara tells the man firmly. 'We're going to find my friend Hala. In Hanover.'

The official tells us to return to the office two days from now to collect a temporary residence permit. In the European Union, there's an agreement which says we have to apply for asylum in the first country we enter. In normal times, other European countries are allowed to send people back to apply for asylum on the borders of the EU. But these aren't normal times. No one is sending asylum-seekers back to Greece right now, the country is too over-whelmed with people. And anyway, we don't want to stay in Greece. We're going to Germany. Only once we have our papers can we buy tickets for the overnight ferry to the Greek mainland. In practice, this piece of paper, this residence permit, is a legal waiver that allows us to move on further into Europe.

We shuffle back out into the glaring sunshine and scan the crowd. Our original group from Damascus, Muhannad and

Blondie and our cousins Majed and Nabih are still with us, as are
the brothers Ayham and Bassem. But we've lost Idris, his boy
Mustafa, and the others from the boat somewhere in the queue. I
look around. We need showers, we need a place to rest, to digest
last night's ordeal. Sara and Bassem volunteer to look for a hotel.
We follow them out to the edge of the car park. There are people
everywhere, some of them have even set up tents on the tarmac.
The late-afternoon sun is still relentless. We find a spot in the shade
to wait and Bassem and Sara wander off into town. An hour later,
they reappear. Sara looks like she's been crying.

'None of the hotels will let us stay because we're Syrian,' says
Sara, slumping down on the step next to me.

'They all want to see that registration paper first,' says Bassem,
flopping down next to her. 'Paper, paper, paper. We tried the whole
city.'

A man in a high-vis jacket walks past. I jump up, wave, and ask
him where we can sleep. He tells us we have to go to a temporary
camp that has been set up for asylum-seekers. The man points to
where a free bus goes from around the corner. We're just struggling
to our feet when we hear a familiar voice.

'Yusra! Sara! You're alive. Thank God.'

We look up. It's Zaher, the dad of the baby I met in the smuggler camp. He walks towards us, arms outstretched. His
heart-shaped face breaks into a wide smile.

'*Alhamdulillah*,' says Zaher and kisses each of us several times
on both cheeks. 'Last night, we thought... We thought you hadn't
made it.'

Zaher won't hear of us going to the camp to sleep. He's heard
it is already so overcrowded that people have to sleep outside on
the floor. Zaher tells us to come with him to a nearby park where
he's been sleeping rough with his family and the others from the
smuggler camp. They've been using the showers and bathrooms at
a nearby private beach. I look at Sara and shrug. It will be good to
be among friends. And it seems sleeping rough is the only choice
on this overcrowded island. Zaher offers to show us a shop nearby
where we can buy sleeping bags. We follow him out of the port car

park, across the road and turn right around a corner. A large harbour opens out before us, forming three sides of a square. In the centre, the calm, green sea laps innocently against the harbour wall.

'We saw the Facebook post last night about your boat,' says Zaher, turning to Muhannad. 'We called the Greek police for you. But when you didn't come... well, we feared the worst.'

My gut squirms with panic at the memory of Ayham's desperate calls from the boat. Our group stares at the floor and walks on in silence. None of us is ready to talk about the crossing yet. Zaher stops at an open-fronted shop along the harbour front. Hanging from the awning is an odd mix of tacky souvenirs and camping equipment. We buy a sleeping bag each, then Zaher leads us back around the corner, along past the port and out towards the edge of town. To the right, on the shoreline, I spot a bronze statue mounted on a stone plinth. A woman in long, flowing robes faces out to sea with one foot forwards. In her right hand she holds aloft a burning torch.

'Hey, isn't that the Statue of Liberty?' I say.

'Yeah,' says Ayham, grinning. 'That boat must have gotten us further than we thought.'

I whack his arm.

'My God,' I say. 'Was that supposed to be a joke?'

The road winds around a corner and we come face to face with several long-haired, mangy-looking dogs. They scratch themselves and lounge lazily on the scorching tarmac. Rusty iron railings run along a wall up to a turnstile on our right. A sign on the gate reads: 'Tsamakia Beach'. Behind it, a tatty stretch of sand runs down to the sea. On the other side of the road, a grassy slope rises under a scattered pine wood. Families and small groups cover the grass, sitting, milling around, and sleeping in the shade. Like us, they're waiting for their papers so they can move onto the mainland and continue their journeys north into Europe. We follow Zaher up some shallow steps. The grass either side of the path is strewn with clothes, rubbish, and blankets. At the top, the steps level out onto a dusty car park. There, bordered by a low brick wall, is a small children's playground.

'Look who I found,' says Zaher, grinning as we approach.

A crowd of familiar faces looks up. The whole group from the smuggler camp is there. The older woman, Mama, is sitting on the floor next to a graffiti-covered slide. Baby Kamar sleeps peacefully in her lap. Mama's face breaks into a wide smile.

'Praise God,' she says. She passes the baby to Zaher and struggles to her feet. 'Thank God you're safe.'

Mama draws me and Sara into a bear hug. Umm Muqtada and her two children are waiting behind, arms outstretched.

'We thought...,' says Umm Muqtada, holding me tight. The Lebanese girl Coco steps up next and kisses me on both cheeks. Ahmad, the man from Latakia travelling with his friend and two sisters, shakes hands warmly with the men. I'm touched. We've spent such a short time together, but it's clear these people already consider us family.

'Ugh, I need a shower so bad,' says Sara at last, once the hugs and greetings are over.

Coco offers to show us the way to the shower block. We follow her back down the slope to the rusty turnstile. She points through the railings to a building beyond. We just have to go in and say we want to swim. There's no charge. Coco takes a bottle of shampoo out of her bag and hands it over. I grin, thank her, and push open the rusty gate. It's the first shower I've had since Istanbul, five days ago. The water runs black with grime. I stand motionless for twenty minutes, staring at the tiles, letting the water rain down on my neck. Outside I find Sara, Coco, my cousin Nabih and the brothers Ayham and Bassem waiting for me by the turnstile. Coco leads us back around the harbour and into a maze of backstreets. She stops outside a restaurant with white tables leading out onto the street. 'Damas', reads the sign above the door. Damascus.

'We're in the right place, then,' says Sara, grinning.

The restaurant is packed with Syrians, eating, chatting loudly, or hunched over phones charging on tangled clusters of power points laid out on the tables. I hear a loud shriek from the back of the restaurant and look up to see Mustafa, sitting with his father,

Idris. The little boy drops his fork, runs over, and wraps his arms around my waist.

'There they are,' says Idris, smiling. 'Our swimming heroes.'

The customers around us look up, begin to nudge each other, and point. Before long, everyone in the restaurant is looking at us, smiling, and murmuring to each other.

'What's going on?' I mutter to Sara.

She shrugs.

'I guess they heard what happened,' she says.

The waves glint and march again. My gut twists.

'Looks like you're famous in Greece now too,' says Ayham, nudging me.

'Shut up,' I say, my cheeks burning red.

We collect plates of meat and rice and wander outside to the tables on the terrace. We eat in ravenous silence for a few minutes. Then, between mouthfuls, we tell Idris about Zaher's camping spot in the park and he agrees to join us. Mustafa grins and bangs both his fists on the table. We finish eating and wander back through the town, around the harbour and up the hill to the camp in the children's playground. The way is lined with hundreds of new arrivals bedding down outside in the summer night. I climb into my new sleeping bag between Coco and Sara. I lie awake, listening to the chorus of barking dogs and echoing music from the tavernas and bars. Cicadas squawk and chirp rhythmically in the trees and motorbikes backfire in the streets. I close my eyes and feel safe for the first time in days. It's good to be back with Mama and Kamar, I think as I finally drift off to sleep. The older woman and the tiny baby will protect us.

The next morning, Zaher and Majed discuss our next move. Zaher and the others arrived earlier, so they're a few days ahead of us in the registration process. They're due to get their papers later that day, but our papers won't be ready until the following one. Zaher says they'll all wait for us, so we can all move on together. It's generous of them and I'm relieved. I'll be glad to travel in a larger group. It feels much safer. Majed turns to me. We have some time to kill, so he offers to replace my lost glasses. I follow him around the harbour, past the tavernas, bakeries and tourist shops into the winding backstreets beyond. At last, we find an optician, but he says it will take at least week to make up my prescription. We can't wait here that long. I'll have to do without them. I'm annoyed. A whole week. They'd have done it in a day in Syria. Majed and I trudge back to the port. On the way we peer into the car park. The crowd looks even bigger than the day before. We spot Zaher and his family emerging from the throng. Zaher grins and waves a piece of paper in the air. Then he points at a huge crowd on the other side of the car park. It's the queue for ferry tickets to the mainland. My eyes widen. It looks just as long as the line to register.

The next day, after a long wait on the baking tarmac, we also pick up our registration papers. I peer at the strange Greek letters on the sheet and wonder what they actually mean. All we know is it means we can get off the island. We join the next queue, the one for the ferry ticket, straight away. A few more hours and we finally buy tickets for a boat leaving the following evening. At last, after another night camping in the playground, our whole group crams onto the ferry to the Greek capital, Athens. Three hundred kilometres, an eleven-hour crossing. The ship is so overcrowded that we have to sleep on tables in the cafeteria on the upper deck. I spend the night battling waves of nausea and trying to ignore the rolling of the sea beneath us. We arrive in Piraeus, a large industrial port near Athens, early the following morning. We don't stop, but follow the crowds past the rusting machinery along the dock. It isn't long before we hit a crowd of smuggler touts.

'Where do you want to go?' says one of them in Arabic as we pass.

'Germany,' says our cousin Majed.

The smuggler laughs. Everyone is heading north, to Germany or Sweden. The man says the next bus goes at midnight, but it'll only take us as far as the next border. From there we walk across into Macedonia, a tiny country along the way from Greece to Hungary. Few of us have heard of Macedonia before, but Majed does a deal with the smuggler and gets us all seats on a bus. We travel all

night and cross the length of mainland Greece, five hundred kilometres north to the Macedonian border. I'm just glad we don't
have to walk it. The smugglers drop us just after dawn at the side
of a road beside an abandoned hotel. Three other buses arrive at the
same time. The crowds stream off them and begin trekking pur-
posefully through the fields in a long, snaking line.

'Yes, this is right,' says Majed, looking at his phone and trying
out the names. 'Idomeni. Gevgelija. The border is over there. This
is the way to the train track that leads to the crossing point.'

'No kidding, I'd never have guessed,' says Muhannad, and
waves his hand in the direction of the stream of people.

Nabih and I giggle. Majed doesn't notice, he's too busy staring
at the screen. We follow the crowds through the long grass until we
hit the train tracks. This is it. The border between Greece and
Macedonia. A huge crowd sits on the tracks, waiting in the sun to
cross. The atmosphere is tense. Ahead, a line of police blocks our
path. We sit down at the back of the crowd to wait. I eat another
chocolate bar and then go into the bushes next to the tracks to
change my clothes. Half an hour later there's a commotion at the
front of the crowd as the police part to let around fifty people
across the border. We stand and join the crush as the whole mass
moves forwards as one, shouting and shoving one another. A Sudanese man topples into me and sends me flying backwards into my
cousin Nabih. Nabih steps forwards to push the man back.

'She pushed in,' says the Sudanese man, pointing to me.

The brothers Ayham and Bassem step up to the man.

'No,' says Ayham. 'You pushed her.'

'You're all pushing in,' says another man, pointing at our group
and stepping up to Ayham.

The argument soon escalates into a shoving match. In the confusion, Sara and I shuffle further forwards in the queue. The crowd
eventually settles down again, but tempers fray more and more as
we wait in the midday sun. Little by little, we inch our way forwards towards the police line. At last, after fifteen minutes at the
front of the crush facing down the police, the officers stand aside

and let us through into Macedonia. We hold hands in a long chain
to keep our group together as we cross.

Just across the border, a policeman points us towards a low
building. We have to go there to register and get a paper granting
us temporary asylum in Macedonia for three days, enough time to
travel through the country. Once we have the paper we can catch a
government-run bus to the next border. If we move fast, we could
be out of Macedonia by nightfall. The border with Serbia is only
two hours' drive north of here. From there, it's another four hundred kilometres to the Serbian capital, Belgrade. If we're lucky we
could sleep there tonight and in the morning begin planning how
to cross the next border, the worst one of all, from Serbia into
Hungary.

Zaher takes one look at the long, ragged queue outside the
building and frowns. Kamar begins to wail in his arms. He hands
the baby to his wife and shakes his head.

'Another queue,' says Zaher. 'Let's not bother with the paper.
We can't wait here forever. We have to move on.'

Zaher and his group are keen to get moving, but Majed is in
less of a hurry. He says we should stay here and wait to get the
transit paper before moving on. Zaher shrugs and says we can just
meet up again at the next border. I don't like the idea of splitting
up, but Majed is adamant. We don't move on without getting the
paper.

'We play by whatever stupid rules they give us,' says Majed. 'I
don't want trouble further down the road just because I don't have
some bit of paper.'

'He's right,' says Muhannad. 'It's a game. We stick to the rules.
If they say we need the paper, we get the paper.'

We join the queue and wait in the sweltering heat. Five hours
later, we find ourselves sitting in front of two policemen. We give
them our names, but no fingerprints. They don't ask to see our
passports, so Sara and I leave them where they are, in our bras. The
police give us a stamped transit paper and usher us onto a bus to
the Serbian border. It's clear the Macedonians want us out of there
as quickly as possible. That's fine with us. We're happy to be moving

so quickly. On the bus into Serbia, Majed gets a message from Zaher saying they've had to double back. Without transit papers, the police turned them back at the border. Zaher says he'll meet us later, in Belgrade.

'Ha,' says, Majed grinning in triumph. 'You see? It's a game, there are rules.'

I stare hard out of the bus window, fighting irritation. Majed grins again when we cross into Serbia and have to show our papers to the policemen. He loves being right. Across the border, another free, government-run bus is waiting to take us the final four-hour stretch north to Belgrade. The Serbian and Macedonian governments don't want us sticking around so they're bussing us quickly north and west towards the wealthier European countries. To Germany, Sweden, and France.

It's late in the evening by the time the bus drops us at Belgrade bus station. We follow the crowd to into a well-trampled park. Crowds of people are camping out on the bare, dusty earth. The lucky ones have tents. Stinking piles of rubbish are strewn across the square and gangs of strange men wander around in the dark. I feel uneasy. Sara reads my thoughts.

'Let's get a hotel,' says Sara, looking around. 'We can meet the others tomorrow.'

We trudge off into the city to find rooms. One after another, the hoteliers refuse to serve customers with Syrian passports. It hurts. I think back to the restaurant on the island that wouldn't sell me water. We have money. Isn't it good enough for them? It's late and the streets feel edgy by the time we find a hotel that will take us without documents. We pay double the going rate, but I'm so relieved to have a room I hardly notice the price. Sara and I bolt our door. I take an hour-long shower and then sink into the crisp, clean sheets. I've been sleeping rough since we left Istanbul. Seven nights now. A whole week. I've forgotten what it's like to sleep deeply, peacefully, in a bed.

We find Zaher and the others in the park early the next morning. They've pitched their tents on the dusty ground. The unofficial camp has no running water and only chemical toilets. I think

Two of the few childhood photos that survived Yusra's escape from Syria

Travelling through Europe, crouching in cornfields at sunset, 2015
(Hien Lam Duc/Agence VU)

Yusra at the head of the group walking on train tracks at the border between Serbia and Hungary, 2015 (*Hien Lam Duc/Agence VU*)

Left to right: Idris, Mustafa, Yusra, Blondie, 2015
(Hien Lam Duc/Agence VU)

Left to right: Khalil, Sara, Blondie, Nabih, Yusra, Majed, 2015
(Hien Lam Duc/Agence VU)

The Mardinis: Sara, Yusra, Mervat, family friend Karoline, Shahed and Ezzat, 2015 *(Hien Lam Duc/Agence VU)*

Coach Sven Spannekrebs talks to Yusra during a training session at the Wasserfreunde Spandau 04 training pool, Olympiapark Berlin, March 2016 *(Alexander Hassenstein/Getty Images for IOC)*

The Refugee Olympic Team join the Parade of Nations in the Maracanã
Stadium during the opening ceremony of the Rio 2016 Olympic Games
(Reuters with permission of the IOC)

The Refugee Olympic Team in front of the Christ the Redeemer statue in
Rio de Janeiro, Brazil, 2016 *(Kai Pfaffenbach/Reuters)*

Yusra swimming at the Rio 2016 Olympic Games
(Benjamin Loyseau/©UNHCR with permission of the IOC)

Yusra speaking at the
United Nations' Global
Goals Awards dinner,
September 2016,
where she received
the Girl Award
*(Markisz/UN032947/
UNICEF)*

Yusra met President Obama and delivered a speech to the United Nations
General Assembly in New York, 2016 *(Pete Souza/Obama Presidential Library)*

Yusra and Sara holding
their Bambi awards
for Silent Heroes
(German media
awards) in Berlin,
September 2016
*(Joerg Carstensen/
picture alliance)*

Yusra met his Holiness Pope Francis, November 2016, to present him with the Millennium-Bambi Prize, a German media award *(Vatican Media)*

Yusra with Queen Rania of Jordan at the 2016 Global Goals Awards dinner in New York *(Michael Loccisano/Getty Images for Global Goals)*

about the clean sheets and the shower and feel bad. I tell myself that's just how it is. Not everyone can afford a hotel room. You buy yourself a safe place to sleep if you can. I sit down between Mama and Zaher's wife. Both are doting on baby Kamar. They coo to her and she gazes up at them with her pale moon eyes. Ayham and his brother Bassem wander over to say goodbye. They are planning to fly to Germany from here using forged IDs. If it works, it'll be a considerable shortcut, saving them weeks on the road. But it's a risk. If they get caught using fake passports, they could be arrested.

'We'll meet you in Germany, then,' says Ayham, pressing my hand. 'Where is it you said you are going?'

'Hanover,' I say. 'We're going to find Sara's friend Hala.'

'Ok, so we'll find you there,' he says.

I wish him luck and we wave them off.

'They'll never make it onto the plane,' mutters Majed as they leave.

I sit listless on the brown, dusty soil. The grass is long gone. Around us sit hundreds of people, groups of young men, families with grandparents and tiny children. They sleep, eat, wait, and plot their next move. Smuggler touts lurk around the edge of the park. Everyone is talking about how best to cross into Hungary. They say the Hungarian police have been cracking down on the border, but it is still possible to get through. Our group is split about the next move. Muhannad says he wants to pay a smuggler to drive him over the border all the way to the Hungarian capital, Budapest. Majed is keen to go with him. Zaher and the others say they'll go to Horgoš, a small village on the Serbian–Hungarian border, and walk across. We could also go with them. Majed asks me, Sara and Nabih what we want to do. Get a smuggler car with Muhannad or walk across the border with Zaher.

'I want to stay with Zaher,' I say. 'Stay with the big group. They're our friends. Let's walk with them. I have a good feeling about them. We're family now.'

As I say the words out loud the feeling grows stronger. These people care about us. They waited for us on the island, helped us, wanted us to camp with them in Greece. They didn't have to do any of that. Sara and Nabih grin and nod. It's decided. We'll walk across into Hungary with Zaher and the others.

Dusk falls in the park and the atmosphere grows tense again. Me, Sara, and our cousins Nabih and Majed wander back to the hotel, leaving the rest to camp. The next morning, we arrive back to the park and find Ayham and his brother Bassem sitting with the group. Security was too tight, they say, they didn't make it onto the plane to Germany. It's clear, the only option is to try to cross into Hungary with us on foot.

'Hey,' says a male voice behind me in English. 'Can I sit with you?'

I look up to see a man smiling down at our group. He wears a khaki shirt and has big, friendly brown eyes and a stubbly beard.

'Err, I guess so,' I say. 'What do you want?'

The man says his name is Steven, a journalist with Belgian news channel VRT news. He and his crew are making a news programme. Steven points to a man standing next to him holding a camera. Behind him, another man holds a furry microphone on a stick. They're his team, he says. His cameraman, Ludwig, and his soundman, Stefan.

'We'd like to talk to you about your journey,' says Steven. 'It's for a youth programme, to tell young people in Belgium about what's going on here.'

I smile. It'll be a welcome distraction from the boredom, from all the talk about borders, smugglers, and Hungary. I stand and look down at the others. The adults shake their heads. They're worried about going on camera. It might bring problems later. I look around. The sun is shining, I'm feeling confident. We've made it this far. What harm can it do? I follow him over to a quiet corner of the park. We pick a spot in the shade of some tall trees. I sit cross-legged on the ground facing Steven. He puts a microphone on me and Ludwig points the camera into my face.

'So, what are you doing here?' says Steven, once the camera is rolling. 'Tell us about yourself.'

I tell him I was on the national swimming team in Syria and that I'm going to Germany because I heard it's a good place to train and study. Nowhere is safe in Syria, we had to keep moving to escape the bombs. There's no future there. I can't study, I can't dream. We're looking for a chance of a better life, I say. Anything would be better than just existing, waiting for death, or for an end to the war, whichever comes first. Steven nods gravely and asks about my hopes and dreams for the future.

'I want to be a professional swimmer,' I say. 'One day, I want to go to the Olympics.'

Steven pauses and shoots me a quizzical look. Then he glances around. Zaher and the others have gathered around us in a circle while we've been talking. Steven gestures at them and asks me who I'm travelling with. I tell him I'm with my sister, my cousins, and some friends who have become like a family. The interview is over, and Ludwig turns the camera to film the crowds in the park. We stand, Steven shakes my hand and thanks me. Sara wanders over to join us.

'It was hard to get here,' I say and point at Sara. 'We had to swim.'

Steven stops dead and stares at us.

'Swim?' says Steven. 'What do you mean?'

'Yeah,' I say. 'We swam from Turkey to Greece.'

Steven raises his eyebrows and shakes his head in disbelief.

'It's true,' Sara chimes in. 'We're swimmers so we had to swim.'

Steven beckons urgently to his cameraman.

'Ok,' says Steven. 'Let's do the interview again.'

I shrug and sit back down. The camera rolls again. I tell Steven about the towering waves and the tiny, overcrowded boat, how low it sat in the water. Sara and I are swimmers, I say, we swam to keep the boat afloat on the waves. We were in the sea for three and a half hours. It was cold and dark, we were afraid, but we arrived, thank God. It's the first time I've told the story out loud to someone else. I struggle to remember the details, it feels faraway and unreal, like a bad dream that fades after waking. Steven smiles and thanks me again. We take a selfie together and I give him my phone number. The journalist says he'll stay in touch.

That night we return to the hotel. Early the next morning

Muhannad leaves to meet his smuggler, leaving his friend Blondie with us. It isn't an emotional goodbye with Muhannad. We think maybe we'll meet him further along the way somewhere. We never see him again, but later I hear from Dad that he made it through to Germany on his own. Back in the park, Zaher says he has found a smuggler bus to take all of us to the Hungarian border the following morning. The plan is to walk across from there into Hungary.

The Hungarian police are different from the others we've met so far. If we get caught at the border, the best we can hope for is to be turned back into Serbia, but they might arrest us instead and take us to prison. We've heard stories of cruel treatment and beatings. But our biggest fear is that the Hungarians find our passports, register us, and take our fingerprints. If that happens before we make it to Germany, we could even get sent back here under EU asylum rules. It's complicated and we're unsure of the legal situation. All we know is we have to avoid the police at all costs.

In the park, Umm Muqtada is fussing, her two small children clinging to her long *abaya* jacket. She looks around at the other veiled women in our group.

'My brother-in-law Ali says we'll need to look European when we cross into Hungary,' says Umm Muqtada. 'They're scared of Muslims there, remember? We can't stand out. That means no *hijabs*. We'll have to cover our hair with hats instead.'

The other women look doubtful, but Umm Muqtada insists. Sara and I go with them to a cheap clothes shop near the park. The veiled women buy big straw sunhats to cover their hair. Sara and I buy shorts and t-shirts. While we're gone, Majed goes with Nabih to a Western Union to get more money for the next stage of our trip. We meet Zaher and the others early the next day on the road bordering the park. A coach is waiting to take us the two hundred kilometres north to the Hungarian border.

The bus drops us on the side of a road near some trees. There are a lot of other people milling around, looking scared and lost and searching for a leader to show them a way to cross the border without getting caught. Zaher leads our group off the road onto a sandy track. After a few minutes, Zaher stops and points into the trees. We have to go up the slope, find the train tracks and then follow them across the border, he says. But there are police are everywhere. If we go with all these people, we'll get caught for sure. We should wait here and pretend to be resting, let the crowd go ahead and wait to see what happens. Maybe the police will be so busy with them that we can sneak across unnoticed.

We sit down in the clearing and let the other lost people stream past up the path towards the waiting police. At last, the crowd melts away, leaving our group behind, slightly hidden out of view. We're alone, like we wanted to be.

13

A little man with almond eyes appears out of nowhere and approaches our group. He has an open, brown face surrounded by a shock of black and white hair. On his nose balance a pair of thick-rimmed, square glasses. Next to him stands a woman with short, curly brown hair.

'Are you going to cross now?' says the man in English.

'Who is he?' says Zaher. 'Does he want money, or what?'

The man says his name is Lam. The woman flashes us a warm smile and says her name is Magdalena. Lam reaches under his jacket and pulls out a camera with a huge lens.

'We're journalists. I take photos,' says Lam. 'I want to come with you across into Hungary and take pictures.'

Sara explains to the group.

'He can do whatever he wants as long as we don't get caught,' says Zaher.

Sara looks up at Lam and grins.

'Ok,' she says. 'You can come with us.'

All of us struggle to our feet. Sara stands, lifts Kamar out of her mother's arms, and slots the baby into a red carrier strapped to her front. Zaher's wife hands Sara a pink shawl and she wraps it around the child to shade her from the midday sun. Lam snaps a picture of our group and then he and Magdalena follow Zaher along the sandy path. Sara and I follow close behind, the others in tow. Zaher turns right off the path and uphill into a small wood. We scramble up the steep slope and emerge from the trees onto a railway track. A pair of parallel steel tracks glint in the midday sun. There are no sleepers between them, only a bare dirt path. We trudge off along it.

'Don't the trains run?' I whisper to Lam.

'Oh, not that often,' he says and winks, ducking to one side to snap more photos as the group files past. After a few minutes, Zaher stops and holds out one hand behind him, his palm facing up towards us.

'Stay very quiet,' he says in a whisper. 'Not a word.'

I signal to the others. Zaher disappears into the trees to the left. We follow him down the slope. At the bottom, the trees open out onto a large cornfield. Zaher stops and raises his hand. I freeze behind him. He leans back to whisper in my ear.

'The border is over there,' he says, consulting his phone and pointing to the end of the field on his right. 'Hungary.'

Zaher draws a line with his finger from left to right to show the main road, where the police are waiting. We'll have to hide from them in the cornfield and try and make it past them. If we stand, they'll see us.

'No one talk, no one smoke,' says Zaher, turning back to the group. 'Keep the kids quiet. And all of you turn off your phones. When I say run, you run. When I say sit, you sit. Ok?'

I nod.

Zaher is off, bending low and scurrying between the corn stalks, his head about level with the tops of the corn. I follow, keeping my head bent down, breathing hard. Lam, Magdalena and Sara are close behind me. Twenty metres into the field, Zaher freezes. He holds his palm out behind him and I stop dead. Then he turns his palm to face the ground and waves it sharply up and down.

'Sit,' he hisses at me over his shoulder.

I crouch down. Behind me, the others do the same. We wait in silence. Minutes pass. Then Zaher stands, beckons to us, and makes a sharp right between the corn stalks. We're heading directly towards the border now. The road runs along the edge of the field around two hundred metres to our left. Police cars are parked nose to tail in a long line along it. If I stand, anyone scanning the field will see my head. Zaher freezes again and makes the sign to duck down.

'They're looking this way,' he whispers. 'Wait here.'

We settle down to wait. The silence drags on. I strain my ears for the sound of police marching through the field towards us.

Nothing. Only the buzz of insects and the birds singing overhead. The kids stay quiet. I keep my eyes fixed on the ground. I can't bear to look the others in the face. The situation is just too embarrassing. We're human beings, not animals. Yet here we are, like criminals, crouching in a field, being hunted by the police. I cringe, pick long blades of grass, and tear them to shreds.

The sunlight is golden, the shadows longer by the time Lam gets to his feet and beckons. We follow him, bending low below the corn. The corn thins out into long grass and Zaher motions to us to sit again. Kamar wails and breaks the thick silence. Sara quickly hands the baby to Zaher's wife, who starts feeding her to keep her quiet. Silence falls again in the field.

Umm Muqtada's little boy stands in front of his mother. His eyes are red and exhausted, his face screwed up in pain. Umm Muqtada strokes his black fringe back to feel his forehead and lets him lie down with his head in her lap. An hour passes in tense silence before Zaher signals to us to get up. The little boy is too exhausted to move. His face creases and he begins to cry, holding his arms up towards Umm Muqtada.

'Shh,' says Umm Muqtada. 'Don't cry, *habibi*.'

She picks him up and carries him in her arms.

We sneak on, following Zaher through the tall grass. Ahead, he breaks into a run. I sprint behind him, bent double and breathing hard. Lam and Magdalena follow close behind. Behind them, Sara, carrying the little boy on her back. Umm Muqtada holds her daughter's hand and jogs along behind them. We stop and start, making slow, silent progress through the grass. The sun is slanting low over the field when Zaher finally sits down and consults his phone. He smiles with relief.

'That's it. We're across,' says Zaher. 'We're in Hungary.'

Lam nods and turns to me, grinning.

'You did good,' he says.

The photographer glances up and snaps a picture of Sara as she lets the little boy down off her back.

'And you, old Antar here,' chuckles Lam. 'What are you, like a war hero or something?'

Sara and I laugh. Antar was an Arab knight and folk hero known for his epic adventures. I ask Lam how he knows about Antar and he says he lived in Iraq for many years. Imagine finding someone who knows about Antar in a field on the border between Serbia and Hungary. I grin at the journalists. Some more unexpected friends to add to our travelling group.

Zaher points over his shoulder at a low building about sixty metres away. The gas station, he explains, where the smugglers gather. We have to wait here until it gets dark. There are still police scanning the area, looking for us. After night fall we'll sneak across the field to the gas station and find cars to take us to Budapest. We settle down again to wait.

The sun is sinking fast into the fields behind us. The light fades to deep pink and grows grainy. The white glare from the gas station forecourt gradually bleaches the colour out of the sky until at last everything is black, white, or grey. Lights from the police cars whir along the road. A blue flashing barrier, barring our way. We sit tight, waiting out the police. Sara sits nearby with Bashar and Abdullah. The men are smoking, their hands cupped over the glowing ends of their cigarettes to cover the light. Once again, we aren't alone. A steady stream of people scurries across the border through the field to join us. Before long, our group has doubled in size.

Just after nightfall, a woman and two men stroll casually across the field from the gas station. There's enough light to see they aren't police: A teenage Roma girl in a long skirt and a t-shirt, flanked on either side by muscular men in black.

'Where do you want to go?' the girl says as she reaches us.

Sara translates between Zaher and the girl.

'Budapest,' says Zaher.

'How many people?' says the girl.

'Thirty,' says Zaher. 'How much?'

'Eight hundred each,' says the girl. 'We will bring enough cars for everyone.'

Zaher's eyes widen.

'Each?' he says. 'No. That's too much.'

'Maybe you want the police to get you?' says the girl, pointing to the flashing blue lights behind her.

Zaher sighs. There's no other way. We need to get out of here. Zaher tells the girl to bring the cars. We'll wait for her here. The girl strolls with her gang back towards the white light of the gas station. For all we know they're working for the police. We're completely at their mercy. Zaher starts planning for the next part of the journey. He counts on his fingers those of our group who can speak English. There's five of us including me and Sara. When the cars come, the English speakers will split up so that there's one of us in each taxi. That means I'll be apart from Sara for the next trip, but I don't mind, I trust the others.

Just then, a commotion breaks out on the road. The journalists look up, then exchange glances. Lam nods at us as he and Magdalena get slowly to their feet, keeping low.

'Farewell, brave Antar,' says Lam and winks at Sara. 'Until we meet in battle once more.'

Sara grins. Lam is off, darting across the field towards the road, Magdalena following close behind. We watch them until they disappear into the gas station glare. I'm sorry to see them go. Without them, our situation feels much bleaker. The presence of the journalists made our cat-and-mouse game with the police seem almost fun. What happens if the girl never comes back? How will we ever get out of here without getting caught? I shudder and push the thought away.

Umm Muqtada looks around at the other veiled women and tells them it's time to change out of their *hijabs*. Their headscarves are just too much of a giveaway that we're Muslim. The women shuffle a little way off into some longer grass. They emerge again, and I have to stifle a giggle. They've tucked their hair under large straw hats and swapped their long, fitted *abaya* jackets for long skirts and denim jackets, lifting the collars to cover their necks. It's a weird look, especially at night, in a field. I put on my new shorts and t-shirt and throw away my filthy, grey jumper into the long grass. I soon regret it. A wind picks up and I start to freeze. But it's too dark and too dangerous to go and find my jumper again now. The hours wear on with no sign of the girl or her gangster friends.

There's no moon, I can't even see any stars, only a low blanket of angry, purple clouds. I try to sleep but I'm too wired. The blue lights flash, round and round. They're giving me a headache. I look at my phone, shielding the light with my hand. I get a shock. It's three in the morning. Umm Muqtada's little boy is crying again. He whines quietly, standing next to his mother. She puts one arm around his shoulders and offers him a plastic bottle of water. The boy scowls and pushes it away. Umm Muqtada draws both arms around him and the little boy buries his face in her shoulder. She murmurs to him soothingly and her eyes fill with tears.

'Don't worry, *habibi,* it'll be ok,' she says and strokes his hair. 'Don't cry.'

Umm Muqtada's daughter is watching her mother and her brother. She looks close to tears herself.

'Hey,' I whisper to the girl.

She looks over to me.

'Do you know how to plait hair?' I say.

She nods shyly.

'You know what? I've been looking for a new stylist,' I say. 'You want to plait mine?'

The little girl shuffles over to sit behind me. She gathers my long hair into sections and twists them over and under each other. When she's done, she pulls out the knot with her fingers and starts again.

'Those smugglers aren't coming back,' says Zaher at last. 'And the police aren't giving up. We should see if we can find somewhere better to hide and maybe get some sleep.'

Ayham and his brother Bassem volunteer to go look for a hiding place. They disappear off towards the gas station, bending low, scurrying through the tall grass. Twenty minutes later they're back. They've found a kind of ditch, like a dry river, behind the trees. We can hide there from the police until morning. Zaher stands, taking Kamar and slotting her into the carrier on his front. The sleeping baby barely stirs. Umm Muqtada gently wakes her son and they get to their feet, holding hands, ready to run. I get up and grab the little girl's hand. A loud beating, buzzing noise fires up in the sky beyond the gas station. A white streak of light beams down from the purple clouds. A helicopter.

'Ok, go,' hisses Zaher to the group. 'Run.'

Bassem and Ayham set off at a sprint across the field towards their hiding place. We follow them as fast as we can. Umm Muqtada's little girl gallops along next to me, her breath coming in panicked rasps. I look behind us. The whole crowd is fleeing across the field, lit up by the blue lights flashing along the road to our left. There must be at least sixty of us, spread out in the long grass, heading for the cover of a small patch of trees ahead. More search beams appear in the sky and the beating buzzing grows louder overhead. I grip the girl's hand tighter and she starts to whimper.

'It's ok,' I whisper to her as we run. 'It's just a game.'

It begins to rain. Fat drops of water fly into my face. The roaring of the helicopters grows closer. I hear shouts behind me, but I don't dare look back again. I focus on the brothers, Ayham and Bassem, up ahead. They duck into the trees, followed by Zaher and his wife. Just thirty metres, twenty, ten. We're there. I haul the little girl into the wood behind me. We catch our breath for a few seconds. Sara is next to duck in under the trees, carrying Umm Muqtada's little boy on her back. I count the rest of our group in, our cousins Nabih and Majed, Blondie, Sara's buddies Bashar and Abdullah.

We set off into the forest. After about twenty metres I reach the edge of a hidden dip. I catch my breath. I could easily have fallen into it in the dark. I slither down the steep, muddy sides into a wide ditch, about the same size as a skaters' halfpipe. I look back up as the rest of our group piles in. Most of the strangers that joined us near the gas station don't find our hiding place. I sit on the muddy floor and listen to their shouts as they run past and out onto the road, into the arms of the waiting police. I listen and hold my breath. The helicopters fly overhead but we're well hidden by the canopy of trees. On the road, the patrol cars are busy. It's a stand-off, there's no way out. All we can do is wait until morning and hope that the police leave so we can escape and find another smuggler on the road. I wonder whether Lam, Mama, and the others made it out.

It's even colder in the trench than out on the field. The rain has stopped but a thin mist swirls along the ditch. I sneak a look at my phone. Four thirty. I need to sleep. I think of my hotel room back in Belgrade. The helicopter searchlight makes another sweep of the canopy. I remember my jumper back in the field.

'I'm freezing,' I mutter to Sara, my teeth chattering. 'I just want to sleep.'

Ayham stands and takes off his leather jacket. He smiles and puts the jacket around my shoulders, then walks off along the ditch hugging himself and rubbing his bare forearms, stopping every few steps to jump or jog on the spot.

'I wish I had my trousers,' moans Sara, rubbing her bare legs, her eyes brimming with tears. 'Why did we put shorts on?'

Just then Sara's buddies Bashar and Abdullah slide down into the ditch, carrying two dirty sleeping bags between them. Abdullah cuts them into strips with his penknife. I try making a bed out of the material, but it is already wet from the rain and the ground is too muddy to sleep on. Sara stands and announces she's going back into the field to get her jumper. I tell her not to be stupid, but she's not listening. She wanders off. I'm too tired to stop her. Five minutes later she's back, grinning and holding up a pair of large black sweatpants.

'Look what that guy over there just gave me,' says Sara, pointing to one of the strangers hiding in the ditch with us. 'I don't even know him, and I could kiss him right now.'

No one gets much sleep. The lights flash, the helicopters circle above. We wait. At last, as night begins to lift, the noise from the road quietens and the blue lights disappear. Zaher wants to leave, he's worried his baby can't take much more of this cold.

It's calmer on the road now. One of us English speakers needs to go out to look for a smuggler. Ayham and Blondie volunteer, scramble out of the ditch and disappear. We strain our ears, listening. All is quiet. Ten minutes later, they slide back down the steep slope. They say they've found a guy with enough cars to take all of us to Budapest. The smugglers have offered to take us to a hotel, Hotel Berlin, where they say we'll find another smuggler to continue to Germany. It won't be cheap: five hundred euros per person. It's an outrageous price to drive the two hundred kilometres to Budapest. But we don't care. As long as we get out of this ditch.

We scramble out of the trench and emerge shivering from the wood out into a weak, drizzly dawn. Along the road wait five dirty, black cars and a black van. I get into the black minivan with Umm Muqtada and her kids, Abdullah and two others. I climb up into the passenger seat next to the driver. He's short and middle-aged, wearing all black apart from a white baseball cap on his head.

'Five hundred,' he says. 'Each.'

His breath reeks of alcohol and cigarettes. I collect the cash from the others and hand it over. We set off and the smuggler whacks the music up full blast. Tinny pop music with a driving beat. I don't care. I fall into a deep sleep, exhausted from my night in the ditch. I wake up in the middle of the morning rush hour. We're crawling through traffic under a motorway bridge. The music is still blasting out. I look behind me. The others are fast asleep.

The driver pulls off the highway and parks up in a layby next to a bridge. Ahead is an out-of-town shopping mall. The others wake up in the back. The driver waves vaguely out of the window and says we should get another car here. We bundle out. The black van speeds off, leaving us lost and alone on the side of the road. There's a screech of tyres and a white minivan speeds across the road towards us. It looks as though it's about to hit us but veers off at the last minute. The driver door opens to reveal a bald man with muscles and tattoos.

'Get in,' he says.

'Are you going to take us to Hotel Berlin?' I say.

He grins, showing yellow teeth.

'Hotel Berlin,' says the man. 'Yes.'

We climb in. The driver turns to me.

'Five hundred,' he says and spits out of the window.

'But we already paid the other guy,' I say.

'Five hundred,' he says again and turns to points at the others. 'Each one.'

My heart sinks. This man has complete power over us.

'But we already paid,' says Abdullah.

'I know, I told him,' I say. 'But err... well, look at him, do you want to take him on?'

Abdullah grunts and bangs his fist on the door. I look out of the window at the urban wasteland. We can't hail a taxi here. And I don't like the idea of walking down the main highway. We'd get arrested. There's no option but to pay again. The others scrabble around in the back seat behind me and produce the cash. I add my share from the stash in my plastic wallet and hand it over, pressing the money into the driver's hand as hard as I dare. He grins and tucks the money away in his jeans pocket. The driver puts his foot down and screeches back onto the highway. We hit traffic and crawl towards the city.

Hotel Berlin squats on a corner in a rundown, industrial part of Budapest. The three-storey building is beige and orange and utterly out of place. On the roof, a scaffold sign advertises the hotel's three stars. It looks like it hasn't seen a real tourist in ten years. I spot Sara as we pull up next to the entrance. She's pacing, looking worried. Zaher, our cousins, and the others are sitting under the trees in a little patch of green to our right. The van stops, I open the passenger door and climb out.

'Yusra. Thank God,' says Sara. 'Where have you been? We all got here an hour ago.'

'I dunno,' I say. 'I guess we got stuck in traffic.'

The others have been waiting for us to arrive before asking at the hotel for a smuggler. We've been told this is a smuggling hot spot and we'll need help for the next part of our journey. It's only a five-hour drive from here through Austria to Germany. But there are two borders in our way. First, we'll have to get past the Hungarian police to cross into Austria. For that, we need smugglers.

Sara and I volunteer to go inside and do the talking while the others wait outside on the patch of grass. We walk up the red-carpeted steps and into the foyer. A man with a shaved head stands behind a counter. More muscles. More tattoos.

'What do you want?' he says in English.

'We want to go to Germany,' says Sara. 'We heard we could get a car...'

'Yes,' he cuts us off. 'Come with me.'

The receptionist comes out from behind the desk and leads us into a bar area on the left. He walks up to a man sitting at a table. The man wears a blue shirt, beige trousers, and black shiny brogues. I blush and look down at my mud-stained shorts. He greets us in Arabic.

'What can I do for you?' he says. His accent is Syrian.

Sara tells him we want to go to Germany.

'Germany,' he says. 'Yes, we can arrange that. You'll take one of our rooms while we find you a car.'

Sara tells him there are more of us outside, about thirty all together and asks him how much the journey will cost.

'All the better,' he says and smiles. 'Let's worry about money later, shall we? Bring the others in and we'll show you to your rooms.'

We walk back towards the foyer. Behind the bar stands a girl in a tiny, red skirt and a tight, white top. She stops cleaning glasses and looks us up and down as we walk past. I stare back at her. Her bleached-blonde hair is sprayed up onto her head and she's wearing full make-up. We reach the steps and Sara calls out of the doorway to the others to come inside. They climb the steps and crowd into the foyer. A group of muscly Hungarian men appear. They're younger and better looking than the drivers. Each has the physique of a bodybuilder and broad arms covered in dark tattoos. The men separate us into groups. One of them approaches us and points at me, Sara, the Lebanese girl Coco, and the brothers, Bassem and Ayham. We follow him out of the foyer and into an elevator. He takes us to the third floor and marches us down a long corridor. We pass two more of the musclemen leaning against the wall. Between them stands a woman dressed like the girl behind the bar. The man catches Sara staring at them as we walk past.

'And where do you want to go next?' says the man.

Sara frowns at him.

'Germany,' she says.

'Mmm,' he says and looks her up and down. 'I'll come and find you there, then.'

I catch Sara's eye. She raises her eyebrows but says nothing. The man stops outside a door and flings it open without knocking. A crowd of strangers look up from five beds. Something is very wrong. There's at least thirteen people in here already. Men, women, and children, two or three to each bed. They sleep, stare at their phones, or gaze listlessly at the floor. I gawp at them. What kind of a hotel is this? The man ushers us inside and tells us to wait.

'Isn't this room kind of full already?' says Ayham.

The man ignores him and slams the door shut in his face. Ayham bangs on the back of the door.

'Hey,' he shouts. 'Can we get something to eat?'

There's no answer from the corridor outside.

'This is really creepy,' mutters Sara, turning to face the strangers in the room. A woman in a white *hijab* headscarf looks up at us. Two younger women sit quietly on the bed beside her. All three of them look scared. The woman tells us she's been waiting on a car to take her and her family across the borders, through Austria and into Germany. At first it sounded like a great deal, says the woman, but she's been waiting here a week already and the smugglers keep telling her the car will come tomorrow. In the meantime, she's running out of money. The rooms here are very expensive.

'This place is messed up,' says Coco quietly from behind us. She addresses the woman slowly, as if talking to an idiot. 'Have you actually seen anybody leave here?'

The woman says some people left the second day she was here, but she hasn't heard from them since then. Coco turns her back on the woman and holds up her phone. Her face is pale, and she speaks in a shocked whisper. Three days ago, Coco tells us, police found a truck on the side of the road just across the border into

Austria. Inside were seventy-one dead bodies. All of them were
Syrians. The victims had suffocated in the back of the truck. The
driver fled, leaving the bodies to rot on the side of the road. They
had already been there a week by the time someone found them. A
wave of nausea hits me as the news sinks in. I realize with a jolt just
how vulnerable we are. We have to get out of here. Sara's hand is
already on the door handle. She opens it a crack and looks outside,
then back at me, her eyes wide.

'That guy,' says Sara. 'He's out there in the corridor, just waiting.
Like a guard.'

'This is creeping me out,' I say. 'They're keeping these people
prisoner here. They could do anything to us. They could kill us and
cut us up and sell our organs. Or make us whores like those women
down there.'

'Don't be so dramatic,' says Coco.

'Then why are they keeping us here?' I say. 'Why can't we meet
them outside somewhere in the city when they have the car ready?'

Coco shrugs.

'They're only making money,' she says.

Sara is typing into her phone. She writes to the others and tells
them to get out and meet us downstairs in five minutes. She finishes her message and opens the door.

'Get inside,' comes the voice from the corridor.

'You can't keep us here,' I call over Sara's shoulder.

'Come on,' says Ayham and barges past Sara out of the room.

We follow him and sprint down the corridor. The guard outside looks surprised but doesn't stop us. We run past the elevator,
find the stairs, and take them three at a time. Three of the bodybuilder guards and the Syrian smuggler are waiting for us down in
the foyer. One of the guards makes a lunge towards Ayham. He
dodges and runs towards the exit. We follow, down the stairs and
out into the car park.

'Who do you think you are?' calls the Syrian after us. 'You can't
just leave.'

We keep running. We turn left around a corner and along the
busy main road. We stop at a bus stop and I look back. They aren't

following us. We wait. One by one, Zaher and his family, our cousins Majed and Nabih and the others come jogging around the corner to meet us. A taxi pulls up. The passenger window rolls down.

'Keleti?' calls the driver across the seats. 'Train station?'

We clamber into the car. It's a lucky escape. Just over a week later, Hungarian volunteers acting on a tip-off rescue one hundred Syrians from Hotel Berlin. All of them had been brought to the hotel by smugglers and charged small fortunes to be kept prisoner there, waiting indefinitely for cars to Germany that never came.

14

The taxi drops us in a square where crowds of people are camping in the shade of a grand, decaying station building. Two large gaps in the pavement open down onto a pedestrianized lower level. Even more people sleep and mill around in the concourse below. It's a sea of tents, towels, and blankets. In the square above stands a row of seven temporary toilets. Next to the furthest toilet is a solitary water tap. These are the only facilities. The air reeks of human waste and desperation. I gaze around in shock. It's the worst camp I've seen.

The people here have been waiting for days. Some of them more than a week. There are no smugglers available, so everyone is waiting to get on a train. Regular international trains run from here across the border into Austria. But the Hungarian authorities keep shutting down the station to non-visa holders, saying they are upholding European law. At this moment the station is out of bounds for us. A line of police blocks the station doors. They carry batons and pistols on their belts. The sun glints off their riot helmets. It's a deadlock, a stand-off.

I feel dizzy. It's mid-afternoon. I try to remember the last time I ate. A Snickers bar just before we met Lam on the Hungarian border. The last meal, breakfast back in the park in Belgrade, thirty hours ago. I look around. Bingo. A Burger King. Right here on the square.

'Let's eat,' I say.

Majed frowns at me. His mind isn't on burgers.

'We can go online inside,' I say. 'And err... work out what to do.'

We all traipse across the road and a little way along a pedestrianized shopping street. The others settle down outside while Sara, Nabih, Majed, and I go inside to order food. The doors open and we're hit with a familiar waft of fried food and air-conditioning.

MTV blares out from screens on the wall. We go upstairs to eat. Burgers. Coke. Wi-Fi. We're in heaven.

Majed soon gets bored and wanders outside to the others. He knows to find us here if anything changes. We sit in the red, gummy booths until the sun begins to set on the square outside the window. Sara gets a call around seven thirty. It's Majed. He says he's found a smuggler who has agreed to meet us in a McDonalds down the road. We file downstairs and out into the street. The sun has disappeared. The night is sticky and warm, the air stinks of diesel fumes. We find Majed and the others and follow them along the busy road. Police sirens wail past us every few minutes. Locals argue on the street in the heat.

A Moroccan man is waiting for us inside the restaurant. I see his eyes widen as he watches all thirty of us file in. The smuggler shakes Majed's hand and motions to us to sit down. We spread out across the room. Majed and Zaher sit down at a table with the man. Sara and I sit in a corner with the brothers Bassem and Ayham and our cousin Nabih.

'I could eat another burger,' I say.

Sara whacks my arm.

'Aren't you supposed to be an athlete?' says Ayham, grinning.

'Shut up,' I say. 'We athletes need to keep up our strength.'

After ten minutes Majed comes over to our table to update us on the plan. The smuggler has gone, he doesn't want to be seen with us. But he's agreed to take us all to Germany tonight and will bring cars here to pick us up. We're to wait here until he gives a signal to come out. I'm relieved and surprised. It was all so easy. We'll be in Germany by the morning.

We wait, play songs on our phones, take selfies, mess around. Every ten minutes, Majed gets up and peers outside into the street. Half an hour passes, forty minutes. At last, Majed loses patience and tries calling the smuggler, but gets no answer. He throws a nervous look at the McDonalds staff. They're staring at us. We've outstayed our welcome. We file out into the street to wait for the smuggler there. At midnight, the McDonalds closes its doors.

Exhausted and disappointed, we give up on the smuggler and trudge back to Keleti station to find a place to sleep.

We pick our way among the thousands of sleeping bodies until at last we find a clear spot to camp in the underground concourse. I lie down next to Sara on a pile of clothes. I'm too tired to notice the noise and the chaos around me. I close my eyes and try to picture the winding streets of Damascus. I see Mum and Shahed once more, shopping in the covered market. Tears trickle out from under my closed eyelids. I lie completely still so no one notices. I don't want anyone to know I'm hurting. I have to stay strong. I wait and drift off to sleep, the soft breeze drying the tears on my cheeks.

I wake the next morning to the sight of kids sifting through garbage from overflowing trash cans. I look at my phone. It's Monday, the last day in August. We've been on the road nearly three weeks. How much longer will it take? I walk upstairs with Sara into the square to join the queue for the toilets. The crowds are waking up outside the station building. The line of police still blocks the ornate doorway, stopping anyone with the wrong skin colour from entering and trying their luck on a train.

Sara's phone rings. She walks a little way off to take the call. Ten minutes later she's back. The toilet queue has barely moved. It was Sara's friend in Hanover, Hala, calling to tell Sara that her former neighbour from Damascus, a guy called Khalil, is also stuck in Budapest. He's just a kid like me, sixteen years old, and travelling alone. Hala asked Sara if she would take care of him. One more won't make any difference to the family. We've got lots of room. Sara says she's told him to come and find us here in the station.

Just then, the journalists, Lam and Magdalena, melt out of the crowd. I couldn't be happier to see them. They'll know what to do.

'What took you so long?' says Lam, beaming at us.

He turns to Sara.

'And how fares brave Antar?'

She grins.

'Good, thanks,' says Sara. 'Do you know how we get out of here?'

'Hmm,' says Lam, frowning. 'That's a hard one.'

We use the stinking toilets, then the journalists follow us back downstairs to join our friends. The rest of our group are awake now. They sit spread out along the wall of the concourse, all frantically working to find a way out of Budapest. Umm Muqtada and her group are still waiting on her smuggler and brother-in-law, Ali. He was supposed to meet her here in the city, but he hasn't been in touch about a meeting. Zaher and his family have spent all morning trying every smuggler contact they can find, but no one is answering their phones. There are thousands of us trying to get out. The smugglers are in high demand.

Getting on a train through to Austria seems our best chance. Lam has heard a rumour the Hungarian police will reopen the station this morning for a few hours and let people on a train across the border. In theory, all we'd need to do is to buy a ticket and get on. But we aren't the only ones trying for that train. The queue to buy tickets is already several hours long. There's no other way, we'll have to try it. Sara and I tramp back up the stairs and around the left-hand side of the station building, Lam and Magdalena in tow. We hit the queue straight away. A ragged line snakes back from a side entrance all the way to the corner of the building.

'My God,' Sara says. 'We'll be here for weeks.'

A girl in a high-vis jacket overhears Sara and stops. We don't have to wait in this queue, she tells us, there are other stations in the city where we can buy international train tickets. The closest, Déli station, is just a fifteen-minute bus ride away. The girl guarantees there will be no queues there. Most people don't know about it. Sara thanks the girl and the volunteer melts back into the crowd. Another station. It's worth a try. Sara heads back downstairs to offer to go there and buy tickets for the others. I sit down on the concrete floor to wait with Magdalena. Lam is snapping pictures of the desperate queue for tickets. He looks up. I must have been frowning at him.

'I was a refugee too,' says Lam with a grin. 'So it's ok for me to take photos.'

I'm surprised. I hadn't thought anything of his taking photos of us. It's a bizarre situation. The world should see it.

'I don't care about you taking photos of anything,' I say. 'Do your job.'

There's a pause as he returns to his work.

'What do you mean, you were a refugee?' I say.

'I grew up in Laos,' says Lam. 'And then I went to France. Now I'm French.'

I don't ask any more questions. Lam raises his camera again and I watch the photographer work. So Lam was a refugee too. That word. Refugee. I guess you never lose the name once you're given it. I stare at him, full of respect and admiration. He already fled once. I'm stunned that he would come back here to live through it again with us. And he isn't only here to get some cool photos, he went out of his way to help us.

Sara returns with one of the brothers, Bassem, and our cousin Majed. Majed goes to the Western Union at the edge of the square. When he comes back he passes Sara a wad of cash, enough to buy tickets for all three of us and our cousin Nabih. Sara reaches down the neck of her t-shirt and pulls an even bigger wad of money out of her bra. She adds our money to it and puts it back.

'Hey,' says Lam and holds up his camera. 'Do that again. I want to get a picture.'

Sara grins and does it again, then sets off with Bassem to find the other train station. I watch them wander across the square. My stomach growls. I'm starving. I'm about to suggest getting food when Lam jumps up without warning and runs off towards the station entrance, Magdalena close behind. I follow the journalists towards the station. A huge crowd has gathered on the steps outside. Hundreds of frantic people, shouting, pushing, and shoving each other. The police stand back along one side and watch the chaos. They've opened the station. They're allowing anyone with a ticket to try and cram themselves onto a train for Austria.

I avoid the crush and duck back downstairs to sit with the others. Another crowd is pushing their way into the station entrance underneath. Mama is standing watching the scrum, hands

on hips. Her son Zaher stands next to her. They both look sceptical. None of us want to try getting onto a train if it means risking
being trampled to death in the process. We decide to wait until it's
calmer. Besides, it might be safer this way. If we let this train go
first, we can see whether it really does make it across the border
into Austria. After all, the whole thing could be a trap. A trick to
clear the station and get everyone off the streets and into a camp.
But then we'd be stuck in Hungary forever, or sent back. We've
heard rumours. Nobody trusts the authorities here. Best to wait
and see.

Sara and Bassem return with the tickets an hour later. The shoving crowd in the underground concourse has melted away. The first
train has departed. Those who didn't get on it have retreated to
their makeshift camps in the station. Sara grins triumphantly and
waves a wad of rectangular papers in the air. The other train station
was completely empty, she says, there was no queue. She hands out
the tickets valid for the next day. It's a gamble. No one can say
whether the station will still be open to us tomorrow.

A teenage boy appears out of the crowd and sidles up to me.
He's pale, with a shock of brown hair. He wears a sleeveless black
puffa jacket, black sweatpants, and white trainers.

'Are you Sara?' he says.

'No, she is,' I say, pointing to Sara. 'You're Khalil?'

The kid flashes a wide, cheeky grin. I like him straight away.

'Hi,' says Sara. 'So you'll come with us? I got you a ticket for the
train tomorrow.'

Khalil sits down next to us, instantly part of the family. I can tell
he's relieved to have company. We're all in this together. That night,
we sit in the Burger King as the square grows dark, posting selfies on
Instagram and chatting online with friends back home. Suddenly
my phone lights up and buzzes with a flood of notifications. New
followers. Lots of them. I scroll through the accounts. All of them
are Belgian. I wrack my brain for an explanation. It must be Steven,
that journalist I met in the park in Belgrade. Could I have been on
Belgian TV? Are these viewers who want to follow my journey on
Instagram? That must be it. I stare in disbelief as the notifications

keep coming. I'm pleased and bewildered by the response. I'm just a girl from Syria going to Germany. There must be thousands of others just like me doing the same journey. Why are they interested in me?

It hits me that Steven might be able to help us get out of here. He's a TV journalist, he must have a lot of life experience. At least he'll know what's going on. I write to him, tell him where we are and about our plan to get the train the next day. He writes back, telling me to stay in touch and warning me to be careful.

Majed comes to find us in the Burger King. He doesn't want to sleep another night in the station. He's right. It's dangerous and filthy. We decide to find a hotel. The new kid Khalil says he'll join us, but the others stay put in the station. We know the hotel will be very expensive. But we're willing to pay to stay safe. We walk down the long, busy street back towards the McDonalds. We try every hotel we pass. All the receptionists want to see our passports or just say straight out they aren't serving refugees. We reach a hotel with an old-fashioned, patterned façade. Maybe if we try a more expensive hotel they'll ask fewer questions. We stride in through the sliding doors and up to the reception desk as if we are just a normal family on holiday. Americans, maybe. The gamble pays off. No passport, no papers. I stare at the extravagant chandeliers in the lobby. The price is very high. But we'd have happily paid more to avoid another night in the station.

We check out of the hotel the next day and go back to the station early to find the others before we get our train. When we arrive, we get a shock. Rows of riot police line both entrances. The station is closed again, but this time they've shut it down completely. They aren't letting anyone in or out; us, locals, or tourists.

We go in search of Zaher, picking our way through the families, blankets, and tents on the underpass floor. As before, I feel a pang of guilt as we approach our friends. The hotel room was very comfortable. I'd have paid for rooms for all of them if I could. Zaher looks depressed. He says we were right to be suspicious of yesterday's train. It didn't make it through to Austria. The police stopped it along the way and took any passengers without valid visas to prison. I look at the grim line of riot police blocking the door, then down at the train ticket in my hand. Even if we wanted to, we couldn't get on our train today. Hundreds of euros, wasted. I fight the rising wave of despair.

Chanting drifts down from the square above.

'Germany, Germany, Germany.'

We follow the brothers Ayham and Bassem up the stairs to see what's going on. An angry crowd, mostly men, has gathered outside the station entrance. Lam is on the edge of the crowd, snapping pictures. Beside him, Magdalena spots us and waves. We join them.

'Germany, Germany, Germany,' the men chant, their clenched fists raised in the air. They bang on plastic water bottles and wave Syrian passports in the air.

'You took our money,' shouts a man next to me in Arabic, brandishing his useless train ticket. 'You thieving dogs. Let us on the train.'

'Open the station,' chant the crowd. 'Germany, Germany, Germany. Angela, Angela, Angela.'

'Who's Angela?' I ask Sara. She shrugs.

'Angela Merkel,' says Magdalena. 'The leader of Germany.'

Oh, that Angela.

A line of riot police forms a wall at the front of the protest, still, menacing. They wear masks over their faces as if they think we carry deadly airborne diseases. The crowd convulses around them. A man breaks out and rushes the police line. The cops jump on him and the whole crowd pulses with movement. Another battalion rushes forwards in formation along the road to my left. Sara grabs me and Khalil by the arm and propels us both back down the stairs into the safety of the concourse. I crane my neck just in time to see the brothers Ayham and Bassem and our cousin Nabih follow Lam deeper into the crowd.

Downstairs, the women sit in silent groups, listening to the chanting above their heads. In a corner, a number of volunteers have set up a screen and are projecting a Tom and Jerry cartoon. Sitting crossed-legged in front is a crowd of young kids. Among them, engrossed in the action, sits Idris's little boy, Mustafa, and

Umm Muqtada's kids. I sit down nearby and get out my phone. I
scroll through my contacts. Who can help us? I'll try the journalist
Steven again. I bring up his contact and record a message.

'There are thousands of people here,' I speak into the phone.
'There's a problem and the police are arresting people. It's dangerous here and we don't know what to do. They're letting people pay
for tickets, but they closed the station. They're stealing our money.
No one will travel from here. Come to Budapest and help us!'

I finish recording and lean back against the filthy wall of the
concourse. I close my eyes and see angry fists punching the air as
the chanting continues above my head. Why won't these people let
us go? We don't want to stay, and they don't want us here either.
But they've got us in a trap. We can't go forwards, can't go back. I
put my head in my hands and press my palms against my eyelids,
fighting back the tears. I feel a hand on my shoulder. It's Sara. She
puts out her hand and hauls me up. We escape the protests and
retreat to Burger King, later to the hotel.

We arrive the following morning to find the demonstrators
already in the square in front of the station, singing, chanting, and
clapping in the air. They hold signs made from scraps of cardboard:
'We love Germany.' 'We heart Merkel,' or simply, 'Help us.' Down
in the underpass, Umm Muqtada is upset. She's still waiting for a
reply from her smuggler, Ali. The group she is travelling with is
growing impatient. None of us knows how long we are going to be
stuck here in this pit. We hole up most of the day in Burger King
while the adults sit in the station below, discussing their next move.
I'm bored. The others are all tapping and scrolling on their phones.
I ask Sara what she's doing. She says she's writing to Mowgli, the
smuggler from Turkey. He's added her on Facebook.

'Are you mad?' I say.

'What's wrong with that?' says Sara, taking a sip of her coke.
'He might be able to help us.'

'Err, did you forget about that time he crammed us all into that
boat and then jumped off and left us to drown?' I say.

Sara raises her eyebrows and goes back to tapping into her
phone with her thumbs. I send another voice message to Steven. I

ask him if he thinks the station will open and we can catch a train, or whether we should try and get a smuggler to drive us into Austria. I tell him we're worried the police will catch us, fingerprint us, and send us back to Greece or, worse, to Turkey. Steven is now back in his newsroom in Brussels and sends me a photo of a news alert that has flashed up on his screen. The station is open again, but no international trains are running. The Hungarian prime minister is in Brussels to discuss the situation with European Commission. I sigh and thank him. It's clear he can't tell us what we should do.

We return to the underpass mid-afternoon to find the smuggler Ali sitting with our friends. Finally, he's arrived. I don't like him on first sight. He looks smug and arrogant. He wears a shirt and jeans and has kept his sunglasses on, even in the shade. Ali is explaining to Umm Muqtada that he'll have the first car ready to leave for Germany tonight. He offers to come back later with a van and take the rest of the group. It would be a storage van, he says, just a cab and an empty compartment in the back without seats. We would have to sit on the floor for the whole five-hour drive through Hungary and Austria to the German border. Majed stands up and motions for us to come with him. Nabih, Khalil, Sara and I get to our feet and follow him around a corner.

'What do you think?' says Majed.

'About the van?' says Sara. 'Or about that asshole back there?'

Khalil giggles.

'About the van,' says Majed, frowning. 'Should we ask Ali to take us too?'

'No,' says Sara. 'No way. Have you forgotten that story about those Syrian guys last week who suffocated in a van like that? We can survive in the sea but not in a van without air.'

I don't trust this Ali guy either, I tell Majed. He'd leave us at the first sign of trouble. Look at the way he treated poor Umm Muqtada, and she's family, his brother's wife. Not replying to her messages for days, leaving her alone with two young kids to cross the sea, to cross the border into Hungary. We're desperate, but not that desperate.

Majed sighs. The trains across the border to Austria still aren't running. The only way is to try and find another smuggler, someone we trust. We rejoin the others. Ali is finalizing his plans with the rest of our group. He'll pick up Umm Muqtada and her kids later tonight and send a van for Zaher and his family as soon as he can. Then he'll send a third car back for Coco and the others, but he can't say when that will be. Ali stalks away through the concourse towards the stairs. Umm Muqtada stands, takes both her children by the hand, and wanders off to gather her things.

'Are you sure about that guy?' Majed asks Zaher when she's gone.

'Don't have much choice,' says Zaher. 'We can't afford to keep spending hundreds of euros on worthless train tickets, hoping to be let on board.'

'It looks like Ali has his hands full with all of you,' says Majed. 'We'll find another way.'

We leave the others and spend the evening following up with some of the smuggler Mowgli's contacts. We arrange meetings with three different smugglers, two Hungarians and another Moroccan. Not one of them shows up. Tired and defeated, we go back to the hotel.

The next morning in the station, we don't find Zaher and his family in their normal spot. The brothers Bassem and Ayham are also gone, as are Umm Muqtada and her children. Only Idris and little Mustafa, Blondie, the Lebanese girl Coco, Ahmad from Latakia, his sisters, and a couple of others are left. I feel strangely alone. I miss baby Kamar and the older woman, Mama. We didn't even say goodbye.

Lam and Magdalena come strolling out of the crowd.

'Your friends left?' says Lam.

I nod.

'So what's your plan?' says Lam.

I shrug. We haven't got one. The situation seems more hopeless than ever. Lam points at the stairs leading up to the station, at the usual crush of people trying to enter the building. Lam says he's heard rumours the police will let a few trains leave for the border today. We could try buying another ticket and see if we can get on one of them. If we're quiet, he says, and don't give ourselves away speaking loudly in Arabic, we might just make it through to Austria. It's worth a try. There's no other way out.

I wait with our cousin Nabih and the kid Khalil in Burger King while Sara and Majed go back to the station at Déli to buy new tickets. We watch through the restaurant window from above as the crowds battle their way in through the station entrance. The police stand by and watch the crush. TV film crews line the edge of the square. It's chaos.

Sara and Majed come back late afternoon with tickets for the eight o'clock train. By sunset, the crowd at the station has thinned out. We meet Lam and Magdalena while Majed is fetching sandwiches for the journey. The journalists carry large bags on their backs.

'We're coming with you,' says Lam.

I grin. It will be good to have them with us. If anything happens, Lam will know what to do. The nerves flutter in my gut as we enter the station, but there are no police around. We walk down the platform alongside an old, green train. Ahead, Majed climbs into the last carriage and sits down at a table. I follow and take the forward-facing window seat opposite him. The others file in behind me. Our cousin Nabih, Sara, Blondie, the kid Khalil, Lam, and Magdalena. Our friend Abdullah, who has decided to join us at the last minute, brings up the rear. I look at the time on my phone. Just before eight. Five minutes to go. I look around. We have the carriage to ourselves. Ahead, the door opens, and a blonde girl enters. She sits down at the far end near the door.

At last, the train begins to move. I grin at the others. We're finally getting out. I gaze out of the window. Cargo trains wait in a depot in front of a neglected warehouse. The rails cross over a road, yellow trams snake along the street below. We trundle over a bridge above a river, wide and shallow and dull green in the twilight.

We're all exhausted. Abdullah gets up from his seat, walks past us to the end of the carriage behind me and slumps into a corner, pulling his sweater over his face. Magdalena looks up from her phone. There's no guarantee we'll get as far as Austria, she reminds us. We could be walking into a trap. Earlier today, police stopped another train heading for the border at Biscke, a town just outside of Budapest. Now there's a stand-off as the police try to force all the migrants off the train and take them to a camp. So it's true. Today's trains were another trick. A trap by the police to clear the station. I look at Majed. He's looking out the window. He hasn't understood.

'Will the police stop this train too, then?' says Sara.

'I don't know. I don't think so,' says Magdalena. 'Their plan backfired on them. All the people are refusing to leave the train. There are loads of TV crews there. I don't think they'll try it again.'

'I guess we'll see,' says Lam.

He turns to Sara.

'You guys have your passports on you, right?' he says.

Sara nods. They're all still in our plastic pouches we bought for the sea crossing.

'I'm just thinking maybe you should hide them somewhere,' says Lam. 'Just in case.'

He's right. If we do get caught and the police find our passports it might cause problems for us later in Germany. Our passports are still safely hidden inside our bras, but I have no idea what the others have done with theirs. Sara translates Lam's suggestion for the others. Majed shrugs and puts his passport onto the table. The others do the same. Sara gathers them up, takes her plastic pouch out of her bra and puts all of our documents inside it. Then she puts the pouch back down the neck of her t-shirt. Lam grins at her.

'Nice,' he says.

I stare out of the window. Trees rise either side of the train as the tracks cut through a small wood. Beyond, fields, a valley, more depots and warehouses. The train screeches and begins to slow. We're stopping. We crawl past the station sign on the platform: Kelenföld.

Magdalena looks up from her notebook and glares at the door of the carriage. She waits, staring intently. A few minutes later we

pull away again and she goes back to writing. The train begins to
clatter as we pick up speed. Outside, a field of a thousand sunflow-
ers, bending their heads in the dying light. I count back. Six days.
Just six days in Hungary. It felt like months.

The train screeches and slows and pulls into a station. Another
sign: Tatabánya. Magdalena puts down her pen and stares again at
the carriage door. Lam looks up from his camera screen and the
journalists exchange looks. Doors slam, voices mutter in the corridor outside, but the door to our carriage stays firmly shut. The train
pulls out again and the journalists return to their work.

We sit in silence. It's dark now and the light from the train
carriage reflects on the inside of the black window. I watch the
others' reflections. Khalil is asleep. Across the table, Majed gazes at
his phone. I catch Sara's eye in the window reflection and she grins
sleepily. At the other end of the carriage, the blonde girl looks out
of the window and talks quietly into her phone. Nabih yawns,
stretches his arms above his head and asks Majed for something to
eat. Majed reaches down and pulls up a paper bag. He empties a
pile of sandwiches onto the table. Sara and I take one. Nabih gathers up four of them in his arms and puts them on the opposite table
for Khalil, Blondie, Lam, and Magdalena.

'Thanks,' says Lam. 'But we've got our own food.'

Nabih insists. The journalists take one to share. Nabih picks up
the extra sandwich and takes it down to the other end of the carriage, where Abdullah is still fast asleep. Nabih waves his hand in
front of Abdullah's face but he's out cold. Nabih shrugs and walks
past us to where the girl is sitting. She watches him warily as he
approaches. He holds out the sandwich.

'You want to eat?' he says in English.

The girl shakes her head. Then, abruptly, she breaks down into
loud sobs. Nabih looks back at us, bewildered as the girl puts her
face in her hands, her shoulders shaking. Magdalena and Lam
exchange glances.

'What's going on?' says Magdalena, standing up. 'What happened?'

At the end of the carriage Nabih is backing slowly away from the girl. Magdalena walks down the aisle towards them. Nabih returns to his seat, looking shaken.

'What happened?' I ask him. 'What did you say to her?'

'Nothing, I swear,' he says. 'I only offered her a sandwich.'

Lam stands and walks to the end of the carriage, where Magdalena and the girl are talking in low voices. The train is slowing again, the brakes screeching. Along the platform, out of the window, I see another sign: Györ.

Majed looks up.

'This is the last stop before the Austrian border,' he says.

The train doors clank open and there are footsteps in the passage outside. I hear Lam's raised voice at the end of the aisle. Magdalena spins around as the carriage door opens. I look up and my stomach sinks. A policeman stands in the doorway.

15

The policeman marches towards us, followed by a female cop and two more officers. They wear navy-blue uniforms and belts strung with pistols and shiny black batons. They reach our table.

'Where are you from?' the policewoman barks at us.

She's young and wears her dark hair drawn up into a long pony-tail. I look at Majed. He looks pale and slightly nauseated. Sara takes charge. She looks the policewoman straight in the eye.

'We're from Syria,' she says.

'Ok,' says the female cop. 'Off the train. All of you. Now.'

I'm too stunned to move at first. Then I see Lam looking at us from over the last policeman's shoulder. He winks at me and I manage a grin. We collect our stuff together, shuffle off the train and down onto the platform. The police surround us as if we're hardened criminals. Magdalena and Lam catch up with us along the platform.

'Where are you taking them?' says Magdalena.

'Who are you?' says one of the policemen, looking at her for the first time.

'We're journalists,' she says. 'If you hurt them, we'll print it.'

'Don't threaten us,' says the policewoman.

Magdalena makes a face at the cop and steps up alongside me and Sara. It was the blonde girl, Magdalena whispers. She called the police on us and told them where we were sitting. The girl told Magdalena she thought we were bad people, terrorists who were going to bomb the train. Then she regretted it when our cousin Nabih offered her some food.

'What an idiot,' says Sara loudly. 'Can't she see we're just human beings like her?'

The police march us off the platform and through sliding doors into a grand station entrance hall. We turn left into a waiting room.

The cops sit us down in a row along a wooden bench. Behind us, a large window opens onto the platform. I turn and watch our train pull out, on towards Austria. We were so close. Wait. Abdullah. I look around. He's not with us. He must be still on the train. He's probably still asleep, riding unaware across the border.

The police line up in front of us. Behind them, Lam is snapping pictures and Magdalena is writing in her notebook. Blondie sits on the end of the bench to my left. One of the policemen steps up in front of him.

'Stand up,' says the policeman and gestures with his hands. Blondie stands and the cop pats him down. The cop demands to see his bag. Blondie hands over his small backpack and the cop empties it out on the floor.

My stomach clenches. What will the police do when they find our passports? Will they take our fingerprints? Register us against our will? They could force us to stay in Hungary, or even worse, send us back the way we came. I look around wildly. We have to cross the border. We have to keep moving. We have to get to Germany.

The policewoman steps up to me next and orders me to stand. She pats me down. I hand over my phone and then the woman empties out my bag. The little I own spills out on the floor. The cop picks up a piece of card and turns it over. It's the business card of the hotel we stayed in in Budapest. The cop asks what it is. I shrug. The woman says something in Hungarian to the other policemen and they all laugh.

'Right,' says Sara in Arabic. 'These guys think they're shit-hot, huh?'

Khalil bursts out laughing.

'Ooh, the big men, so scary with their little plastic sticks,' says Sara. 'I bet their wives beat them with them when they get home. Ooh, I'm so scared.'

Nabih and I start giggling too. I know it isn't appropriate, it could even be dangerous. But I can't help laughing. The situation seems too absurd. Blondie and Majed both stare at their feet in humiliated silence. They aren't laughing. One of the policemen steps closer to Sara. He demands to know what we're laughing at. Sara looks him in the eye.

'We were just saying we aren't scared of you,' she says.

'Why not?' he says. 'You should be.'

'You know what?' I say to the policewoman. 'What's the worst you can do to us? Take us to jail?'

The woman looks at me in surprise.

'We survived the sea,' I say. 'What can you do to us now?'

The woman says nothing. Lam grins and keeps snapping photos. Nabih and I pull silly faces for the camera while Magdalena looks on, utterly horrified. Another policeman steps up to Majed. He's sitting on the other side of me, staring at the floor. The policeman orders him to stand. I nudge Majed and he gets to his feet. The policeman pats him down and empties his bag on the floor. Majed hands over his phone.

Sara is next. She has our papers. It's almost over. My heart is beating hard. This is it. What if they send us home, back to face the bombs? Just then, a phone rings. The cop who searched Majed says something in Hungarian and marches out of the waiting room. The female cop turns to her other colleagues.

Sara takes advantage of the distraction. She holds her backpack up to her front and begins fiddling with something around her neck. Then she coughs loudly. Majed raises his arms above his shoulders as if he's stretching. Sara lowers her head down to her backpack and lifts her left hand to her ear. I can't believe it. She's holding up the packet with the passports. Majed takes it and slips it into his pocket. We're in luck. No one has noticed.

The first cop comes back into the waiting room and the policewoman turns back to check Sara. She orders Sara to stand and the cop pats her down. Sara hands the cop her phone and the woman empties her bag. No passports. I breathe a sigh of relief. Nice move, Sara. It's all I can do to keep a straight face.

A blue flashing light whirs through the waiting room from the road outside. The tall policeman orders us to stand. I cram my few belongings back into my bag and follow the others through the entrance hall and out of the station doors. A white police truck is waiting for us in the car park. The cop leads us around to the rear and opens the double doors. Two rows of white plastic chairs face each other inside the vehicle. At the back, a fold-down chair is mounted on the divider to the driver's cabin. Through the gloom I can just make out a man sitting on the chair at the back. We pile into the truck. Outside, Lam and Magdalena watch in horror as the double doors slam shut behind us.

'Hello,' says the man on the seat, grinning and flashing his white teeth in the dark.

I jump out of my skin. Sara giggles. In the light from the cabin window I can just make out the man's multicoloured t-shirt and red trousers. The engine starts. The man points over his shoulder towards the two policemen in the cab.

'Look, look, look, look, look, look,' he says in a thick Afghan accent.

I stifle a giggle. The truck turns a corner and rolls down the road. The man pulls out his phone and grins again. He fiddles with the phone until a wheedling pop song blasts out of the tinny speakers. He raises his hands in the air.

'Look, look, look, look, look, look,' he says over the music.

We're all laughing out loud now. Hysteria takes hold inside the van. It's like a release. The laughter gives me courage and strength, makes me feel as if I can take on whatever might be coming next.

'Tell him to shut up,' says Majed. 'He's going to get us all in trouble.'

The man points at me.

'Where from?' he says.

'Syrian,' I say.

'Ah,' says the Afghan.

He reaches into his pocket and pulls out a dark red passport. He opens it on the photo page and holds it up to the light from the cabin. It looks nothing like him. It's clearly a cheap fake. He points to himself.

'Italian,' he says, grinning.

The truck slows and stops. We hear doors slamming, then the double doors open and light floods the van. The female cop orders us to get out one at a time. I wait in the truck as the others file out into the night. Then I climb out and look around. We're in a farm-yard, surrounded by tall barn buildings. The policewoman grabs my arm and marches me towards a one-storey temporary container between the barns. We step inside into a small office with a desk, a filing cabinet and two chairs. In the corner stands a beige machine that looks like a photocopier. The woman points at the machine. Stepping closer, I see it's not a photocopier. There's a square glass plate with a small screen above it.

'Name, date of birth, place of birth,' says the cop.

'Yusra Mardini, 5 March 1998, Damascus.' I say. 'That's in Syria.'

The cop looks at me, trying to work out if I'm being cheeky. She turns back and types into the machine. Then she orders me to hold out my left hand and presses the tops of my four fingers down onto the brightly lit glass. Four dark splodges appear on the screen. She takes each of my fingers in turn and presses and rolls the fin-gertips across the scanner. She does the same with my right hand. My fingerprints. Recorded, in their system. My heart sinks. What will that mean later? The cop reaches into a drawer in the desk, pulls out a camera and takes my photo. Then she produces a grey, plastic tray.

'Shoelaces,' she barks.

I shrug, pull the laces out of my trainers and hand them over. She points at the string bracelet on my wrist. I take it off and put it in the tray. The cop grabs my bag and puts it in a corner with the others. We're done. She seizes my arm and hauls me out of the office and into the barn building on our left. Inside it smells faintly of animals. Both walls are lined with three-metre-high railings marking out a series of stables. The stables are open at the top. A gap runs all the way up to the barn's corrugated iron roof.

The cop marches me to the end of the row and stops outside the last stable. Through the bars I see Sara and our cousins Nabih and Majed already inside. The cop unlocks the door and I step inside. Six white plastic sun loungers take up most of the floor space. A few strands of hay lie scattered on the floor. The cop locks the door behind me and strides off.

'So, that was fun,' I say once she's gone. 'What was all that about the shoelaces?'

'Yeah, she took mine too,' says Sara. 'As if I could kill myself with a shoelace. What a joke. I told her if we wanted to kill ourselves we would have stayed in Syria. Like I'm going to come all this way and commit suicide in this dump of a country.'

The stable door opens again and Khalil and Blondie step in. A policeman locks the door behind them and throws a large bundle over the top of the railings. I pick it up and peel off a piece of fabric, a grey fleece blanket. I open it and read the white lettering: 'UNHCR. The UN Refugee Agency.'

The policeman is back, holding a cardboard box in both arms. He lifts a small, oval package out of the box and throws it over the top of the railings. It lands on the concrete floor with a soft thud. A second package flies over, followed by a third, a fourth, a fifth. The last one lands in the hay at the back of the stable. I walk over and pick it up. It's a sandwich, wrapped in cling film. I unwrap the plastic and I'm hit by a foul stench of rubbery processed chicken. Ugh. I'm not eating that. The others don't even look up. We leave the food where it landed.

I sit down between Nabih and Khalil on one of the sun loungers. They both look depressed. My mind races. Tears prick my eyes. Our friend Abdullah must be in Austria by now. Maybe he's even already on another train to Germany. That blonde girl. Why couldn't she have just left us alone? They fingerprinted us. Does that mean it's all over? Will they send us back to Turkey, to Syria? Even if we get to Germany, will they send us back here to Hungary? It might still be ok. My cousin Nabih and I are under eighteen, so we're classed as minors. Sara and Majed are our legal guardians. We've heard that European countries don't deport minors and their guardians. But we aren't sure. That's all we have to go on. Rumours and half-understood laws.

Sara looks down at me, then at Khalil. We're both close to tears, starving, scared, and confused.

'Hey,' says Sara, smiling. 'Don't worry. They can't keep us here forever.'

Sara paces to the other end of the stable, turns, and walks back.

'You know,' she says. 'You've got to say *Alhamdulillah*, praise God. This morning we were eating burgers in Burger King. Last night we were sleeping in an expensive hotel. Now we're sleeping in a stable and they throw sandwiches at us that a dog wouldn't eat. And tomorrow, who knows? That's life.'

'She's right,' says Majed. 'We're safe, no one's hurt. Thank God for those things.'

A man appears at the railings and introduces himself in Arabic. He says he's a translator, on our side, here to help us. Majed asks him what will happen to us now. The translator tells us the police will keep us here for the night. Then, in the morning, we'll be processed and given a transit paper allowing us to leave Hungary. After that we'll be free to go. I catch my breath. Maybe things aren't as bleak as they seem. Majed is sceptical, but the translator insists. We can cross the border to Austria tomorrow if we like, go to Germany, wherever. The translator leaves us, and we lie down on the plastic sun loungers underneath the grey blankets. No one is in the mood for talking. All we can do is wait for what tomorrow brings.

I'm woken by a loud female voice telling me to get up.

I open my eyes. It's morning. I struggle to work out where I am. My back hurts.

'Time to go,' says the voice.

I look up. The female cop is at the stable door. Two policemen are with her. The others are already standing. I peel the blanket off my legs and struggle to my feet. The woman unlocks the door and we file out. The cops lead us out of the stables and across the courtyard into the second barn. Instead of stables, this barn has a large metal cage on one side. Through the bars I see a crowd waiting inside. About forty people, all men by the look of it. Those nearest to the door look up as we file in. They stare at me and Sara. We sit on the concrete and do our best to ignore them.

It's late morning by the time the policewoman comes back. The translator is with her. They lead us into the reception building and give us back our things. The translator tells us a bus will pick us up from here and take us wherever we want to go. Hope rises in my chest as I battle to thread my shoelaces back into my trainers. Can they really be setting us free? The translator warns us not to get caught by the police again. If they find out we're already on their system they might take us to a real prison, he says.

The policewoman appears again at the office door and beckons. Outside, a large, black truck is waiting. The cop leads us around to the back and opens the double doors. Inside there are no windows, only a small hatch at the back that leads to the driver's cabin. My eyes adjust to the gloom as the cop fiddles with a key. She steps back and swings open an inner door I hadn't spotted before. My stomach drops. It's a steel cage.

'Get in,' says the cop.

'But the translator said we're free to go,' says Sara.

'In.'

We climb inside. The cop slams the cage door behind us and locks it. Then the truck doors crash shut. It's dark, the only daylight comes from the hatch to the front cabin. My heart is beating hard. Where are they taking us now? I look at Sara. I can just make out her face in the gloom. She's furious. The cop climbs into the driver's cabin and closes the hatch, plunging us into total darkness. The engine starts, the truck pulls away. It's so humiliating. Why are they treating us as if we're hardened criminals? That translator. I don't understand. Why did he say they would let us go? The hurt deepens and turns to anger. We trusted him. He betrayed us. Couldn't he have just been straight with us?

We sit in gloomy silence in the dark as the truck swerves and chugs along. After twenty minutes it slows to a stop and the engine dies. Moments later, the back doors open and light floods in. I screw up my eyes against the sun as the policewoman reaches in to unlock the cage door. I clamber out after the others and look around. We're in a camp. Rows of off-white, pointed tents stand in lines outside a long, grey building. Outside each tent sits a large refuse bag, overflowing with trash. It smells bad. There are people everywhere, men, women, and children, walking between tents, carrying laundry, or sitting under trees in the shade. Behind us, the cop climbs back into the truck. The engine fires up and the vehicle beeps, turns and drives off, past an open metal gate. We're alone. There's no sign of any staff.

A woman in a red and white *hijab* is staring at me. I walk up to her.

'Excuse me,' I say. 'How long have you been here?'

'Three months,' she says.

'And what are you waiting for?'

'I don't know. No one tells us anything,' says the woman. 'I want to go to my husband in Germany. But then I came here. They say I'm supposed to stay here six months. I'm with my three children. So, well, I just wait.'

I look at her in pity and horror.

'We want to go to Germany too,' I say, looking around, trying to keep the panic out of my voice. 'Right now, today. If we leave now we could be there by tonight.'

I turn and rejoin the others. Majed has found a camp resident who knows a smuggler in a nearby village. The smuggler might be able to take us across into Austria. We're only an hour's drive from the border. Majed arranges for the smuggler to collect us from here. We're to wait for him outside on the road. Apparently, there's no fence keeping us in here. We can just walk out.

We turn and wander back towards the metal gate. There's still no sign of any staff. Majed tugs the gate and it swings open. We file out onto the road outside. I grin at the others. That was easy. But we know we can't get caught again. None of us wants to find out what a real Hungarian prison is like. We hurry further down the road away from the camp.

'I'm so done with the smugglers here,' says Sara as we walk. 'They always say they'll do something for you and then they disappear. Let's go back to Budapest.'

We all stop walking and stare at her. We're so close to Austria already. The border is only an hour's drive from here. Why would we go back to Budapest? But Sara is adamant. She wants to try again on the train. She's sick of dealing with unreliable smugglers.

We know people in Budapest, she says. We know a hotel we can stay in. But Majed and the others want to try the smuggler, see if we can make it across the border right away. The argument drags on as we wait for the car to pick us up. A few cars pass but no one stops. Over an hour later, a minivan appears on the road ahead. It slows as it passes us and pulls up. Sara marches up to the driver's window. We follow. The driver is a man in his mid-thirties with an open face and a kind smile. He seems harmless, almost normal. Sara tells him we've changed our minds and want to go Budapest. The driver names a price and Sara opens the sliding door along the side of the van. We're all gawping at her.

'What?' she says. 'Come on, let's go.'

I shrug and get in. The others climb in behind me. Before we know it, we're speeding back towards Budapest. Sara's won. Khalil brings out his phone and says he's found another smuggler we can try. Sara frowns, but Majed thinks it's worth a go. Half an hour later, Khalil's phone lights up again and buzzes. The smuggler has two cars and says he can take us all the way to Germany. But we have to get back to Budapest, fast.

'Tell him we're coming,' Majed tells Khalil. 'Tell him we're going as fast as we can.'

I stare out the window, wondering what's coming next. There has to be a way out of this country. I'm exhausted. Tired of running, tired of being on the road. I just want to arrive somewhere. Feel safe. Settle down. For the first time since leaving home it hits me how far I am from Mum, from Damascus, from everything and everyone I love. I turn my head, stare hard out of the window, and hope nobody notices my tears. We've been driving about an hour and a half when I spot blue flashing lights ahead on the other side of the road. A police van, parked right in the middle of the opposite lane. Behind it, a huge crowd of people are walking down the highway towards us, away from Budapest. At the front, a man waves a huge, blue flag with yellow stars on it. The flag of the European Union.

'Look at all those people,' I say. 'What's going on?'

No one speaks, we all stare out of the windows to the left as we drive on past the crowd. Thousands of men, women, and children, walk slowly, exhausted, along the highway. Some of them don't even have shoes. The cars speed past them. Further back, a few families sit, resting on the side of the road. We drive on towards the city.

The driver drops us by the square in front of the station building in Budapest. The crowd has thinned out, leaving piles of rubbish strewn across the concrete. The police guarding the doorway are also gone. We step inside the station building and find a row of people sleeping inside against a low wall, pairs of jeans hung out to dry on the wall above them. I wonder if any of our friends are still here. We walk around the sleeping crowd and down into the concourse underneath. There, in the same spot as before, sits our friend from Latakia, Ahmad, and his sisters. Idris sits a little way away, Mustafa lying next to him, his head in his father's lap.

'What are you doing back here?' says Ahmad. 'I thought you got the train.'

Majed fills the others in on our prison adventure.

'Why did you come back here?' says Ahmad, shaking his head. 'Some thugs were here earlier. They threw fireworks at the crowd and we had to hide down here. Then a guy came around saying he was going to walk to Austria. A load of people went with him. They're all mad. It's at least three days' walk.'

So that was the crowd we saw walking along the highway. I wonder if they'll make it through. I glance around the ravaged station. Maybe we should start off on foot too, back in the direction we've just arrived from? Just then, Khalil's phone rings. It's the smuggler, telling him he'll meet us at the McDonalds down the road. My heart sinks. That's if he turns up. We're going around in circles. Will we ever get out of this trap?

We leave Ahmad at the station and walk down the busy main road to the McDonalds. There's no sign of the smuggler when we arrive. Khalil calls and calls but the smuggler doesn't answer. We wait for two hours and then wander back to the station. We try another of Mowgli's contacts and wait for his reply in Burger King. Our last glimmers of hope seep away as dusk settles on the square outside. At nine thirty in the evening, we finally give up. It begins to rain and we trudge back down the road towards our old hotel. I hardly notice my hair getting soaked. I can't believe we'll ever get out of this place. None of us talks. We all just want to sleep.

Sara's phone rings.

'What?' she says into the handset. 'Wait, what, really? Ok, we're coming now. Yes, we'll run. Tell them to wait.'

Sara hangs up and turns to me, her eyes shining.

'That was Ahmad,' she says and grabs my shoulders. 'He says he heard the government are sending free buses to the border, to Austria. Tonight. Now. From the station. He heard soon. He said we should hurry up. We've got to go back. Right now.'

'Is he sure?' I say. 'I just want to sleep, to be honest.'

'It could be a rumour,' says Majed doubtfully. 'Or another trap.'

'Do you really care at this point?' says Sara. 'What more can they do to us? Let's run.'

Sara sets off back down the road towards the station. I follow her at a sprint, my bag bouncing on my back as I weave past the pedestrians through the hazy drizzle. Ahead looms the station, below the cars' red tail lights glint off the black oily puddles. We arrive on the square to find the crowd swelling again. Two rows of ancient navy and yellow buses are parked up along the road. We run between them, dodging through the throng, and scanning for Ahmad. I hear him shout and spot him standing with his sisters next to one of the buses. As we get closer I see Idris standing nearby. He grins at us as we approach.

'Where's Mustafa?' I ask him.

Idris points over his shoulder towards a woman in a headscarf and a long flowing skirt. She stands with her back to us, Mustafa in her arms. The boy looks at me over the woman's shoulder and waves. The woman sees and turns around. I see her face and burst out laughing.

'Oh hi,' says Magdalena. 'You lot coming to Austria?'

'Hope so,' I say. 'Nice disguise.'

'That's nothing,' she says. 'You should see Lam.'

A little way off I see Lam standing awkwardly next to a Kurdish woman and her small son, pretending he belongs to them. The photographer waves and opens his jacket for a second to reveal his sixteen-thousand-dollar camera.

'Still got my *habibti*,' says Lam, grinning. Then he turns to Sara. 'Old Antar survived a night with the police, I hear. Everything ok?'

'It will be if we get to Austria,' she says. 'You coming too?'

'Wouldn't miss it,' he says.

The driver of the bus opens the doors and the crowd nearby begins to surge. It could be a trap, another trick by the government to get us all into camps. There's no time for second thoughts. The crowd is already fighting its way onto the bus, sweeping us along with it. We'll have to take the gamble. Maybe this time we'll win. I grab Sara round the neck and jump up and down.

'We're going to Germany!' I shout.

The bus is old, made to hold about forty passengers. We're easily more than a hundred, crammed in three to a seat and sprawled on the floor. Sara and I find a corner of the floor up against the back doors, crushed in between strangers. The bus chugs off noisily in a cloud of diesel fumes. I fall asleep with my head against the shuddering door. After an hour, I wake to shouts. The bus has pulled up on the side of the highway. The bus door behind me opens and I tumble out onto the side of the road. Black, toxic-smelling smoke billows out of the back of the bus. Sara clambers out behind me, coughing. I put my hand on her shoulder.

'This is just your luck, Sara,' I tell her, grinning. 'We're finally getting out of Hungary and the bus breaks down.'

We wait two hours on the side of the road in the pouring rain until another bus comes to pick us up. It arrives already full of people. Somehow, we all squeeze in, even more tightly packed than before. I can barely breathe, let alone get back to sleep. Cramped up against the doors, I pull out my phone and leave the journalist Steven a voice message telling him we're all on buses going to Austria. He replies saying he and his film crew are also on their way to the border. Maybe we'll see each other there. I mutter a silent prayer to myself. Please God, let this really be happening. We're really getting out.

The bus shudders to a stop and we pile out onto the road into the grey early morning. It's still raining, and a light wind is up. I can't feel my legs from the cramp. We follow a snaking line of people along a path towards a low building. As we cross the border into Austria, Sara breaks down in tears. She stops walking and puts her hands over her face, her shoulders shaking.

'What's wrong with you?' I say.

It's so unlike Sara to break down like this.

'Now you cry?' says Lam. 'After all that? You were such a badass and when you're finally safe, you cry?'

'I'm just glad to be out,' says Sara between sobs.

We all look away, leave her to calm down. Rows of modern coaches line the concrete forecourt, sent by the Austrian government to pick us up and take us to Vienna. All we have to do now is find ourselves a space on one of them. I look back at Sara, still sobbing with relief at my side. Lam opens his bag and pulls out a bunch of bananas, snaps one off and hands it to me. I eat in the rain and watch my sister pull herself together.

PART SIX

The Dream

16

I step down from the bus and gaze around. It takes a few moments to register what I'm seeing. Crowds of people line the forecourt of Vienna's main train station, smiling, clapping, and cheering us. I scan the colourful banners and homemade posters and read my very first German words. *Flüchtlinge*, refugees. *Wilkommen*, welcome. I can't believe it. These people want to help us. They've come here to welcome us into their country. Tears prick my eyes. I'm overwhelmed by the gesture. I stumble with Sara past the cheering strangers. Volunteers hand us tea, sandwiches, and bottled water. One man hands us each a rose. Sara takes the flower, looks at me, and grins. Relief washes over me. We made it out of Hungary. We're in Austria. We'll take the train across the final border to Germany in the morning.

Sara's phone buzzes. It's our friend Abdullah, who made it to Austria on the train ahead of us. He's been staying here in Vienna with his cousin and offers to put us up for the night. It'll be a squeeze in the small apartment, but Abdullah's cousin says our whole group should come. Lam and Magdalena decide to stay in the station and work. They want to take photos and interview the thousands of new arrivals and the locals who've come to welcome them. Before we part ways, the journalists promise to visit us wherever we end up in Germany. I watch them disappear off into the crowd and wonder if I'll ever see them again.

I look down at my rain-soaked, purple hoodie and muddy, grey sweatpants. I need new clothes. I don't want to arrive in Germany looking like this. We stop at a clothes shop on the way to Abdullah's cousin's apartment. It's a Saturday and the shop is crammed with people. My phone buzzes in the queue for the till. It's the journalist, Steven. I tell him I'm in Vienna and agree to meet him later for another interview.

We find Abdullah's cousin's apartment and take turns to shower. I change into my new clothes and throw my old stuff away. I write to Mum and Dad, telling them we're safe and relieved to be out of Hungary. It's late by the time Steven writes to me again. He and his crew have finished working on the border and have made it to Vienna. I meet them in a McDonalds in the city centre. I'm too exhausted to do an interview, but we agree that the TV crew will come with us and film the next day on the train to Germany.

That night we sleep draped over sofas and on the floor of the apartment living room. Nobody minds the crush. It feels almost comfortable after two nights camping out on the road. The next morning we're up at dawn to catch one of the trains the Austrian and German governments have organized to take us to Germany. We find Steven and his team, Ludwig and Stefan, waiting for us in the train station and we all cram onto a packed train. We find an old-fashioned carriage, with two rows of three seats facing each other, just to ourselves. I gaze out of the window as the train pulls away from the station, gathers speed, and rattles out of the city. Soon we're trundling past dark-green pine forests, rolling fields and small towns.

Ludwig turns on his camera and begins filming. Steven asks me how I'm preparing to adapt to life in Europe. The question takes me by surprise. I haven't really thought about it before. I know it'll be a culture shock, that they'll do things differently in Germany than in Syria, but I'm not sure how exactly. I tell Steven it won't be easy, but I'll manage. I'll have to. Next Steven asks me what I learned on the journey. That's easy. I learned perspective. Back in Syria I wasted time worrying about petty things. Now I know what real problems are. My eyes have been opened.

'And do you feel like anything is possible now you've done this journey?' says Steven. 'Like going to the Olympics, for example?'

I look him straight in the eye and smile. Yes. I'll make it. I've never felt so sure of anything. The train chugs on past lush, green fields. On the horizon, mountains rise above the morning mist. Ludwig shuts off the camera for a while and I stare out of the window. I see Mum and Shahed, our lost home in Daraya, the winding streets of Damascus. I think of Dad and try to picture us all together again. Our journey is almost over. What's coming next?

It's several hours before we cross the border into Germany. I can tell by the shouts of celebration from the other carriages when we do. Butterflies flit in my stomach. It doesn't seem real. We made it. We're here. It doesn't matter if the police catch us now. We're in the right country. We just need to ask for shelter. Ludwig starts filming again as I watch the large, pointed-roofed villas and green hills of Bavaria speed by. Steven asks what I think of Germany, whether I think it's too clean. I smile into the camera.

'No,' I say. 'I love it.'

'Don't you think it looks a bit boring?' says Steven.

'We're going to make it fun,' I say.

We chat and laugh until the train slows and draws into Munich. Sara comes into the carriage and fills me in on her plan. When we get into the station, she says, we'll run away from the crowds and find a train going to Hanover, to her friend Hala. The train screeches and stops. We file out of the carriage, along the corridor towards the train doors. Steven and his crew go down onto the platform first to film us stepping out of the train. Two large male policemen are waiting at the train door. Sara steps down in front of me and goes to dodge out of their way. The nearest cop puts out his arm to stop her. He raises his index finger.

'Where do you think you're going, *habibti*?' the cop says and gently pushes her back into the stream of people. 'This way.'

I wave goodbye to Steven over my shoulder as the police escort him and his crew firmly off the platform. It seems we won't get to go to Hanover after all. We'll go where we're told. We don't mind too much. After all, we aren't the only new arrivals. That first weekend in September 2015 alone, twenty thousand people arrive on buses and trains from Hungary through Austria into Germany. Sara and I are just two of them. Germany has taken us in. For all of us, it's over. No more borders, no more smugglers, no more sleeping rough, no more danger, no more war. We follow the crowds to a row of waiting buses. At the station entrance, more people are clapping and waving 'Refugees welcome' signs. I grin at Sara. It's unreal. All these strangers, come to cheer and offer us a chance for a future. Who are these people?

We get on a bus that takes us to a reception camp. There is a big open tent with a restaurant. Above the canteen, a sign in Arabic: 'welcome.' We eat and are given a medical check-up, then we're ushered onto another bus. We drive for eight hours with no idea where we are heading. At last, the bus slows and turns off the motorway, then winds through dark city streets and pulls into a courtyard. We file off the bus as another crowd cheers and holds up homemade signs in Arabic: 'Welcome to Berlin Spandau.' So, we're in Berlin, the German capital. I look at my phone. It's very late, these people have waited up to greet us. A warm feeling spreads in my chest. We did it. Three in the morning, Monday 7 September. We've arrived.

Behind us, more crowds spill out of a whole fleet of buses. There must be several hundred of us arriving at the same time. This is a brand-new camp, opened spontaneously to house the new arrivals from Hungary. Here in Germany people refer to a camp like this as a *heim*. It translates as home, but the Germans also use it as shorthand for refugee housing. We soon adopt the word too.

We join the queue that leads inside the courtyard. Ahead, in what looks like a car park, sit rows of rectangular white tents. At the front of the queue stands a man in uniform. The man points at me, Sara, our cousins, and Khalil and asks us if we're a family. Sara points at me and tells the man we're sisters. The man takes our names and ages and points at Khalil.

'He's underage, does he have a legal guardian with him or is he alone, unaccompanied?' says the official.

'Khalil stays with us,' says Sara.

'So you're his guardian?' says the man.

Sara shrugs. The man points to a blonde woman waiting at his side who leads us to one of the white tents. Inside, there are three sets of black, steel bunk beds with white mattresses. A large camping lamp hangs from the ceiling and the floor is made of grey plastic matting. There is a small, white electric heater in one corner.

After the train station floor, or the prison stables, it feels like luxury. A five-star tent. I climb onto a top bunk, lie down, and close my eyes. We can stay. No more running. I repeat the words over and over to myself in my head. I can barely believe it. I fall into a deep sleep.

In the morning, I send a photo of the tent to Mum and Dad and tell them we're in Berlin. Then I step outside to find the bathrooms. The long, red-brick building is divided into several houses. Each house has two toilet blocks and separate showers. Outside the shower block stands a trestle table piled high with donated soap, shampoo, shower gel, razors, towels, and flannels. I take what I need and go inside to wash. The water runs black as the grime rinses off my feet. I look at myself in the mirror and grin at the chronic t-shirt tan on my upper arms.

I find the others in the canteen, eating a breakfast of bread rolls and cheese. No one talks about leaving Berlin and setting off for Hanover. We're all too tired to think of more travelling. All of us are just glad to have arrived somewhere we can stay. Sara writes to her friend Hala and tells her that her old neighbour, Khalil, is safe and well and with us in Berlin.

After breakfast, Sara and I go to look through the second-hand clothes the Berliners have donated to help us out. Let's be honest, no one wants to pick through someone else's old clothes. But I swallow my pride and tell myself I'm lucky. People here have been so generous. Besides, I don't have a choice. It's only September, but Berlin feels freezing after the heat of Budapest and I only have one change of clothes with me. Inside the building, a group of volunteers has hung up the donations in a kind of walk-in wardrobe to save us from scrabbling through boxes. Sara and I browse through the strange mix of jackets, shirts, jumpers, and a pile of shoes. I pick out a pink scarf, a white t-shirt, a white jumper, some black shoes, and a pair of second-hand Ugg boots. I spot a box of donated teddy bears laid out for the kids. I take three.

That afternoon, Sara and Khalil and I are wandering around the *heim* when there is a commotion at the entrance gate. More buses are arriving. Hundreds of people spill out of them and start milling around the entrance, waiting to be given somewhere to sleep. We wander over to take a look. I hear a shout from the queue and spot a crowd of familiar faces. It's our friends, the brothers Ayham and Bassem, and Zaher and his family. Zaher grins wide and steps towards us with open arms. We all kiss each other on both cheeks. The others arrived in Germany a few days ahead of us with the smuggler Ali. They were transferred from Munich to a camp in a town called Eisenhüttenstadt outside of Berlin before being brought here. It's great to be back with the people we shared so much with on the journey. Now we'll start our new lives all together in the same place. That night we eat together in the canteen.

'So have you been to Arab street yet?' says Ayham as I pick at my food.

'What's Arab street?' I say.

'All the other Syrians in the other camp are talking about it,' says Ayham. 'It's this place in Berlin somewhere, a whole street full of Arab restaurants, shops and supermarkets.'

We ask the volunteers at the *heim* about it the next day. They tell us Berliners know Arab street as Sonnenallee. We have to get a bus from the end of the road to the train station, then get on the underground train for another forty minutes. We're all missing home. We decide to go straight away. We emerge from the subway onto a square at a busy intersection lined with dark-grey, concrete buildings. We turn right off the square and stroll down Sonnenallee, past a bus stop, a few newsagents, and electronics stores.

'This is Arab street?' I say to Sara. 'Doesn't look very Arab to me.'

At last, we hit a small Arabic supermarket on a corner. Ayham wanders inside with his brother Bassem and the others. I stop at the door. I nudge Sara and point over the road to a pizza place. We're both starving, we decide to try it out. We walk in and order in English. The guy behind the counter is sullen and we sit down to wait in gloomy silence. Now we've arrived, the reality of what has happened begins to sink in.

'We left our beautiful country for this?' says Sara when our pizzas arrive. 'We should be blossoming young women in Damascus, enjoying the time of our lives. And now we're here.'

I feel a gnawing emptiness in my chest. I thought Germany was supposed to be heaven. Surely heaven is prettier than this? I'm glad to be here, but I can't help thinking about all we've lost. Sara and I decide to go shopping for clothes to cheer ourselves up. The problem is we're running out of money. We need to talk to Dad, ask him to transfer us some more. We finish our food, walk back to the square and buy German SIM cards with data. Then we cross the road and go into a department store to look at clothes. Everything seems very expensive, but I find a pair of cheap black sweatpants. When I'm done, Sara hands me a plastic bag. Inside is a large fluffy brown teddy bear.

'In case you get homesick,' she says.

I grin. At least I have my sister with me. I wander off to buy Sara her own bear. I wait until we're back in the *heim* to call Dad. I ask him to wire us some more money.

'What do you need money for now you've arrived?' says Dad.

'For clothes, Dad,' I say. 'And you know, for food and transport.'

'I've just spent ten thousand dollars getting you both to Germany,' he says. 'I don't know how you managed to spend so much. You'll just have to live on what they give you.'

I understand. Dad spent a lot of money getting us here. But it's still a shock. I wonder how we'll manage. Once we are registered as asylum-seekers, the German government will give us an allowance of one hundred and thirty euros every month. From that we have to buy everything except food and accommodation. It's going to be tough. Things are expensive here.

There are a lot of misunderstandings about money. It's hard for some people to accept, but anyone who made it to Europe must have been reasonably well off at home. Everyone I know who did the journey from Syria spent at least three thousand dollars. Many of them sold everything, their houses, their cars, all they owned to get this far. We're the lucky ones. The ones with enough money to travel. Those who have no savings or nothing to sell end up in camps in Jordan, Lebanon, or Turkey. But then we arrive, the money runs out, and we have to rely on charity. I'm grateful that people here in Germany are so generous, that they treat us like human beings, want to help us. But it's hard not to feel bad about having to accept donations from others. Lots of us, me included, never wanted to take anything from anyone.

Getting support money isn't as easy as Dad makes out. First, we have to register as asylum-seekers. In Berlin that means going to the social affairs office, a huge complex of buildings in west Berlin which everyone knows by its acronym, LaGeSo. We aren't the only ones trying to register. Every day hundreds more of us arrive in Berlin. But there's a bottleneck. The office only gets through forty people a day.

Sara, as acting legal guardian to me and Khalil, goes to the office on behalf of all three of us. The crowds are so big, she has to wait several days just to get a number to get into the real queue for an appointment to register. Then, once she has a number, she has to wait for it to flash up on the screen outside the office. There's no way of telling when that is going to happen. It could be today, tomorrow, three weeks from now. Sara spends most days staring at the screen, too afraid to leave the office in case we miss our slot and have to start the whole process again. She soon gets bored waiting and decides to join a group of volunteers handing out food and emergency medical aid to the crowds. Keeping busy does her good. Every night she comes back late to the *heim*, looking happy but exhausted.

'I just had the weirdest conversation,' says Sara one night, sitting down on her bunk bed in the tent. 'This volunteer girl. She couldn't believe I was a refugee because I have a phone and I do my hair and I wear jewellery.'

'What?' I say.

'Yeah,' says Sara. 'Then she was surprised when I mentioned I had a laptop at home. Says she didn't know we had computers in Syria. Like we all live in the desert or something. I had to tell her we had a normal life before.'

We both laugh. It's clear there are some Europeans who are confused about the world we come from. We're going to have a lot of explaining to do. I go along with Sara to the office once or twice, but mostly I sit in the *heim* with the guys and daydream. The days drag on and I begin to sort through everything that's happened since I left my home. The change of pace catches me out. The last days, weeks and years have been so full of drama that it takes a while to understand that it's really over. I'm safe. Bombs aren't going to fall on the street or crash through the roof. I don't have to hide from the police, sleep rough in crowds of strangers, or deal with criminal gangs to smuggle myself across borders. But as the emergency subsides, I begin to realize the price of my newfound safety. I've lost my home, my country, my culture, my friends, my life. I sit in the *heim*, listless and disorientated. I have to fill my life with purpose. I have to find a way back into the pool.

One morning a few weeks after we arrive, Sara and I join the crowds behind the railings at the door to the LaGeSo office. A screen above our heads flashes up numbers, calling people in one by one. A male volunteer walks past carrying sandwiches in a plastic pallet. Sara waves at him.

'I'm going to say hi,' says Sara and slips out between the metal railings. 'Wait here. Watch the screen.'

I look around at the crowds. Some people haven't been given a *heim* yet, so they are sleeping rough in the office grounds. I stare at them in pity. Men, women, children, families, their journeys not quite over. The only authorities in sight are the security guards, most of them locals with Arab backgrounds. I watch them shouting at everyone in Arabic, enjoying their new power over us. Sara comes back. I tell her I need to go to the toilet, it's her turn to wait. I squeeze out of the crush. My foot gets caught on the railings. I trip.

'What's the matter with you?' says a male voice in Arabic. 'Can't you see, beautiful?'

I look round. It's a guard. He looks like a bodybuilder.

'What's your problem?' I mutter. I stalk off to the toilets, fighting back tears of hurt and anger. Who do these guards think they are? Gods? I breathe and tell myself to be patient. This is just the situation we're in today. It won't last forever. I squeeze back through the railings to join Sara in the queue. We settle down to wait, staring longingly at the office doors and watching the numbers flash up on the screen in random sequence. A cheer goes up from the front of the crowd every time anyone actually gets inside the building.

It's five hours before our number finally flashes onto the screen. Sara grins, grabs my arm, and hauls me up as the crowd cheers our turn. We step inside, walk upstairs and into an office. A woman beckons to us from behind a table in the middle of the room. We sit down. The woman asks if we have our passports. Sara puts our documents on the desk. The woman inspects them. Then she takes our fingerprints and our photos and notes down our names, dates of birth, places of birth and what languages we speak. Then she hands us each a piece of A4 paper with our photographs in the top-right corner and tells us the paper is a certificate to prove we've registered as asylum-seekers. We'll need it to officially apply for asylum and to collect our support money. But to get the money we have to get another appointment at the office.

'Wait,' says Sara. 'We have to do all that again?'

'*Ja*,' says the woman and smiles grimly.

The next morning, we're eating breakfast at the *heim* when a man comes to sit with us. He tells us he's from Egypt and that his name is Abu Atef. He asks us if there's anything he can help us with. Sara and I tell him we'd like to be given our own room. We're still sharing with our cousins Majed and Nabih. We're girls, and we'd like some privacy. Abu Atef disappears and returns ten minutes later with one of the camp operators, who says they have a room for us. They follow us back to the tent to get our stuff, then lead us along the red-brick building and through a door with a stone relief above it that looks a bit like an eagle. As we climb the stairs, I ask Abu Atef about the building. He tells me this place is called Schmidt-Knobelsdorf-Kaserne. I laugh at the silly-sounding German words.

'It used to be a military base,' says Abu Atef. 'The British used part of this complex as a prison. A famous Nazi was held in a building near here once. Ever heard of Rudolf Hess?'

'No,' I say. 'Never heard of him.'

We walk up to the second floor and into a sparse room with three beds and a closet. I plonk my new teddy bears onto one of the beds. The big, fluffy, brown bear Sara gave me takes pride of place on the pillow. Abu Atef lingers in the doorway and asks us how we're finding Berlin. We tell him we're still thinking of leaving, of going to Hanover to find Sara's friend Hala.

'No, don't do that,' says Abu Atef. 'Stay here in Berlin. It's better for you. You want to study? There are more universities here.'

I look up. This is my chance.

'And swimming clubs?'

'That too,' says Abu Atef. 'Why?'

'We're swimmers,' I say. 'Can you help us find a place to train?'

17

'Go ahead,' says the blonde woman. 'Swim.'

I shiver and step onto the block at my feet. I put my right foot forwards, wrap my toes around the steel edge and grab it with both hands. Beside me, Sara does the same. I stare at my knees and wait, battle the fluttering in my stomach. I tense my muscles and rock back slightly. Go ahead, Yusra. Just swim. A whistle blows. I push with my right foot, straighten my body, and launch forwards, reaching for the other side of the pool. I fall, fingertips, arms, head in line, and slip through an imaginary hoop in the water. I power a dolphin kick with my core, hips rising, legs straight, hips falling, knees bent. My lower body works as one, my ankles flick and push the water back behind me. Rolling, rolling. I rise, break water, gasp. My shoulders whirl and bring both arms around in front. I dive my head and my hands crash down into the water like paddles. I drag and scoop the water towards my stomach, draw a keyhole shape with my hands. My legs roll again. The power isn't there. My muscles are nothing. Stop thinking, Yusra. Swim.

The whistle blows again halfway through my eighth length. I swim the final strokes, grab the edge of the pool, and flip off the goggles, breathing hard. The blonde woman grins from the poolside. Beside her, a man with blonde hair and glasses nods encouragingly and tells us we can get changed.

Sara and I climb out of the pool and walk into the changing rooms. I wonder what they thought of our technique. We're trying out at Wasserfreunde Spandau 04, a swimming club based in Berlin's Olympic Park, known locally as Olympiapark. It feels as if my whole future rests on what these strangers say. We walk back to the poolside in bare feet, carrying our shoes and our swimming stuff. Abu Atef, the translator from the camp, is chatting to the man and the woman.

'Well done,' says Abu Atef as we approach. 'It turns out you really can swim.'

'I told you,' I say. 'We were in the national team, we won medals for Syria.'

I hand the goggles, swim cap and swimming suit back to the woman.

'It's ok,' says the blonde man. 'We get a lot of people saying they are swimmers and then they drown when they get in the pool.'

I laugh. The man says his name is Sven and holds out his hand for us both to shake. He points at the woman and introduces her as the club's head coach, Renate.

'Call me Reni,' she says and smiles warmly. 'I think we can find space for you both here at Wasserfreunde.'

My stomach flips. I can swim. Reni says we can start off training with our own age group, the over-sixteens, and see how we get on. She asks if we can come back in a few days' time, a Friday, for our first session. I nod enthusiastically. I'd start right away if I could. It was so good to swim.

'Also, it would make sense for you to stay here if you're training,' says Reni. 'And I imagine you'd like to get out of the *heim*? We've got space in Alfreds, our clubhouse. Shall we look at the room?'

I draw breath. I hadn't been expecting to be offered somewhere to live. We follow Reni out of the pool and around a corner. Crispy yellow leaves blow across the path in front of my feet as we walk towards a one-storey building. Renate tells us this is Alfreds. Inside is a small hotel the swimming club uses for competitions. Sometimes swimmers stay here overnight. We step inside and turn left down a corridor lined with old pictures of swim teams and framed medal displays. Reni leads us into a cafeteria lined with dark wooden benches. I glance around, my eyes fall on the trophy cabinet and the ancient shop till in the corner. On the ceiling, a toy wooden aeroplane hangs next to a chandelier with fake candles. To our left a middle-aged woman with red hair stands behind a wooden bar.

'*Morgen*,' she says.

'Hallo, Sibel,' says Sven.

He continues in German and points to us both.

'Hello,' says Sibel in English. 'Welcome.'

We smile back at her. Then Reni leads us past the bar and on through some double doors into a white dining room fitted with square, wooden tables. She turns and opens a door in the left-hand wall that leads onto the rooms. We turn right down a corridor and stop at the end. Reni opens a door and ushers us into a small room. There's a pine bunk bed, a chest of drawers, a wicker chair, a cupboard, and a sink. Reni shows us the toilets out in the corridor.

'If you stay here,' says Reni, 'you'll be on your own, no one else lives here permanently.'

Technically, we're supposed to stay in the camp for three months before we can move out. But tens of thousands of people have arrived in the city in the past weeks, and there's a shortage of refugee housing in Berlin. We're sure the authorities would be glad to have two fewer people to worry about. We back out of the tiny room and start back along the corridor. Abu Atef turns to me and murmurs something in Arabic about my glasses.

'What it is it?' says Reni.

I turn to Reni. We've been very lucky to be offered a place to live. I'm embarrassed to ask for more when these people have already been so generous.

'Erm, it's just that I lost my glasses on the way here,' I say. 'I'm short-sighted and I get kind of dizzy without them. I just thought if I'm going to start swimming again...'

Reni doesn't blink. She offers to take me to the opticians after training the following Saturday. We walk together back past the football pitches and long red-brick buildings to the Olympiapark entrance. Reni and Sven stop and turn to us.

'So we'll see you Friday?' says Reni. 'We'll see about getting you some new training gear. And then you can move your stuff in over the weekend.'

Sara and I grin and thank them, then walk to the bus stop and catch the bus back to the *heim*. I stare out of the bus window as we chug through the grey streets. I'm bewildered and overcome by

Sven and Reni's generosity. I can hardly believe our luck. I just wanted somewhere to swim. I never imagined the try-out would turn into an apartment viewing. Sara and I get off the bus, cross the road and stroll down the avenue under the yellow, autumn trees. In the *heim* we find our friend Abdullah and the brothers Ayham and Bassem smoking shisha in the small playground outside the entrance to our building.

'Hey,' says Ayham, looking up as we approach. 'Where have you been?'

I sit down on one of the chairs the guys have brought out from the rooms. I tell them we've been to a try-out at a swimming club and that we can start training again. I hesitate, then I drop the bombshell. The club is going to let us move into their clubhouse. The others fall silent.

'I mean, I can't train and stay here in the *heim*,' I say quickly. 'I'll be getting up very early and I need to sleep. It's noisy here, there are so many people. The security guards shouting all night. It's not great for athletes.'

Abdullah snorts and raises his eyebrows.

'It's not good for anyone,' he says.

Abdullah leans down and picks up an old wooden tennis racket off the floor under his seat.

'Hey,' he says. 'Seeing as you're an athlete, you should check out the new game I invented. Soap tennis.'

He brandishes a dirty bar of soap and throws it over to me.

'Grow up,' I say, catching it.

'Your serve,' he says and stands, bobbing like a tennis player.

I stand and throw the soap at him. He hits it hard and it explodes, showering soap fragments over my sweatpants and shoes.

'My God, Yusra,' says Sara. 'What are you doing?'

I'm laughing too hard to answer. All the pressure of the past weeks evaporates. I'm going to start swimming again. I feel like anything is possible.

I get up far too early the following Friday, nervous and excited for our first training session. Sara and I get the bus to the Olympia-park and find Sven and Reni waiting for us outside the pool. With them is another man with ash-blonde hair and stubble who introduces himself as Lasse. He and Reni coach the oldest group, the over-sixteens. Reni says they've left us swimming gear out in the changing room. The rest of the training group is already inside. We thank the coaches and go inside to get changed.

I'm nervous. How will I swim after my two-month break? I remember how hard it was when I returned to swimming after more than a year's break in Syria. And anyway, the training is more intense here than in Syria. In Germany, swimmers get two training sessions a day. We only had one a day growing up. It'll be a challenge, but maybe with some work I'll be able to reach an even higher level than before. Despite the nerves I can't wait to get in the water. A row of teenagers stares at us as we walk out onto the poolside. I stare back. All the guys have huge shoulders and six-packs, the girls are toned and muscular.

Lasse tells the group to warm up, speaking in English for our benefit. The other kids jump into the pool. Sara and I follow. Even warming up I can tell they are faster than us. I try and ignore them, focus on my stroke. Lasse and Reni have us sprint 50m and 100m races against the others. Sara and I are about the same speed as each other, but we're both a long way behind the rest. We get changed and the rest of the group goes to their lessons at the elite sports school also based in the Olympiapark. None of them speaks to us. No one says hello in the second session in the evening either. Nor at Saturday-morning training the next day. Afterwards, Reni drives us to see an optician who is a friend of the swimming club and gives discounts to members. He tests my eyes and tells me to come back in a week to pick up my new glasses. Reni settles the bill.

'The other kids in the group are good, huh?' I say to Sara on the bus back to the *heim*.

'Don't worry, we haven't swum in ages,' she says. 'We'll catch up again.'

'I shouldn't have smoked all that shisha in the year I wasn't swimming,' I say. 'Or eaten all those burgers on the way here.'

'I know what you mean,' says Sara. 'My shoulders are killing me.'

Sara's old injury. I feel bad for her. Our ordeal in the sea can't have helped. It's clear she won't be returning to competitive swimming any time soon. The next day, a Sunday, there's no training. Back in the *heim,* we pack up our few belongings. Khalil sits on my bed and watches as I stuff the clothes and the teddy bears into my pink backpack. I'm sad to be leaving my friends here, but I know we'll come back to visit them now and then. We haven't told the camp operators we're moving out. Besides, Sara might need to come back to sleep here if she decides not to carry on swimming. I doubt anyone will even notice we're gone.

We get the bus to the Olympiapark early the next morning and dump our luggage in the room in the clubhouse before training. Sibel smiles and waves at us from behind the bar on the way in. In training I swim ok, but I'm worried that the coaches, Reni and Lasse, are disappointed with our speed. How can we keep up with the others when they've always had two training sessions a day, twice as many as we had? That night after evening training I lie down on the top bunk bed in our new room and give myself a pep talk. Don't ever give up. Ever. No matter what. Just swim.

There's a knock on our door. It's Sven, asking if we want to eat with him. Reni has to go home, he says, but he can stay here for dinner. It's good of him to stick around, make sure we're settled in. Sara, Sven, and I file down the corridor and out into the little dining room. We sit down at one of the round tables and Sibel brings us plates of chicken and rice.

'Can I ask why you left Syria?' says Sven when we've finished eating. 'Was it the war?'

'Yeah,' I say. 'And to carry on training. I had to stop swimming in Damascus. There were bombs falling all around the pool.'

Sven looks at me wide-eyed. It wasn't only the war, I tell him. I wanted to go to a place where I could have a swimming career. Women aren't likely to be swimmers after a certain age in Syria, I explain. They're expected to marry and stop training. That's what happened to our aunts. And I said no, I want to swim.

'So you left your home to swim,' says Sven. 'And what is it you want to achieve in swimming?'

I look him in the eye.

'I want to go to the Olympics.' I say.

Sven looks surprised.

'You mean that?' he says.

'Absolutely,' I say.

We sit in silence for a minute. Then Sven asks me about my role models. I tell him about watching Michael Phelps power through to all those Olympic golds and about Therese Alshammar's win at the World Aquatics Championships. Those are my sporting heroes. Then I tell him I'd love to meet Malala, the Afghan teenager who survived being shot by the Taliban and still campaigns for girls' education. That's courage.

Sven asks about Syria. I don't know where to start.

'I've never been to the Middle East,' says Sven. 'I don't know anything about it. Tell me what it was like.'

'I don't know,' I say. 'Should I give you some facts? Damascus is one of the oldest capitals in the world. Syria is big on cotton exports. That kind of thing?'

'No, ok. I get it,' says Sven, laughing. 'So tell me about the journey.'

Sara and I tell him about the smugglers and the sea and the engine dying and the waves and the borders and the creepy hotel and the station and the prison. I realize I haven't thought about any of it in weeks. It's another chapter. It's hard to explain, but parts of the journey seem genuinely funny, looking back. It wasn't that bad. We made a lot of friends on the way.

'I don't know how you can sit here and laugh while telling that story,' says Sven at last, his eyes red with emotion. 'Most full-grown men would sit in a corner and cry after what you've been through. And you're laughing?'

'I don't know,' I say. 'The sea and Hungary were bad. But the rest of it was kind of fun.'

'Fun?' Sven shakes his head in disbelief.

I look out the window at the dark October night. The club-house is quiet now Sibel has left. There's no one else but me, Sven, and Sara in the building. There's probably nobody else but a security guard for a kilometre. Sven shifts in his chair.

'I mean you did everything right, you got here in one piece,' he says. 'But now you have to deal with what happened. Maybe you should see a psychologist.'

I shake my head. That isn't the way we do things where I'm from. Sven looks at his watch, stands, unhooks his kit bag from the back of the chair, and puts it on his shoulder. He looks concerned, reluctant to leave us in the empty building. We tell him we'll be fine, so he says goodnight and walks out of the dining room. I look at Sara. We're alone in a Nazi-era Olympic park. Outside, beyond the statues of Aryan athletes and proud imperial eagles, a monumental stadium looms. There's no shop, no supermarket, no life, nothing. There's nothing to do but go to bed. We open the door to the corridor. Sibel has turned out all the lights. I feel with my hand along the wall but can't find a switch.

'This place is creepy,' says Sara. 'Like living in a school during the zombie apocalypse.'

We run at full speed down the dark corridor towards our new room. After a few steps the automatic light flickers on above our heads. We both collapse on the bottom bunk bed in our room, giggling with relief. I clamber onto the top bunk.

'Just think,' says Sara from the bottom bunk. 'There's no one for miles around. If someone attacked us now we'd be dead by the time the police get here.'

'Thanks for that,' I say and turn over on my side.

I'm up early for training. Sara skips swimming to go back to the LaGeSo office to start the battle for our next appointment. Today, Lasse's group is doing additional weight training in the gym. I join them, scowl, and push as hard as I can. I've got a long way to go to regain my fitness.

That night, Sven eats with us again. The following day, a Wednesday, there's only one training session in the morning, so we have the afternoon free. Sven says he wants to take us shopping. He says his mother, along with Reni and a few others from the club, have given him some money to buy us new training gear. I look down and toy with the pasta on my plate. I'm embarrassed. There's somehow a difference between picking out donated clothes from an anonymous pile and taking money from people you know. Back in Syria, we never gave anything directly to anyone. We'd give to a charity and then they'd make sure it got to people in need. That way no one felt looked down on. I remind myself how lucky we are to have found such generous new friends. I try to push the uncomfortable thoughts away, but I can't help it. It's charity. And it hurts.

The following afternoon, Sven takes us on the train to a sportswear store near Alexanderplatz, a grey, windswept square in the east of the city. The sky is wide and empty apart from a looming tower topped with a glass orb that rises above the concrete prefab buildings. In the store we buy running shoes, sweatpants and some everyday clothes. I just need the dryland training gear. Sven says the club has offered to donate me goggles, swimsuits, and swimming caps. We're heading back to the train when Sven stops outside a women's clothes shop. He clears his throat and looks at us awkwardly.

'So,' says Sven. 'Reni told me I should ask you...'

'What?' says Sara.

'About, well, whether you need anything else,' he says. 'I can leave you and you can maybe take a look.'

'Uh-huh,' I say, deeply embarrassed.

I can sense Sara trying not to laugh. I avoid her eye. Sven presses some cash into my hand and Sara and I wander into the shop. We turn a corner and Sara splutters with laughter.

'He meant underwear, right?' I say.

'Yeah, I think so,' says Sara. 'But I don't need any underwear.'

'I know,' I say, giggling at the memory of Sven's face. 'Me neither.'

Sara and I look around the shop for ten minutes and then go out empty-handed. Sven clears his throat again and says we should go and find some food. We get on the train to Potsdamer Platz, a cluster of glassy tower blocks further to the west. We eat at an Italian restaurant. Afterwards, Sven takes us up in an elevator to a rooftop viewing platform with black bars like a cage. The flat, grey city stretches on as far as I can see. Nothing is very high, nothing very old. To the left, a golden angel rises out of a large patch of brown and yellow trees. Sven points out a square building with a glass dome on top. The *Reichstag*, the German parliament building. I stare out at the view and try my best to love it. A piercing wind blows and stings my eyes. I close them and see Mount Qasioun looming above the ancient streets. I miss Damascus.

The next week, I'm consumed with swimming. I'm up at six every morning and finish training at eight in the evening. Sara is busy with paperwork and doesn't always make training. One morning, she asks me to come to the LaGeSo office to switch with her after she's waited all night in a queue. I'm devastated. I don't want to miss training. I only want to swim. In between sessions, while the others are in school, I wander around the Olympiapark grounds or sit alone in the clubhouse. Most days, Sven joins me in the dining room. We talk for hours, about our families, about swimming, about Germany, Syria, and the war.

Sara and I come to rely on Sven for everything. He and Reni pay for our meals in Alfreds every night or take us out for dinner. Often, Sven ends up staying in one of the other free rooms along the corridor. Sometimes he's up at four in the morning to help Sara with our paperwork before he starts his coaching job. The admin is horribly complicated. Sven asks around the club for advice. Michael and Gabi, the parents of one of Sven's swimmers, volunteer to help. They have intimate knowledge of the situation at the LaGeSo office through their work. Soon, Sven is calling Gabi for guidance every time Sara has a question.

I talk to Mum on the phone every few days. After Sara and I left Damascus, Mum and Shahed moved out of our old apartment and went to live with relatives. We're all focused on getting her and Shahed out of Syria and safely over to Germany. But the sheer volume of new arrivals means everyone's paperwork is taking a very long time. Sara and I have been in Berlin more than a month and we haven't even applied for asylum yet. Mum misses us badly and she often cries when we talk. I distract her by telling her about our new life, about swimming, and about Sven. Mum struggles at first to understand why I'm spending so much time with my new coach. I'm also amazed at how much he's helping us. Back home, it's only family that would give so much. No one else does anything for anyone, at least not without expecting something back. One night, when Sven and I are eating dinner in the clubhouse, I decide to ask him.

'Why are you doing all this for us?' I say. 'Buying us meals, taking us shopping, helping with the papers? I mean, what's in it for you?

Sven looks surprised. He shakes his head.

'There's nothing at all in it for me,' says Sven. 'I feel good helping. That's just the way I was brought up. When I was a kid there was a war in Yugoslavia and a lot of people came to Berlin. My family helped them, too. My Mum taught me it's a big world out there, not just Spandau, not just Berlin. I have to be open to it.'

I'm staring at him. He smiles.

'And anyway, it's easy to help,' says Sven. 'You and me, we're the same. We're swimmers.'

I fall silent and think about what Sven has done for us. All his free time, his energy, even his extra money, goes towards helping us settle in. It's inspiring. I promise myself I'll do the same for someone else one day. I'll pass on Sven's generosity.

That week I swim on, struggling to keep pace with the others. I know I'll get better. It's only a matter of time. The following Saturday, Sven comes to find me after training. He says my coaches, Reni and Lasse, want to talk. We sit down all together at one of the wooden tables in the clubhouse cafeteria. Lasse clears his throat.

'We think you should train with Sven from now on,' he says.

I'm shocked. Sven's training group are thirteen and fourteen years old. I'm seventeen. That's two age groups down from mine. Sven sees my face and tries to comfort me.

'It'll be good for you,' says Sven. 'You missed out on some key years when you had your break in Syria. We need to build up your strength. Better to come into my group where the training is more general.'

I stare hard at the table, fighting tears. I'm crushed. I think back

to breaking that record at the World Championships in Istanbul. I
need to be pushed if I'm going to get back to where I was then. If
I go back down now it might take years to shave just half a second
off my times. I take a few deep breaths and the panic subsides. Sven
is helping with so much anyway, I guess it makes sense if he coaches
me too. I look up and manage a weak smile. It's settled.

I start training with Sven's group the following Monday morning. The girls in the group stare at me as I get changed. The eldest
are four years younger than I am. After the warm-up, Sven blows
his whistle and says something in German. The group moans in
response. Sven turns to me.

'We'll do a time trial,' he says. 'Three times 800m freestyle, one
after another.'

Ok, I think. I'm ready. I can do this. I dive in. By the end of the
third length I'm slightly behind, by the end of the sixth I'm lagging. I can't believe it. These little kids are faster than me. Stop
thinking. Just swim. I push but it's no good. The others finish the
trial a good two minutes before me. I grab the poolside and look
up at Sven to hear my time: 12:32. I'm devastated. I should be
closer to eleven minutes. Once I swam it in 10:05.

We start the next trial. Don't think, swim. With each sideways
breath, I see the others pushing ahead. After the second length, I'm
last again. One hundred fifty metres down. Just keep going. It's no
good. At the end of the fourth length I stop and grab the pool
edge. The others are already halfway onto their next lap. I haul
myself out. Sven frowns at me.

'What's wrong?' he says.

'Nothing,' I say.

I walk off to sit at the poolside and put my head in my hands.
I'm suddenly furious. Those little kids, training twice a day their
whole lives. It's not fair. I'm going to get faster than them if it kills
me. I stare at the tiles, breathing long and deep. The anger cools
and leaves me more determined than ever. I'll get back to where I
was, then I'll climb higher than ever. I'll go to the Olympics. Sven
starts the group on their third time trial, then he sits down beside
me.

'I know it's hard for you,' says Sven. 'There's a lot going on, you've been through a lot. But you'll only get back to where you were if you keep going. You can't let it get to you.'

I sigh. I know he's right. I have to keep going, however hard it is. I stand and join the training group in the pool. The other kids in Sven's class are sweet. They're curious about me, but they have some funny ideas. A few of the boys from the group stop me after training. They want to know if I swam in a pool in Syria. I stifle a laugh and explain that I didn't live in a tent in the desert somewhere. I trained in a pool, I tell them, I had a swimsuit, at home I even had a TV and a computer. They stare at me wide-eyed. I sigh. I've got a lot to explain.

That evening, Sven takes Sara and I out to his favourite Italian restaurant for dinner. Our pizzas have just arrived when Sara looks up and announces she's stopping swimming for good.

'I can't do it anymore,' says Sara. 'My shoulders hurt too bad. I want to swim but just for fun maybe.'

'You'll get better,' says Sven. 'You had a long break.'

'I'm trying my best, but it hurts when I swim,' says Sara. 'That's why I'm getting blown out of the water by these thirteen-year-old kids.'

It isn't easy, for either of us. Once we were both on top, winning medals for our national team. Now these younger kids are faster than us. Sven suggests Sara should go to the doctor and look into getting some physiotherapy, but she shakes her head. She's worried a doctor will tell her she can never swim again. Sven says Sara can come to the pool and swim for fun whenever she likes.

Just then a loud crash comes from the kitchen as a load of plates smash onto the tiled floor. Sven and the other customers jump out of their skin. Sara and I carry on eating. Sven gazes at us. I look at Sara and burst out laughing.

'What's so funny?' says Sven.

'This one time in Syria,' I say. 'A weapons store exploded. *That* was a real shock. The whole sky was red.'

Sven gawps at us. I giggle, but as I laugh it hits me again that I'm safe. No bombs are going to crash into the street outside and blow out all the windows in the restaurant. I don't have to be ready to take cover when the mortars screech overhead. I realize it's hard for Sven and others to understand why we can laugh about all that happened to us. It's not that we don't care. It's just easier to laugh than to cry. If I cry, I'll cry alone. But if we laugh, we can do it together. I guess no one knows how strong they can be until it's their turn to deal with tragedy.

For the next few weeks, Sara comes along to training when she feels like it. She's out a lot, at the office trying to push on with our paperwork, visiting the others at the *heim*, or exploring Berlin with her new volunteer friends. Our routines are very different. Often Sara stays out late and wants to sleep in. That can be a problem when I get up at six for training. I tell Sven I think it's best if me and Sara have separate rooms. He talks to Reni, who organizes us a room each along the corridor in the clubhouse.

Each room starts off exactly the same, plain and functional, with a window looking out onto the football field. There's a cupboard, a chest of drawers, a single bed and bedside table, a shelf, and a sink. Before long, Sara's room looks more like an antiques shop – a clutter of pictures, books, jewellery, make-up and perfume. Every week she changes the posters, pins up a different-coloured Palestinian *keffiyeh* scarf or a new mask she's made in her volunteer-run theatre group. I tell her it's a mess. She thumps me on the arm.

'At least my room doesn't look like a sports shop,' says Sara, 'with sports gear everywhere, neatly folded like it's on display.'

She's right. My room is very different. The only thing on my wall is Sven's training programme. In the margin along the top I write the words: 'Never stop, keep going.' And along the bottom: 'You will win one day.'

One day in early November, I hear from my old swimming friend Rami that he's left Istanbul. He tells me he has crossed the sea and made it to his brother in Belgium, in a small town near Ghent. It's amazing news. I'm so glad he's in Europe too. Now we can both work towards our dreams. I ask him if he's swimming and he tells me he has a try-out at a club. I wish him luck. I know he'll smash it.

I'm happy to be swimming, happy to be safe in Germany, but I can't help feeling lonely. Sven does his best to keep me company, but I don't have any friends my age. Sara often stays away from the clubhouse, sleeping in our old room at the *heim* or at friends' houses. The kids in my training class are nice but there's a big language and age barrier. Not long after I hear from Rami, some of the kids from the group are due to swim in a regional competition at a pool in east Berlin. Sven takes me and Sara along to watch. I'm sitting on the pool deck when two girls from our training group come and join me. They introduce themselves as Elise and Mette. I smile at the girls. Elise has long, blonde hair and bright blue eyes. She asks why I came here and if I'm going to stay in Berlin.

'I came because there was a war and I wanted to swim,' I say. 'I hope I can stay.'

'Are you going to come to school with us?' says the other girl, Mette, who has long, mousy-brown hair pulled back in a bun.

'I don't know yet,' I say.

We chat for a little while. Some of the others in the group watch us as we talk. The conversation breaks the ice. One by one, over the next few days, the other kids in the group introduce themselves to me. I get on best with Elise and Mette. That weekend, Elise invites me to her home to meet her family. I'm nervous at first, but Elise's family welcomes me as if I'm kin. Elise has a younger sister, Aimee, and an elder brother, Fernand. All three of them swim at the club. Over dinner, Elise's mother, Katrin, asks me what it's like living at the clubhouse. I tell her it can be a bit lonely when Sara isn't there. The next day Elise comes to talk to me after training and invites me to stay with her family for a while. I grin as a warm feeling spreads through my gut. What a lovely gesture. After the journey, the *heim,* and the clubhouse, it'll be great to be in a normal family home. I move some stuff into Elise's house the next day. I stay with her family for the next three weeks. I do everything I can to fit in and Elise's mother treats me just like her own daughters.

All the while I push myself hard in the pool. My muscles are destroyed after every training session. I never dreamt it would be so hard to get back to a competitive level. Sven says nothing, but I can tell he's watching closely. Week by week, I'm getting slimmer, faster, regaining my old strength. Sven suggests we contact my old coaches in Syria and get my personal bests. Then we'll have a benchmark to aim for. The coaches reply with my best times: 200m freestyle 2:12, 100m freestyle 1:02, 100m butterfly 1:09, 800m 10:05. I'm a long way off achieving those times now.

'I can see you're serious about swimming,' says Sven one night. 'The way you're committing to training. Well, I couldn't wish for a better athlete. So the question is, are you doing that because you just like swimming, or because you really want to achieve something?'

'I told you already,' I say. 'I want to go to the Olympics.'

'Good. So let's talk about a training plan,' says Sven. 'You won't make it to Rio next summer. But there's nothing to stop us aiming for Tokyo 2020.'

I stare at him. He means it. My heart jumps. I'm so ready for this. He's taking me seriously. At last, here's someone who sees I'm ready to do anything to swim. And he's ready to fight for it just as hard as I am. Sven explains we need long-term goals. We'll work on getting my power and stamina back, concentrate on my aerobic foundation until the summer. I need to keep working on building up my muscle mass and reducing water deposits, he says. I still need to lose about four kilos if I want to stop going so deep in butterfly. I know he's right. Damn Burger King. We won't focus on technical drills just yet, he says, because my technical foundation is very good. That's a big part of getting faster, but it isn't everything. Sven says I should aim to get back close to my personal bests by the end of this season. Then next year I can aim for five per cent improvement on that. And then another three per cent the year after. And if I do that, Sven says, I could make the B cut for Tokyo by spring 2020. That's assuming I'll be able to start for Syria.

'Details,' I say, grinning wide. 'The main thing is we aim for Tokyo.'

A week after we start work on our long-term plan, Sven comes to see me after training. I can tell he's excited. He can barely stop grinning as he tells me his news. It all started when Sven was watching the news on TV one night a few weeks before. Thomas Bach, President of the International Olympic Committee, made a speech to the United Nations, announcing help for refugee athletes who can't compete at the Olympics because they've fled their countries.

'So I wrote an email to the IOC about you,' says Sven, grinning. 'I told them we'd be interested in any help they want to give you. And today they wrote back saying they're thinking about how they can support you.'

I stare at the table. I'm deeply confused. Getting help from the IOC is an amazing opportunity for any athlete. But to get help because I'm a refugee? It feels a bit like charity. If I compete at the Olympics, I want it to be because I'm good enough. Not because people feel sorry for me.

18

It is still dark when we arrive. Our appointment isn't until eleven, but Sara says we should be here at the office by five to join the queue. We're hit with a sharp stench as we enter the high-ceilinged waiting room. Someone has thrown up in a corner. We find seats along one of the rows of maroon chairs. By six, the room is packed with miserable people huddling against the cold. An army of mus-cled security guards scowl at us from along the wall. Sven has come along with us for moral support. He's horrified, this miserable reception isn't what he expected. Sara tells him not to worry. We wait, we go in, we apply for asylum, then we're done.

Eleven comes and goes. It's past one by the time our number is called. We file into an office. A man behind a desk gives us some forms to fill in. Then he gives us each a piece of paper and says we've now submitted our asylum claims. I'm confused. I'd thought they would interview us about why we left Syria, but the official explains that part comes later. We have to wait another three to five months until the interview stage. After that it's another four to six weeks until the final decision.

I'm shocked. We already waited two and a half months for this appointment. And now they're saying it could be another six months before we know if we can stay in Germany. We have to wait to be granted asylum before we can apply to fly Mum and Shahed out of Syria to join us. But by then it might be too late. Family unification is only for minors and I'll be eighteen in March. It's now the end of November. At this rate, I'll be granted asylum in the summer, but I'll already be too old to get my family over. Sven stares at the official as he explains. I can tell he's angry. Sara pushes back her chair and stands.

'Ok,' she says. 'Let's get out of here.'

That evening, while Sara is out with her volunteering friends, I break the news to Mum on the phone. Our plan to bring her and Shahed over to Germany probably isn't going to work.

'But Yusra, *habibti*, I didn't think it would take this long,' says Mum. 'I should have come with you when you left. It's not enough to just talk on the phone. I miss my daughters.'

'Maybe it'll still work out,' I say. 'Maybe the process will go faster than they say.'

'But I can't do anything without you,' says Mum. I can hear she's crying. 'What's the point of working or shopping if there's no one to buy anything for? Nothing has any meaning any more. I feel empty. I can't wait any longer. I'm coming to Germany now with Shahed. If you did it, so can we.'

I tell her not to cry, that we'll work something out. But I know she's right. There's no other way for us to be together again. But Mum and Shahed can't do the journey on their own. I call Dad in Jordan. I tell him the paperwork is taking too long and ask him to bring Mum and Shahed here to Germany. Then we can all be together again. Dad is worried about leaving his coaching job, but I tell him he can start again here. Maybe Sven and the club can help him like they helped me. As I talk, I realize how much I need him here with me. To train, to improve, to really achieve something. Only Dad knows exactly what I need to do to get better, to get faster.

I tell Sara my plan when she gets back later that night. Sara doesn't like the idea of Shahed crossing the sea on a boat like we did. I don't like it either. Neither of us can stomach the idea of Shahed clinging onto a dinghy in the sea. But I've heard stories about people getting onto a yacht from Turkey to Greece. Maybe Dad can pay a bit more and get a better boat. Still, it's hard for either of us to imagine Mum and Dad sleeping rough in the street, or waiting all night to cross borders. But Sara eventually agrees, there's no other way of getting them here. Everything moves quickly after that. Mum and Dad arrange to meet in Istanbul in Turkey and follow the same route as we took to Germany. They both quit their jobs and send some of their stuff ahead in the post. The day before Mum and Shahed fly out of Damascus, Sven and I are eating in the clubhouse. He's toying with his food.

'Come on, what is it?' I say.

'Ok,' says Sven. He puts down his fork. 'So the IOC are now talking about doing something at Rio 2016. They're making a new Refugee Olympic Team and they've hinted you might be on it.'

'A what?' I say. 'A refugee team? What's that?'

The IOC are planning a team of refugee athletes, says Sven. People who can't otherwise compete at the Olympics because they've fled their country. He doesn't know anything more. The IOC have been very vague on the details.

'Wait, but they mentioned me?' I say, pushing my half-eaten plate of pasta away across the table.

Sven says it was Pere Miro, the IOC deputy director. During a press conference he told journalists about the team and said the IOC are searching the whole world for refugee athletes. Three refugees were already in the running. A Congolese guy in Brazil, an Iranian in Belgium, and a female swimmer from Syria now living in Germany. I raise my eyebrows. Me. They meant me. A shudder of excitement runs down my spine. I'm thrilled, but also a little bit appalled.

It's too late for second thoughts, says Sven. The journalists have already found us. Sven's Facebook account went into meltdown overnight. He's received eighty interview requests from journalists wanting to talk to me. Most of them are convinced I'm already on the refugee team, that I'll compete at the Olympic Games next summer in Rio. I'm reeling. This is crazy. Sven said himself there's no way I'm ready to swim in Rio. Suddenly it hits me. If I compete it will be because I'm a refugee.

'Ok, yes, I admit it, I'm a refugee,' I say, holding my hands up. 'But refugee isn't my team, is it? That word doesn't define me, does it? I'm Syrian. I'm a swimmer. I'm not starting for a refugee team. It's so... well, it's a little bit insulting.'

Sven looks at me like I've just slapped him.

'Huh?' he says and shakes his head. 'You don't make sense.'

He leans towards me, looks me square in the eye.

'Tell me again what you want,' he says.

'Swimming,' I say. 'I want to swim at the Olympics.'

'Swimming, right,' says Sven. 'At the Olympics, right. So tell me this. Does it really matter who you swim for?'

I sit in silence, struggle with myself for a minute. It's that word. Refugee. It's the bomb and the sea and the borders and the barbed wire and the humiliation and the bureaucracy. And yes, it's the painful charity too.

'Yusra, think about it,' says Sven. 'This is your chance to do what you want most in the whole world. You can swim. You can compete. And not just in any competition. It's the Olympics. Your dream.'

I tell Sven I need some time to think about it. Training the next day is a write-off. My head is full of the refugee team, full of that word, full of the Olympics. The more I think about it the more unsure I am about the whole idea. Then, just when I've decided against it, I change my mind again. Could it be my chance to change things for the better, even if only a tiny bit? Maybe I could be a role model for people. Show them that even if a bomb rips apart your life, you get up, you dust yourself off, and you carry on.

By the end of the day I'm as confused as ever. I tell Sven I still think the idea of a refugee team is a little insulting. If I get to the Olympics one day I want it to be because I'm good enough, because I worked for it. But then I think about Malala, the activist for girls' education. She has a message and she's out there, changing the world. I know I'm not Malala. I didn't grow up wanting to change the world. I just wanted to swim. That's all I want now. But I'm working hard to build a new life, training every day to reach my goal. That has to count for something. For the first time I see how I could inspire people. I tell Sven I've made up my mind. I'll do it.

Sven beams.

'It's the right thing to do,' he says.

Nothing is set in stone, Sven reminds me. There's no fixed plan about the team yet, how it might work, or whether the athletes have to qualify in the normal way. For the team, if the IOC even go ahead with it, there'll be a longlist, and then a shortlist. We're still working for Tokyo.

The next day Sven gets two calls from the DOSB, the German Olympic Sports Confederation. The first is from a man named

Michael Schirp, one of the people in charge of press relations, offering to help us coordinate all the media requests. Then a woman called Sandra Logemann calls from the German arm of Olympic Solidarity. She tells Sven that the DOSB might be able to intervene with the Interior Ministry to speed up my asylum claim. And Sara's too. I'll need the whole process to go faster if there's a possibility I'm going to travel to Rio in the summer.

I catch my breath when Sven tells me. If my claim goes faster, won't that mean we can get Mum, Dad and Shahed over here on a plane? Then they won't have to risk the sea crossing. After training the next morning, I get a message from Dad saying they've arrived safely on the Turkish coast. They are waiting in a hotel for the sea to grow calmer, then they will take a yacht to Greece. For a moment I'm back on the shore in Turkey, staring at the churning waves. I'm terrified for them. In a panic I write a garbled message to Dad telling him not to do the crossing, to go back. I might be going to the Olympics, the government are speeding up our asylum claims, and we'll be able to get them here legally after all. Don't worry, Dad writes back, it's all arranged. They're coming.

The next afternoon, Sara and I are sitting in Alfreds, trying desperately to think about anything but the sea. We try chatting, distracting ourselves, but every time we fall silent I see the glinting, marching waves flash before my eyes. After what feels like hours, my phone buzzes. It's Dad, saying they've made it to Greece. Sara calls him back straight away.

'Thank God you're safe, Dad,' she says. 'Give me Mum. I want to hear her voice.'

'Mum! *Alhamdulillah*, are you ok?' she says.

I wait for a minute then reach out for the phone. Sara hands it over.

'We're fine, Yusra, thank God,' Mum says. 'We're very tired.'

'Ok Mum, we're praying for you,' I tell her. 'Kiss Shahed for me.'

Dad writes again the next day to tell me they've arrived safely in Mytilene, the city on Lesbos island, and are waiting for their papers to move on. They travel quickly over the next days, up through Greece and into Serbia. I get a message saying that

Hungary has closed the border and they're getting on a free bus through Croatia. That week, Sara and I get a visit from the journalists Lam and Magdalena. They want to interview us and take photos for a magazine story. It's good to see them, but they remind me of our nightmare in Hungary just when I'm trying not to worry about my family. Steven contacts me too. I write him an update on what's going on with me and he publishes it online.

'I want to say a message for all the people in Belgium and all over the world,' I write. 'Don't you ever give up on something you want. Try and if you fail you have to try again and fight to the last breath you have.'

As always, the best distraction is training. I can now swim three 800m time trials, one after another, each one in under 10:30. I've shed almost all the weight I put on during my time out from swimming. I'm making progress, but I can't wait to have Dad's guidance and drive behind me. Training finishes for Christmas and I'm left with only thoughts of my family's journey.

The day before Christmas Eve, Sara and I are sitting in Alfreds when Sara gets a call from an unknown number. It's Mum. She's borrowed a stranger's phone to say they've made it to Germany and that they're sitting on a train heading for Berlin. Within the hour I'm standing on the platform at Hauptbahnhof, Berlin's main train station. I stare at the screen glowing bright blue above my head. The train is on time. They'll be here any minute. My stomach churns. Mum, Dad, Shahed. In Berlin. The station's layered platforms loom above us, stretching up to a colossal glass dome roof. Christmas lights twinkle. It's cold. I can see my breath.

I look at Sara. She's biting her lip. A crackly announcement in German echoes off the glass and concrete. An off-white train snakes along the platform towards us, the front lights two red eyes on a pointed snout. I scan the long windows as the carriages grind past. I can't see them. The brakes screech. Then, through a door window, Mum. Her anxious face breaks into a wide grin as she spots us. The train stops, the door opens. Shahed skips down onto the platform, runs over, and wraps her arms around my waist. Then Mum, she clasps my shoulders, kisses my cheeks and my forehead.

Behind her, Dad. I run into his arms. He holds me tight for the first time in three years.

'Yusra, *habibti*,' he says in my ear. 'I thought I... After you were at sea two hours... I hadn't heard anything. I started to pray.'

I feel strangely numb and far away, like I'm looking down on us from one of the platforms above our heads. Mum and Dad look exhausted. They both have deep, dark circles around their eyes. Shahed gazes up at me and Sara, her face wet with tears.

'We didn't think we'd make it here today,' says Mum. 'We got to a city called Mannheim and they wanted to keep us there. But we told them no, our daughters are in Berlin. We have to go to them.'

Mum smiles and draws me and Sara into another hug. I look down at Shahed. She's shivering. They'll need some warmer clothes. The following day all the shops will shut for the holiday, I tell them, so we should go shopping now. Shahed gazes out of the glass elevator as we float up to the ground floor of the station. There, in the main concourse, stands an eight-metre-high synthetic Christmas tree. It's fluffy and tacky and gold. Mum takes our photo in front of it. Then we go into a clothes shop in the station, where they buy jumpers, hats, and scarves. Sven has arranged for Mum, Dad and Shahed to stay with us in the clubhouse over Christmas. We get some food and then go back to the Olympiapark. I call Sven on the way and he comes to help Mum, Dad and Shahed settle into their rooms. They take long showers and go straight to bed. They sleep deeply, well into the next day.

The next morning, Christmas Eve, I wait with Sara in the deserted cafeteria. We watch snow flurries swirl outside and melt on the window pane. Mum wakes up just before noon and wanders in, blurry-eyed. She hugs us again and then sits down on one of the wooden benches.

'So how was the journey?' I ask her.

'Oh, the crossing was terrible,' says Mum. 'They said they'd have life jackets for us, but they didn't. The yacht was so crowded. It was only because a good man offered us a seat that me and Shahed could sit down.'

'Was the sea rough?' says Sara.

'No, it was still,' says Mum. 'But at the end we hit some rocks and for fifteen minutes I thought we would all drown. But we got on shore in the end. *Alhamdulillah*.'

'And you didn't go to Hungary?' I say.

'No, there's a fence there now,' she says. 'The soldiers put us on buses through to Serbia and Croatia. Then to Austria, then to Germany. We just went from bus to bus. It all went very fast.'

'Uh-huh,' I say and give Sara a meaningful look.

Sara laughs.

'Sounds alright to us,' she says.

Christmas Eve is deathly quiet in the Olympiapark. I spend the evening with Elise and her family. We eat a huge feast and exchange presents. The next day, Christmas Day, Sara takes Mum and Shahed to visit a friend of hers, and Sven invites me and Dad to his place. It's crowded at Sven's apartment. His whole family is there. The language barrier doesn't seem to matter at all. Dad smiles around at everyone as we eat German potato salad and chicken fricassee. I'm very happy. When I arrived in Germany just months before, I never dreamed I would spend my first European Christmas like this, surrounded by friends.

The following evening Sara says she's going out. She comes into the cafeteria to say goodbye in full make-up and a short dress. I wince, waiting for the argument. Mum looks up calmly and tells her not to be late. I stare, open-mouthed. I look at Dad. He doesn't even look up from his phone. I can't believe it. Are things really going to be that different now we're in Germany? Or has the journey changed us in their eyes? Yes, that's it. We've proved ourselves. We were brave. We never crossed any red lines, we just protected ourselves. We've shown we can look after ourselves, that we knew what we were doing. We're adults now, we have power with our parents. What do they care if Sara goes out to see her friends?

A few days later, Mum and Dad say they are going to 'turn themselves in' and get themselves assigned to a camp with Shahed. Sara calls our friend Ayham, who is still living in the *heim* in Spandau. Like Sara, he's been volunteering at Moabit Hilft, a citizens' initiative helping newcomers settle into Berlin. Ayham helps see to it that my family go into a *heim* that isn't too crowded. They end up on the other side of the city, about an hour from us on the train. Two days after Christmas, Dad comes to Alfreds, and Sven and I take him to the pool to swim. Sven suggests Dad comes along and helps with our training group. I'm truly happy for the first time in weeks. My family are here. We're all safe. I can swim, and Dad can help me improve.

I spend New Year's Eve with Elise and her family. Everyone wants to teach me about German traditions. At midnight we watch out of the window as hundreds of fireworks explode over the city. Then we melt tiny scraps of thin metal into a bowl of water. Elise tells me the shapes are meant to predict the future, but I get no answers about what's to come.

Early in the New Year, Sven starts worrying about my education. He organizes a private German tutor for me, a friend of his called Corinna. She comes twice a week for an hour and we study in Alfreds. Learning German is hard work, but already having English helps a lot. One day in early January, Sven walks in at the end of my lesson as I'm reading out my homework. The exercise was to write in German who my best friends are. I look down at what I've written.

'*Meine beste Freundin ist Elise*,' I read out slowly. '*Mein bester Freund ist Sven.*'

I look up at Sven and grin. He's standing in the doorway, his eyes are red. He manages a smile, clears his throat, turns, and walks out.

Maybe it's just the start of a new year, but everyone seems to be thinking a lot about my future. At dinner with Sven that night, Dad asks if I'm planning to study at university. Of course, I tell him. But Sven frowns and shakes his head. Studying in Germany isn't as simple as I think. I left Syria before finishing school, so I don't have a graduation certificate. Sven says that no German university will take me on without it. Sven offers to talk to the headmaster of the Poelchau school, the elite sports school here in Olympiapark and see if they'll take me on.

'Just for the final year?' I say.

'Well, no,' says Sven. 'You'd have to start back with the kids in our group, I guess. Lessons are in German, so you'd need to learn the language first. Then after four years you'd do your *Abitur,* the German school-leavers' exams. After that you can study.'

My eyes widen.

'Four years?!' I say. 'Don't be ridiculous. I'm not going back to school for another four years. I only needed one more year in Syria to graduate.'

My head spins. It's like a nightmare. I want to go forwards. Not back to the ninth grade. I'm already training with fourteen-year-olds, now Sven wants me to go back to school with them? I translate for Dad. Surely he won't expect me to go back to school. But to my surprise he agrees that's what I should do.

'Swimming won't last forever, Yusra,' says Dad. 'You need an education.'

I roll my eyes and sigh. Back to school it is. One bit of good news is that Olympic Solidarity, an arm of the IOC that supports athlete development, has granted me a scholarship. The money is for training facilities, coaching, and travel costs to competitions. It isn't dependent on whether I make it onto the refugee team. They've offered it to me whatever happens. It's a great opportunity.

I can't wait to get back into the pool. I'm excited when training starts again after the Christmas break. Dad joins us for our first session, but he mostly stays quiet and watches Sven at work. One day, not long after training restarts, Richie, one of the boys in the group, stops me on the way back into the changing rooms. He tells me his dad is a drummer in a rock band and invites me along to a concert the following Saturday. Thomas from the group is coming too, he says, and Richie's dad has already asked Sven. I'm touched and surprised. It will be a lovely change to go out and do something different. At last, after a long week of challenging work, Saturday comes around. Sara is also going out and we both get dressed up. Sven drives me to the venue, where we meet Richie, Thomas, and his parents. I'm relaxed and happy. It's the first time I've been out in months.

We get drinks and sit in a corner, waiting for the gig to start. I'm scrolling through Facebook. There on my timeline, a post: 'RIP Alaa.' They can't mean Alaa, my school friend from Damascus? A wave of nausea hits me in the gut. No. It's a joke. It must be some kind of sick joke. I scroll down. Another post: 'RIP Alaa.' I flick down. A third post. This time from Alaa's cousin.

'Sven,' I say, feeling the panic rising.

Sven's brow wrinkles with concern.

'What's wrong?' he says.

I stand, the room is spinning. It can't be true. Alaa can't be dead. She was there, just months ago in the café in Malki, cute, crazy, and very alive. I step away from the table and duck behind a curtain. I dial Sara's number.

'Sara, did you see?' I say. 'They're saying Alaa is dead.'

I barely hear her reply. She tells me she's going back to Alfreds, that she'll meet me at the clubhouse. She hangs up. The walls are crashing down. The tears come. I duck out from behind the curtain. Sven is standing, watching me.

'My friend is dead,' I say. 'I saw on Facebook. I have to go.'

Sven downs his coke and grabs our coats from the cloakroom. I can't speak as Sven drives me home. I study Facebook and cry. It wasn't even the war. Alaa and her elder sister had left Syria already. It wasn't the sea either. They didn't get that far. Both sisters were killed in a bus crash on their way from Istanbul to Izmir. The bus was travelling too fast around a corner in the hills. It flipped and burned.

We're back at the clubhouse in twenty minutes. Sara is there, waiting at one of the tables in the dining room with her friend. I still can't speak. I walk past them into my room and shut the door. I throw myself on the bed and weep. Sven stands outside the door and knocks. I don't speak. He calls my name. I don't answer. I just want to be alone.

'Yusra?' It's Sara this time. 'Come out and talk to us.'

'Please,' I say. 'Just leave me. Just go.'

'Come on, Yusra,' Sara tries again. 'Alaa and her sister are in a better place now. I know it's sad. But at least they're at peace now.'

I ignore her. I can't speak to anyone right now. At last, she gives up and goes away. I pick up my phone. Maybe it's all a mistake? Maybe they survived. Only seven people were reported killed. The other thirty were only injured. Maybe Alaa is in hospital somewhere in Turkey? I write to Alaa's cousin. Is she dead, really? Because there are survivors from the bus. Go and check, I tell her. Maybe they survived. The reply comes straight away: No, *habibti*. I'm sorry. Really. They're both dead. I break down again in sobs.

There's a hard knock at the door. It's Dad. I tell him to leave me alone. The grief comes in waves. I sob for minutes on end, then I stop and stare at the wall, breathe deeply, try to calm myself down. But then I think of their mother, losing both her girls at once. The tragedy screws my insides again and I break down. Breathe, wait. The next wave hits. The pain she suffered, the way she died. The hope they felt on their journey, the fear. I weep again, pray for their souls. The night is lifting outside by the time I lie down on my bed, exhausted. Falling asleep I see Alaa's face. My tears soak into the pillow.

I'm in an apartment in Damascus with Mum and Shahed. A whistling screech rips through the air above. Impact. The walls shake and crumble, masonry falls around us. Shahed screams as the building collapses.

Blackness. I'm in the rubble. I dig myself out, coughing in the beige dust. No Mum, no Shahed. I dig for them, panic rising as I scrabble through the stones. I hear moans from under the broken concrete. A voice calls my name. I turn and see Mum, calm and smiling, carrying Shahed in her arms.

Blackness again. I'm in the pool in Berlin, treading water and holding onto the side. A deep voice echoes off the water and around the hall.

'Yusra, you've got a choice to make,' it says. 'You don't have long to make it. You can stay here. Or you can go back to your country and suffer with the rest. You have to choose, Yusra. Only you can choose.'

I wake up crying.

PART SEVEN

The Storm

19

Dad comes to all my training sessions for the first few weeks after Christmas. He watches me swim, gives me tips, drives me on. Mostly he sits quietly in the background, too shy to comment or contradict Sven. As the weeks go on, Dad gradually withdraws from the pool. I understand, he has other things to worry about. Discovering Berlin, submitting his own asylum claim, learning German.

Sven comes with me and Sara to our asylum interviews at the end of January. Our case worker oversees special cases: spies, celebrities, sports personalities. She's surprised when we ask if Sven can come into the interview room with us. We're the first women she's seen bring a man with them. I grin and tell her Sven doesn't count. He's practically family by now anyway. The interview itself is quite straightforward. The woman asks us questions about our backgrounds, whether we were politically active in Syria and how and why we came to Germany. It takes around thirty minutes. At the end, the case worker tells us we'll get our final decision within six weeks. We're another step along in the asylum process. Just six weeks until we'll know for certain whether we can stay in Germany.

I'm relieved, but on the bus back to the Olympiapark, I can't help but battle with pangs of guilt. The special treatment doesn't feel right. We got our interviews much faster because I might be on the refugee team, because the DOSB intervened with the Interior Ministry. I look out at the grey streets and wonder what the asylum process feels like for everyone else. The government holds all the cards. It can send you running from office to office, queue to queue. You can jump through every hoop and in the end an official can still say no, tell you to leave, go back to face whatever you ran from. Even crossing closed borders is better than that. You can use your wits to get through a physical barrier. Here, if the government says no, there isn't much you can do about it.

I remind myself the special treatment is just a timing thing. The DOSB intervened with the Interior Ministry to speed things up for me so that I can travel. It's not just that we might be going to the Olympics in Rio. Sven has also arranged for us to travel to Luxembourg for a competition, the CIJ Meet, at the end of April. It's one of the official qualifying events for Rio. The IOC has been vague about whether I'll need to qualify for the refugee team in the normal way, but they've said it can't hurt to swim at a qualifying event.

The following Monday I go back to school. A month before my eighteenth birthday, I find myself back in the ninth grade. Sven is overjoyed. Me, not so much. I'm grateful for the opportunity and I know everyone only wants the best for me. But to be honest, the only plus is sharing the same routine as the fourteen-year-olds in my training group. Lessons are torture. I've heard it all before. I sit in the back, drawing and writing and staring out the window until it's time to swim again. 'My name is refugee,' I write in the back of my exercise book. 'At least, that's what they call me.' By the end of the first week, I'm already in trouble with my teachers. They tell Sven I'm not appreciative of the opportunity for an education. They get me all wrong. I want to study. But not like this.

At least there are plenty of distractions from the joys of ninth-grade maths. All the media requests, for one. Just before I start school, IOC President Thomas Bach visits a refugee facility in Athens and confirms to reporters there will be a refugee team at the Rio Olympics. Sven's inbox explodes once more with interview requests. I read a lot of them myself, but leave everything for Sven to answer. Before long he's getting more emails than he can read.

'It's weird that they only want to talk to me,' I say to Sven. 'What about the other refugee athletes the IOC mentioned as being in the running? The Congolese guy, the Iranian woman?'

'I'm not sure the journalists have found them,' says Sven. 'You speak English. And you're Syrian, too. Lots of reporters want to talk about the war. On top of that, there's your amazing story.'

'Which story?' I say.

'The boat story, silly,' he says.

'Oh that,' I say. 'But we told that story already to those reporters last year. Why does anyone want to hear it again?'

Sven shakes his head.

'I don't think it works like that,' he says.

There's no way I can grant all the requests for interviews, so Michael Schirp from the DOSB suggests we hold a press conference. That way, I can talk to all the reporters at once rather than interrupting swimming and school for each one. At first, we plan a small event in the clubhouse in mid-March. We think maybe twenty or thirty journalists will come. Sven and Michael draft a press release announcing a media day in March and asking everyone to please leave me alone until then. I invite my journalist friends, Steven, Lam, and Magdalena, to come along. I know I'll feel better on the day if they are there. And anyway, they're a big part of my story.

Not long after we put out the press release, I get another message from my swimming friend Rami. He says he's swimming again with a club in Ghent and he's also found a great coach to mentor him. Rami asks about the refugee team, he wants to know if Sven can help him get in touch with the IOC. I tell him his coach can do it directly. I'm excited that Rami is going to try for the team too. Just imagine if we both get to go to Rio. Everything will be so much easier if my old friend Rami is there too. We'll be able to laugh our way through it.

The weeks pass. I swim. I sit bored in lessons. Sara and I spend most Sundays with Mum, Dad, and Shahed. They aren't happy in their *heim*. There are thefts and other security problems. Mum says the food is terrible and the bathrooms are dirty. We promise to get them out of there as soon as possible. As soon as the paperwork comes through, we plan to find an apartment where we can all live together. As the press conference draws nearer, I start worrying again about the refugee team. I'm an athlete. Why should I go to the Olympics just because I'm a refugee? I tell Mum about my doubts one Sunday in late February.

'Don't be silly, *habibti*,' says Mum absent-mindedly. 'You deserve it. You've worked hard for swimming your whole life.'

'No really, Mum, I don't know whether I should do it,' I say.

But Mum isn't really listening.

'Just think,' she says. 'All that time I spent sitting at the pool or watching your competitions, it wasn't for nothing.'

I understand why it's hard to get through to my family. Both Mum and Dad have a lot on their plates. They're busy with their own paperwork, their own asylum claims. In mid-March, Sara and I get a letter saying we've both been granted asylum. We can stay for a minimum of three years in Germany. It's a big relief. I think of Sven, of Mette, Elise and her family, of Reni, the club, and the school. Everyone has been so generous. They've helped me come such a long way already in my new life. Now we know what we've been building isn't only temporary. I know I can stay, can continue working towards my dream.

I don't see much of Sara. She's out a lot, doing her own thing. One evening I come into the clubhouse after training and hear traditional Syrian *Tarab* music coming from her room along the corridor. I knock on the door and find her standing at the sink, doing her make-up, getting ready to go out. I sit down on her bed and gaze around the walls at her latest collection of mad posters.

'Do you ever think about going back?' says Sara, staring in the mirror and applying eyeliner to her eyes.

'To Syria?' I say. 'Sure. But only when this is all over.'

'I think I'm going to go back,' says Sara.

'What?' I say. 'Now? Are you mad?'

'Don't you miss it?' she says.

Sara pauses to paint two streaks of dark red lipstick onto her mouth.

'Don't you feel bad about all the people who are stuck in Syria?' she says.

'Of course,' I say. 'But how would I help them by going back?'

Sara takes one last look in the mirror and turns to face me. She changes the subject abruptly and asks if she can borrow my black jacket. I shake my head.

'No,' I say. 'It's my favourite. You'll probably rip it, or lose it.'

'My God,' she says. 'You know you're turning into such a pain in the ass.'

'What?' I say. 'Because I won't let you have my jacket?'

'Just because you have a scholarship, it doesn't mean you're better than anyone,' says Sara. 'Or is it because you're so famous now?'

I stare at her. I stand up, walk out, and slam the door behind me. I go to my room, lie down on my bed and cry. If my own sister thinks that about me, what are the others saying? I open Facebook. One of my friends in Damascus has changed her profile to a picture of a stormy sea. On the picture, in white italics, the words: 'After the storm come calm days.' I stare at the picture for a long time. The storm has gone on too long. When will Syria have calm days? When will I?

'I don't need hand-outs,' I tell my bedroom wall. 'I don't want to be famous. I want peace, so I can rebuild my life.'

In early March, three days before my eighteenth birthday, the IOC makes the team official. The IOC puts out an announcement. This summer, a Refugee Olympic Team, ROT, will march behind the Olympic flag at the opening ceremony. Up to ten athletes will be on the team, chosen from a longlist of forty-three potential team members. I'm on the list. So is my swimming friend Rami.

It's the first time the IOC mentions me by name. Sven's phone rings so much he has to put it in the fridge to get some peace. My private social media accounts go into meltdown. Ordinary people start writing to me. There are insults among the encouraging words. Of the good messages, one stands out. A young guy writes to me from inside Syria. He says his mother was killed in the war, leaving him as the only one left to look after his family. Food is so expensive they hardly ever eat. 'Thank you,' he writes. 'My life is hard, but you've inspired me to go on.' I read his message over and over again.

Others write to warn me about Sven, questioning his kindness, asking what's in it for him. It seems no one can get their heads around our friendship. Even my parents can't understand why he is helping me so much. They think he must be after something. Fame. Money. Whatever. I tell them all they're being ridiculous.

And then there are the journalists. I had no idea there were so many of them. Sven tells me to turn off all notifications on my phone and to stop checking my emails. He says that he and Michael will deal with it. It seems most of the reporters don't understand what a longlist is. They think because I'm on it, that means I'm definitely going to Rio. But nothing has been decided for certain. We're all surprised by the level of interest in the press conference. A few weeks before the big day, Michael tells Sven on the phone that we're going to need a larger room. There are now sixty different media outlets coming, some of them TV crews that need more space. We won't all fit into the clubhouse.

My birthday draws near, my first in Germany. I think about the party Sara threw for me with Leen in Malki in Damascus the year before. Where are all my Syrian friends now? I decide I have to mark the occasion and ask Sven to organize a small party in Alfreds after training for my swimming friends. Sven can't be there with me on the day itself, he has to fly to England for a family event. But he calls me from England the evening before. In Germany, he says on the phone, everyone celebrates at midnight the night before their birthday. It's five minutes before midnight. Sven grins on the screen and says he's got a surprise for me. He tells me to go to my room and open the wooden box. In my room I find a box on the bedside table. Inside, there's a key. Sven tells me to use the key to open the door to the largest room along the corridor. The key fits, the lock clicks, and I push open the door. I draw breath. Sven has decorated the whole room with bright streamers and birthday banners.

'Wow,' I say, grinning wide. 'Sven, this is amazing.'

'Have you found your presents?' says Sven.

I look around. Three packages lie on the bedside table. I unwrap the first one and gasp. It's an expensive-looking compression suit to help muscle recovery after training. Inside the second package is a pair of white Adidas sneakers. The third, the smallest package, feels like a book. I rip off the paper. It's Malala's autobiography. I grin. What an amazing friend I've found. Without Sven, where would I be now? It's only later that I understand that Sven wasn't the only one. All over Germany, thousands of volunteers were supporting newcomers. We had arrived, we had survived the nightmare, and now us lucky ones had found friends to help us carry on.

A few days after my birthday, the IOC and the UN Refugee Agency, UNHCR, send camera teams to the pool to interview me. I say a lot about the Olympics, how it's always been my dream and how exciting it is to be given this incredible chance. The teams take photos outside the stadium with the Olympic rings in the background. The IOC photographer has me jump for joy in the air. Over and over and over again. When they leave, I can't help wondering why the IOC would bother sending a film crew unless I'm definitely on the team. Sven plays it down, says we can't know anything for sure. Anyway, I'm still not sure about the whole idea of the team. Each day, I find myself swinging between wild excitement and crippling doubt.

Despite all the things I have to be grateful for, it's a tough time. I don't like school. Elise, Mette, and Sven are great, but I have no friends my own age. I miss Syria terribly. And the media interest means the pressure is building. I want desperately to compete in the Olympics, but at the same time I don't want hand-outs. I'm getting faster in the pool but there's no way I'm going to qualify in the normal way for Rio. My swimming starts to suffer. We stick to Sven's Tokyo plan, aiming to get back to my personal bests by the summer. I try not to think about the qualifying standard times for Rio: 1:00 for 100m butterfly and 2:03 for 200m freestyle. Even my personal bests are nine seconds off in both disciplines. The last thing I want to do is talk to journalists about all this at a press conference. About my times, or the Olympics, or being a refugee. Or about the boat. Least of all that. Sven knows it isn't easy for me. He's worried that it's too much pressure.

'Yusra, you say the word, and everything stops,' says Sven one night, a week before the press conference. 'You just have to tell me if we're not going to do this. We can cancel everything, pull out of the whole thing. I'll talk to the DOSB, the IOC. We can make it all go away.'

I stare at him. He's serious.

'But if we do that, it'd be final,' says Sven. 'It'd all be over. No going back. No Olympics. Dream gone.'

I stare at the floor and struggle with myself. It's always been my dream to compete at the Olympics. But as an athlete I'm not there yet. My thoughts are still raging by the time I go to bed that night. I've just switched off the light when my phone buzzes. It's a message from Sven.

'I think you should know why I'm doing all this,' he writes. 'Sometimes I get the feeling – and I've heard it said too – that people think I'm doing all this just for my own benefit. I need to know that you don't think that. From the first day you and Sara arrived, I just wanted to help. For what? Just to help. I don't want anything, not money, or fame.'

My eyes widen as I read his message. I know Sven, he isn't like that. He helps because that's who he is, it's the way he was brought up. It is in his nature to help others without expecting anything in return. I read on.

'The first thing you told me when you arrived was that you wanted to go to the Olympics,' writes Sven. 'And now you can. If not this year, then in 2020. You can prove doubters wrong. All those people who threw rocks in your way. Remember, I'm here to help you have a future, Yusra. Good night.'

I smile and think back to how far Sven and I have already come together. He's right. Competing at the Olympics has always been my dream. And now, with Sven's help, it's within touching distance. But somehow it still feels wrong.

A few days before the press conference, Sven gets a call from Michael saying that IOC deputy director Pere Miro is going to attend in person. Sven thinks he might want to come along to confirm I'm on the team. But I'm still torn. I don't want to go to Rio if I haven't earned it or if it's just because I'm Syrian, because I'm a refugee. And anyway, why does it have to be me? I'm sure lots of other people would love to have this chance. All at once, I'm decided. I won't do it. I'll wait and go to the Olympics when I'm ready. I tell Sven. I can't do it. That night I call Dad and tell him my decision. I don't want hand-outs. I don't need people to feel sorry for me. And anyway, what athlete wants to go to the Olympics out of charity?

'Maybe you're right,' says Dad on the phone. 'But maybe you're also thinking about this the wrong way. Think how hard you worked to swim. All those hours, all that sacrifice. Why not take this chance? And afterwards you can use your voice to help people.'

I think of the horrors I see every night just scrolling through my newsfeed. The suicide bombings, the gas attacks, the starving, bloodied children. The desperate escapes, the prayers at sea, those stuck indefinitely along endless barbed-wire borders. Help people. Yes, I'd love to do that. But how? If I go to the Olympics it won't stop the war, or open the borders, or even reduce the queues at the LaGeSo office in Berlin. But Dad says I could help people in a different way.

'Very few Syrians get this kind of chance to speak up,' he says. 'You can be their voice. You know a big part of their story because you've been through it too. It's an opportunity for all of us to be heard.'

Later, I lie in bed thinking it over. I'm sick of watching helplessly from the sidelines while my people suffer. If I go to Rio, I'll certainly have more power than I do now. Besides, the whole thing has a momentum of its own. In a few days' time, I'll be speaking to the world. Journalists and TV crews from Japan to Brazil, the American news networks, the global wires, newspapers and magazines from all over Europe and America. Dad's right. I should tell them our story. For all of us.

The day before the press conference, Sven and I are sitting in Alfreds, killing time before evening training. I ask Sven what will happen if I do end up going to Rio. Sven says he thinks all this media interest might make me a little bit famous, but he warns me not to rely on that long term. The media always move on to the next thing, he says. But we can use that as a start, as a platform for my voice. And I can use that voice to inspire young people, aspiring athletes, kids in schools, that kind of thing. Sven pauses and looks at me.

'You do still want to be a voice for change?' he says. 'Like Malala?'

I look him in the eye.

'If they ask me, I'll do it,' I say. 'Anyway, if you get the chance to go to the Olympics, you go.'

'That's your final decision, right?' says Sven. 'It's fixed. We're not going to talk about it again?'

Yes, I tell him. And I'll do all the interviews. But I want to get better at talking to the media. If I'm going to have a voice, I want people to listen. Sven lists on his fingers what the journalists will want to know. They'll want the boat story. They might ask about Syria. And they'll ask about swimming and why I want to be on the team.

'I'll just tell them the truth,' I say. 'I'm doing this to inspire people to do what they believe in, no matter what. And to show them that if you have problems it doesn't mean you should sit around and cry like a baby. I want to make all the refugees proud of me and show that even if we had a tough journey we can achieve something.'

Saying the words out loud to Sven gives me courage. I'm surprised at how calm I feel. I think about the message from the guy in Syria. Maybe it's all worth it if I can help people like him carry on.

Just then, I hear voices coming from outside the clubhouse. I go to the window and see Dad standing at the bottom of the steps. With him are a camera crew and the translator from our old *heim*, Abu Atef. It's clear they're looking for me, but no one told me about any interviews today. My phone buzzes in my pocket. I take it out. Abu Atef is calling. I throw the phone on the bed. No, I'm not talking to a news crew. I'm talking to a hundred journalists tomorrow and I've got training in ten minutes. But we're stuck in the clubhouse. We can't get to the pool without walking past them. I duck below the windowsill and peek out as a security guard approaches the group. I catch my breath. Maybe he'll send them away. But the guard strolls off again and the crew stays on, waiting to catch me on my way out. My phone buzzes again. This time it's Dad.

'My God,' I say. 'Sven, you have to do something. We can't get to the pool without them seeing us.'

Sven pulls his phone out of his pocket and calls Peter, the vice president of the club. He'll know what to do. Peter says he'll come and distract the news crew so we can get out to training. Sven hangs up and we wait. We watch from the window as, a few minutes later, Peter comes striding around the corner towards the clubhouse. He says something to Abu Atef and the whole group follows him back towards the Olympiapark entrance. A few moments later, Sven's phone rings. It's Peter, telling us the coast is clear. I grab my kit bag and we run along the corridor, out of the clubhouse door and down the steps. We sprint around the corner that leads towards the pool. No Dad, no Abu Atef, no film crew. Just a tall man with dark hair in a suit, looking lost.

'Sven?' says the man.

He holds out his hand and introduces himself. Michael Schirp from the DOSB. In person, for the first time. Michael shakes hands warmly with Sven, then he looks at me and smiles.

'And you must be the famous Yusra?' says Michael.

'That's me,' I grin.

Sven puts a hand on Michael's shoulder and ushers him towards the pool entrance.

'We're in a hurry to get to the pool,' says Sven. 'We just got trapped in the clubhouse because a film crew were looking for us outside.'

'Oh no,' says Michael, his face screwed up with concern. 'I wish I'd got an earlier train. I might have been here to help you fight them off.'

The next morning, I'm up early. Sven and I meet for breakfast with IOC deputy director Pere Miro and Michael before the press conference. I'm nervous at first, but everybody is very relaxed and easy-going. We chat about my childhood in Syria and my new life here in Berlin. Pere tells us about the IOC's plans for the team.

They're planning on setting up a real Olympic team just like the others, with physiotherapists, doctors, press attaché and team leaders. It's clear everyone in the IOC is very excited about the project.

After breakfast, we go to the large room we've borrowed from the Berlin Sport Federation, which also has premises in the Olympiapark. We wait in a small side room with Pere and other guests of the German Olympic Sport Confederation. Lam and Magdalena come and find us backstage. Lam is in a great mood, fooling around, joking and taking photos, which helps me calm my nerves. When it's time, Sven pulls open the door and we step into the packed press conference. The first person I see is the Belgian journalist, Steven. I grin and hug him. It's so encouraging to have my friends here with me among all these strangers. I scan the rows of chairs. Exactly 126 journalists from all over the globe. Eighteen camera teams film from the back. Their cameras follow me as I make my way to the first row and sit down between Pere Miro and Dad. A crowd of photographers slump at my feet. Their shutters clatter over the sound of IOC President Thomas Bach's pre-recorded video message.

'We help them to make their dream of sporting excellence come true,' he says. 'Even when they have to flee war and violence.'

I block out the nerves, focus on my message. Michael sits ahead on a small, raised platform, giving a short introduction before Pere, Sven and I come on stage. Behind him, projected on a screen above his head, is a series of Lam's photos. The images flick up one by one. Sara and I walking down the train tracks on the Hungarian border. Our group crouching in the cornfields, hiding from the police. Did all of that really happen? It doesn't seem real. Michael finishes his introduction and Sven, Pere and I stand up. The cameras click and clatter again and the room stirs. The reporters sit up in their seats, raise their pens, open their laptops. A hush falls as I step on stage. The journalists gaze at me, take in my hoodie, my trainers, my unmade-up face. I stare back at them as Pere gives an introduction about the IOC's plans for the team. What are all these reporters doing here? I'm not even on the team yet. I guess it must be that word. The one they'll all use in their headlines. Refugee.

I scan the crowd and spot my friends, Steven, Lam, and Magdalena. All three of them are beaming, willing me on. My throat feels tight and my chest heavy. My stomach is churning. I wonder for a mad moment what would happen if I told them the honest truth. If I told them what it feels like to be reduced to that one word, tried to explain what that word means to those forced to wear it as their name. Refugee. An empty shell, barely even human. No money, no home, no background, no history, no personality, no ambition, no path, no passion. Our past, present, future. All of it deleted and replaced by that one devastating word. I smile as the cameras flash. I'm calm. I know my message.

'So,' says Michael, 'we'll just open it up for questions.'

A forest of hands reaches up to the ceiling.

20

I look around the cluster of camera lenses. The reporters want to know what happened on the boat. I smile and tell them my story politely, but I speak without emotion. My heart closes, shuts out the vision of marching waves. Only my head is working. We swam from Turkey to Greece. After fifteen minutes, the engine died. We're swimmers, so me and my sister got into the water and held onto the rope. After three and a half hours we got to Greece. I do five group interviews back to back. I say the same words, over and over again. It's impossible to relive the horror of the crossing for each reporter. My heart stays shut, I lock the calm smile onto my face.

IOC deputy director Pere Miro is first to leave the press conference. His last words are that he'll see us in Rio. I look at Sven and raise my eyebrows. I'm definitely on the team now, right? But Sven says we still don't know for sure. Nobody has told him anything definite. It's all very mysterious. I guess if the IOC wants me on the team, they'll put me on the team.

In the days following the press conference, hundreds of articles and videos appear telling the boat story in all manner of imaginative ways. Some have me pushing, others pulling the boat to shore. Some mention Sara, others don't. Some mention the other guys in the water, others don't. The most ludicrous ones have me, alone, with a rope tied around my waist, swimming freestyle, and pulling a boat crammed with 150 people to safety. Like a cartoon. Like superwoman. But the hands-down weirdest version is a headline in an Arabic newspaper: 'Syrian sisters swim from Greece to Germany.' I get a trickle of messages calling me a liar and a fraud. I realize for the first time that whatever you say, journalists get the story they want. I guess they wanted a hero. All I ever wanted was to swim.

If we'd hoped the press conference would satisfy the media, we were wrong. Sven's inbox explodes like never before. He's now fielding 300 emails a week. We get offers to make my story into a book or even a film. Those behind the proposals are very persistent. One guy from a production company in New York is calling Sven every five minutes to pitch a huge film project. He's always talking big money and boasting about his connections in Hollywood. Sven tells him we're focusing on the Olympics, but the producer keeps saying if we want to do a film it has to be now, that no one will be interested in me after the summer. I wonder if the guy is right, but Sven insists we should take things very slowly. We have enough to deal with, working things out about Rio. And I don't need to worry about money for now, I have the Olympic Solidarity scholarship.

I try and focus in training, but the pressure keeps on building. In the back of my mind I'm still hoping for a miracle. I dream about qualifying for the team in the normal way and going to the Olympics not because I'm a refugee but because I'm fast enough. I imagine getting through all the heats to the final. I picture myself winning an Olympic medal. If not this summer, then in Tokyo in 2020. Sven is careful to remind me we're only aiming to reach my personal bests in Luxembourg at the end of the month. I don't have to get a qualifying time for my races. The IOC just want me to swim at a qualifying event as a formality.

One night, a few weeks before the Luxembourg competition, I'm lying on my bed, scrolling through Facebook. My news feed is a horror show of videos about the invasion of rebel-held Aleppo. Some of the images are graphically violent. I screw my eyes shut and take a few deep breaths. Then I open my messages. I'm hit with a barrage of tragic stories, pleas for help for dying children and starving families. A young student writes from inside Syria to say he wishes he could escape like I have. I shut off my phone in horror and switch out the light.

I'm in the clubhouse with Mum and Shahed. Mum stares into the distance, her eyes glazed and faraway, her cheeks swollen and wet with tears. I wave my hand in front of Mum's face. She doesn't move.

'Mum!'

She turns her head towards me but doesn't see. She looks through me. Then she sighs and stands, puts her arm around Shahed, and they walk away. I hear laughter. It's Dad.

'Dad! Why can't Mum see me?'

'Because you died, Yusra. You and Sara. Didn't you know?'

Blackness.

A train carriage. Above my head, blurry symbols flash across a blue screen. I screw up my eyes, try to read the destination.

'Where are my glasses?' I shout to the empty carriage. 'Where are we going?'

Blackness again.

I'm standing alone in the house. Then, inevitably, the screech from the sky, the impact, the walls fall, and I'm scrabbling desperately through the rubble. I wake up, my cheeks already wet with tears.

I swim badly in training the next day. My head is full of the devastation in Aleppo. When will I lose another friend, a relative? Sven wants to know what's wrong. I tell him about my dream. He looks worried and says I shouldn't go online before bed. But I can't just let the war go. I have to know what's happening to my country. And I have to read the messages, the horrific stories, the pleas for help. After all, these are the people I want to give voice to. It's not fair. I'm safe while they starve in the bombed-out ruins of their cities, without food or electricity. I feel so helpless. Sven says it's survivor's guilt. He offers again to take me to a psychologist, but that isn't my style.

Instead, Sven keeps me busy. There are always things to plan. Media appointments, competitions, training camps, admin, travel. Sven often shoots me a concerned look and asks if it's all too much. The question makes me squirm. Does he think I'm that weak, that I've reached my limit? I'm used to being challenged to succeed. Dad's style was high standards, high expectations, high rewards. If you suffer, you suffer alone. You fall alone, you stand alone. I tell

Sven I can take it. I know I'm strong. I remind him I'm still standing after going through much worse.

In mid-April, Sven and I go to the office to pick up my official
residence permit. The paper also serves as a travel document. It's
come through just in time for the competition in Luxembourg.
The official hands me a little blue book and tells me I can use it as
a passport for any country in the world, except my own. I look
down at the document in my hands. The initial relief gives way to
a deep sense of loss. I'm free to go anywhere. Apart from home.

That night at dinner, Sven tells me there are a lot of people, big
names, wanting to make documentaries about me. He asks how I'd
feel about a camera crew following me around constantly for a few
days. I tell Sven I'd be fine with that, but he looks sceptical.

'I was thinking we could do a trial run,' says Sven. 'With someone you trust. We could get Steven and Ludwig to film you for the
weekend when we go to the competition in Luxembourg. Like a
reality show, a fly-on-the-wall-style thing. They'd follow you everywhere. Then we can see how you get on.'

'Ok,' I say. 'It'll be fun.'

We fly to Luxembourg on the last Thursday in April. It's my
first international competition in four years. I'm on the start list for
four races in butterfly and freestyle, spread across Friday, Saturday,
and Sunday. Steven and Ludwig are due to arrive early on Saturday
morning and film me for the rest of the weekend. On the Friday
evening, I swim my first race, the 50m freestyle, in twenty-nine
seconds. I come twenty-eighth out of fifty-three swimmers. It's
an ok result. Neither Sven nor I say anything about it. Next morning I'm woken in the early hours by a twisting pain in my lower
abdomen. I'm ill. Typical timing. The next hour I spend on my
hotel-room floor. I can hardly move. Gnawing cramps follow waves
of nausea. Over and over. I battle downstairs into the hotel restaurant for breakfast. I grimace at Sven. It's his birthday.

'Happy birthday,' I say and plonk a small package on the table.

He opens it and smiles. It's a framed photo of us at the pool. I
grab my swimming things and Sven and I set off on the ten-minute

walk to the pool. Another cramp twists my gut. I stop and bend double, waiting for the waves of sickening pain to pass.

'How are you feeling?' says Sven.

'Good,' I say, fighting tears.

The pain dies. I stand, take a deep breath, and carry on walking. We find Steven and Ludwig waiting for us at the pool entrance. I put on my best smile and hug them both.

'How are you doing?' says Steven. 'Ready?'

'Of course,' I say, grimacing as we walk together into the pool.

Steven tells us he's also being pestered by the guy in New York. The producer wants all of his B-roll from the filming we did in Belgrade and Vienna, every single second of film he has on me. Steven keeps telling him no, but the producer won't let up. And he isn't the only one, says Steven. There are four or five other networks on his back for the footage of my journey. I'm stunned again by the interest in my story.

'All I'm saying is it's obviously a golden moment for you, Yusra,' says Steven. 'You know, if you guys wanted to make some money.'

Sven shakes his head.

'No,' says Sven. 'We're thinking doing a film or anything else would be too much right now. We've got a lot on with preparing for the Olympics.'

Steven turns to me.

'So you're going to Rio?' he says. 'For definite?'

'We don't know yet,' I say. 'They're releasing the final team list in June.'

'I think it's likely,' says Sven. 'After all she's done for the project.'

I leave the others and go into the changing rooms to change into my FINA swimsuit and warm-up gear. I barely notice the huge swimming-pool complex. I'm focused on my times, worried about how being ill will affect my swimming. I know I don't need a qualifying time, but achieving one would make everything so much simpler in my head. The kids around me are talking German, French, and Dutch. It's strange for there to be no friendly faces at a competition. If this was Syria, I'd know absolutely everyone.

Back at the poolside, Ludwig starts the camera running. I put my headphones on, swing my arms to warm up, and try and block out the camera. Around me, the other swimmers are staring. No one else has a film crew following them. I put my goggles and swim cap on. I play it cool and easy-going for the camera. I warm up in the pool and have a last-minute chat to Sven. My first race of the day is the 200m butterfly. Ludwig films as I take off my warm-up jacket and put it in the box next to the start block. The camera is there behind me as I climb onto the block. My stomach is rolling, clenching.

'Take your marks.'

Beep.

I dive. Roll my legs. Break the surface. Whirl my arms. Scoop towards my twisting gut. Let muscle memory do the work. The race passes in a blur. But as I touch the wall I know it's not enough. The camera is on me as I haul myself out. I take my goggles off and walk towards Sven.

'Ok, 2:34,' he says, reading from his clipboard. I can do much better than that. I turn away in disgust, ignoring the camera's relentless gaze. I take my swim cap off, walk off along the poolside after the other swimmers. I look up at the board: 2:34. Twenty-one seconds slower than the qualifying standard for Rio. The worst thing is, I've swum fast enough to get me into the final for my age group. It means I'll have to do it all again later this afternoon.

The echoing announcements sound muffled and far away as I walk down the stairs into the locker room. Sven, Steven, and Ludwig are there waiting, camera still running. I'm horrified. I'm in no mood to talk into a camera. Leave me alone. I'm up for the 100m freestyle in an hour. I ignore them and walk back out to the poolside to wait for my next race. Sven comes out to find me. I'm relieved to see Steven and Ludwig have given up on the fly-on-the-wall treatment. They take the camera and retreat to the viewing area.

I swim the 100m freestyle in 1:05. Three seconds slower than my personal best. I come eleventh of the thirteen in my year group. In the younger group, the top twenty kids are faster than me. And at the Olympics no one cares about age. It's the time that counts.

It's a hard realization. If I go to Rio I won't even get into the second round.

Sven wants to talk but I'm not in the mood. I put my headphones on, retreat into my head, and wait for the final. The hours drag on. The pain in my stomach spikes and recedes. At last, it's time to swim the 200m butterfly final. Just let this day be over. There are only two others in my age group. The race is just to determine medals. I swim it in 2:40 and come second. The winner touches in with 2:28. I've won a silver medal, but it's a hollow victory. I can do better. I haul myself out of the pool. I can't stop the tears. Sven puts his hands on my shoulders. I freeze up, tense my whole body, and twist out of his grasp. I pull on my warm-up jacket and jam my headphones on again. I sit at the side, staring at the tiles until it's time for the medal ceremony. Before long, Sven is in front of me. I don't take my headphones off, but I know he wants me to go and collect my silver medal. I sit motionless, staring at the floor.

'Yusra, are you a sportswoman or not?' says Sven. 'Please go and get your medal.'

Tears roll down my cheeks. Sven grabs my shoulders and wiggles them gently. I don't move. I have to go to the ceremony, says Sven, it's part of the competition. Standing on a podium is the last thing I want to do, but Sven isn't giving up. I stand and march over to the raised platform where a man with white hair is waiting for me. I shake his hand and he places the medal round my neck. Next to me, the gold- and bronze-medal winners grin widely for the photographers. It's all I can do to force a grimace. I step down off the platform, take the medal off, and walk back to Sven. He's watching, stony-faced, hands on hips. I grab my stuff and walk out of the pool back to the changing rooms, wiping my eyes with my towel. It's over. Let it be over. Sven is waiting for me at the lockers. This time without the camera crew. I stare at the floor as we walk down the stairs towards the warm-down pool.

'What's the matter?' says Sven. 'Weren't you happy with the time?'

I stop on the stairs and gaze at him in surprise. Not happy? That's an understatement.

'Happy?' I say. 'With the time?'

His forehead creases with concern. The frustration builds in my throat.

'Are you ok?' says Sven.

'The way I swam today,' I say, choking back the tears. 'I can do much better. I want to get better. I've got options. I could train in America and study there. And get away from... from all this.'

Sven frowns again and shakes his head.

'Ok,' he says. 'Do that. Go to America. Try handling all this on your own.'

Sven strides off. I'm shocked. It's the first time I've seen him angry. I stand staring at the stairs for a second, then head down towards the warm-down pool. I warm down, change, and find Sven and Steven waiting for me by the front door. The camera is filming again. No one speaks as we step outside. Sven heads back to the hotel alone and I climb into the back of Steven's car next to the camera equipment. The shock of my argument with Sven hits me again and I start to sob. Steven turns back from the passenger seat and asks me what's wrong.

'I'm just sick,' I say. 'Can we talk? Just you and me?'

Back at the hotel Steven leads me to a quiet table in the bar. We sit down. I take a few deep breaths. I tell Steven I don't know what to do. I tell him I sometimes dream of going to America, where the university system would allow me to study and train at the same time. I'm impatient to get on with my future, but Sven says I should stay in Germany, take it slowly, stay in school. Sven and the club have done so much for me. I'm confused.

'If you want to go to the Olympics you should stay where you are,' says Steven. 'Right now, it's not about your swimming, Yusra. It's all very political. You telling the world your story seems more important than you swimming a certain time.'

I frown.

'But I'm a swimmer,' I say.

'You remember when we met in that park in Belgrade?' says Steven. 'You told me you had swam across to Greece and you wanted to swim in the Olympics?'

Steven spreads his hands.

'Well, back then, I never thought you'd go to the Olympics,' he says. 'And then, seven months later, I'm standing in your press conference, watching it happen. Really happen. Refugee girl goes to the Olympics. Yusra, you should know, this is a one-in-a-million story.'

I shake my head. I never thought it was such a special story until now. To me it was just a journey. But Steven tells me I have something unique. When I talk, he says, people listen, they relate to me. I've touched them and that's worth keeping. All I have to do for now is tell my story. I don't have to win an Olympic medal just yet. I should concentrate on having a voice, he says. I sit in silence. His words whirl around my head. I've lived my whole life for swimming. How can I put it to one side and just talk? I need space to think, to get my head around it. I thank Steven and tell him I'm going to sleep. I go upstairs to my room and lie on my bed, exhausted. Another cramp hits me. I pick up my phone and write to Sven, asking him for painkillers. Ten minutes later, Sven knocks on my door and passes me a packet of paracetamol. Our argument is already forgotten. He smiles and says goodnight and tells me he's going out with Steven. We both decide it's best if I don't swim my races scheduled for the next day.

I open my eyes the next morning and feel like a switch has flipped in my head. I don't have to race today, I only have interviews. I don't need to win a medal, I just need to tell my story. The relief washes over me as I shower and make up my face. At breakfast, I joke with Sven and Steven as if yesterday never happened. I'm excited for my interview with Steven. I'm ready. We find a quiet corner of the bar and Ludwig sets up the camera and pins a microphone onto my t-shirt. Once the camera is running, Steven asks me what my hopes are for Rio.

'I will make everyone proud,' I tell him. 'It's a big responsibility. I think I'm going to be ready for it. I always wanted to be someone who inspired a lot of people. Who tells people that you can keep moving no matter what. And I think it's amazing because not everyone has this opportunity.'

I'm calm, I know my message. I focus on my voice. All the confusion of the previous weeks has melted away overnight. I meet a

German journalist in the hotel lobby and do one more interview. Afterwards, we still have a few hours to kill before our flight home, so Steven suggests we go sightseeing. We drive into Luxembourg city and Ludwig films me at a funfair. I throw darts at balloons at a stall and win a toy. I think about nothing at all. Steven buys me a waffle with piles of whipped cream. Sven and I are completely back to normal, even alone on the plane back to Berlin. It's clear, we're still here, we'll continue on together as before. But I never hear anything more from him about any fly-on-the-wall documentaries.

The day after we get back from Luxembourg, Sara and I move into our own place, a one-bedroom apartment one train stop east of the Olympiapark. It belongs to the sister of the headmaster of my school, who offers to let us sublet it. We're very lucky to get it. Many Syrians are finding it almost impossible to find an apartment in Berlin. Sven helps us with the paperwork and tries to get the Berlin authorities to help us pay the rent. But the guy at the job centre says we have to wait for Mum and Dad to get out of the *heim* before the state will support us. He says the rules state that refugees can't live alone until they're twenty-six years old. In the end, Sven sorts out an arrangement with the IOC that they'll contribute towards our rent. Again, we're very lucky.

It's good to have some space from the clubhouse, as things are a bit awkward at the club. For one thing, only one athlete has gone to the Olympics from Wasserfreunde in the last ten years. It's hard for some people to get their head around the refugee team, and for them to see what I've now come to accept: this whole thing is about my story, my voice, not about my swimming.

The big day, when the IOC is due to announce the final line-up of the refugee team, is drawing closer. Nothing is certain yet, but everyone expects I'll be on it. I feel calmer after my revelation in Luxembourg. I don't need to achieve impossible times. I just need to tell my story, get my message out. But that isn't always easy. Sven and Michael organize interviews with two big American news networks. They want footage to show after the team is announced. We do the interviews in my school lunch hour. As I leave class I gaze longingly at all the other kids, messing around, taking selfies, and playing music on their phones. And here's me, telling the same story for what feels like the millionth time. I come to dread telling the boat story. Always the boat, often the first question. It's a mystery to me why every journalist seems excited to hear it again.

A few days before the announcement, Sven comes to see me after training. He says he's been warned by IOC deputy director Pere Miro to lock his phone on the day. It's clear there's going to be a lot of media interest. I'm certain that can only mean one thing. But Sven is still playing it cool, saying it doesn't mean anything for definite. The day before the announcement, I get a call from my old friend Rami. He says he had a dream we were both on the team. Imagine, I tell him, if we both go to the Olympics, how much fun it'll be. I promise to call Rami as soon as I hear anything, and he says he'll do the same. The day comes around at last. I force myself to go to morning training as usual. Sven and I are due to travel to the North German Championships in Braunschweig later that evening. After training, I go home to pack and wait for news from the IOC. The doorbell rings. It's Lam and Magdalena, come to record the moment I hear about the team.

'Did you hear anything yet?' says Magdalena.

'No,' I say.

'Open your emails,' she says.

I tell her I haven't read my emails in months. Magdalena grins.

'You want me to do it?' she says.

I give her the log-in to my email account. She sits down and types into her laptop. I hold my breath. The silence crackles.

Magdalena grins again.

'You're in,' she says.

I gasp and peer over Magdalena's shoulder at a list of names on the screen. She scrolls back up to the top. The first name: Rami Anis. I squeal and grab my phone. Come on, Rami. Pick up. My gut is doing backflips. I'm happier for him than I am relieved for myself. He worked so hard and now, the reward.

'Yusra?' says Rami.

'Rami! You're on the team. We both are. We're going to Rio!'

PART EIGHT

The Rings

21

The front door opens and Sara steps into our apartment. I jump up from my bed.

'Sara!' I say. 'I'm going!'

Sara says nothing as she closes the door behind her and takes off her shoes.

'I'm going to Rio,' I say again. 'To the Olympics.'

'Huh?' says Sara. 'Oh, right.'

Oh, right. Is that all she's going to say? My cheeks burn as I wait for her to react. Sara fusses with her bag, steps into our shared room, and sits down on her bed. At last, she lifts her head and looks me in the eye.

'What?' says Sara. 'Really, it's not such a big deal. I've watched you swim in a lot of competitions.'

I'm stunned. This can't be just another competition for her. It's the Olympics. It's our childhood dream. My eyes fill with tears.

'Is it because it's a refugee team?' I ask her.

'Don't be silly, Yusra,' says Sara. 'I'm really proud of that.'

What, then? She could have been on the team with me. I wanted to have her there in Rio with me, I tell her, but she stopped swimming. She stares at me hard.

'You know why I stopped,' she says. 'Because I couldn't swim any more. My injury. My shoulders hurt too bad.'

We sit in gloomy silence for a minute. I wonder when we grew so far apart. Then Sara says she's leaving Berlin. My stomach tightens. Not to Syria? But Sara says no, she's going back to Greece. A friend of hers is volunteering with refugees there and invited her along. Sara sighs and spreads her hands. She has to get away from all of this, she says, be herself again. She tells me a lot of journalists write to her, but all they ever want to talk about is me. They never ask who she is, what she's doing. She says she gets messages from people asking why I'm so successful and she's nothing. She feels like she's shrinking. Pretty soon she'll be nothing but my sister.

'Well, I'm not nothing,' says Sara. 'That's why I'm leaving.'

I stare at her. Why didn't she tell me all this before? I frown and shake my head. I don't understand. What does she want? Fame? Success? Recognition?

'No, of course not,' she says, her eyes filling with tears now too. 'I just want people to stop asking me about the boat. And about you. I want them to stop labelling me with that story. I'm so much more than that. This story happened to both of us, all of it, but now it's only ever about you.'

I'm shocked. I had no idea she was feeling this way. I never thought me being on the team would hurt her like this. Maybe I can help her, I say. Maybe Sven can do something. She cuts me off.

'Just listen, ok?' says Sara. 'I'm going to Greece, to do this thing on my own. Without you.'

Sara grabs her bag from the bed, slips on her shoes, and walks out. The front door shuts behind her and I throw myself on the bed. I've never felt so alone. I see me and Sara on the sofa in the apartment in Daraya with Dad, willing Michael Phelps on to his next gold medal. The Olympics meant so much to us back then. Has she forgotten all that? I stand up and look around. I have to get ready. In a few hours I've got to leave for the competition in Braunschweig. It hits me again. I'm going to Rio. My stomach churns with waves of excitement and unease. Everything has gotten so complicated.

That weekend I swim ok. I don't achieve my best times, but there are no disasters. The pressure is off. I'm on the team. And so is my friend Rami. I try not to think about Sara and manage to silence my nagging doubts about the team. After the competition finishes on Sunday, I speed back to Berlin in time for my very first live-TV appearance. I've been invited to appear on *Mensch Gottschalk*, a star-studded talk show with German TV host Thomas Gottschalk. I'm nervous when we get to the TV studio, but it helps that Sara has agreed to come along for moral support. She helps calm my nerves while I wait to go on stage. I'm due to share a slot with then-President of the European Parliament, Martin Schulz. I meet him backstage and he's very friendly. When it's time, I sit next to him on the on-stage sofa, blocking out the bright lights and the studio audience. I smile and focus on my message. No one chooses to be a refugee. We're human beings, just like everyone else. We too can achieve great things.

Later, back at home, Sara acts like our argument never happened. I'm careful not to bring up Rio and she's busy planning her trip to Greece. She'll leave in August, around the same time I'll travel to Brazil with Sven for the Games. Mum and Dad are also acting like me swimming at the Olympics is the most normal thing in the world.

'That's nice, *habibti*,' says Mum when I tell her. 'You worked hard, you deserve it.'

I push on in the pool and at school. Elise and Mette are excited for me when I tell them about the team. But none of it seems real yet. A week after the team is announced, Olympic partner Visa ask me to appear in a commercial. The producers say they want to tell the boat story in a one-minute short film and want to add in shots of me diving and swimming. Michael and Sven organize a one-day shoot in the pool for the following week. The day of the commercial shoot, Sven and I meet the producers in the dining room at the clubhouse. They show us a storyboard of ten frames. The scenes chop and change between me swimming in the pool and an actress in an overcrowded dinghy at sea. My part in the pool is just diving, swimming, and putting goggles on. The part set at sea shows the actress getting into the water and later a group of people struggling to pull a boat on shore. There's no silliness. It looks alright to me. The shoot is done in a few hours and afterwards I do a couple of TV interviews at the poolside.

A few weeks later, Sven flies on his own to Switzerland for a coaches' meeting with the IOC to work out logistics for the team. He comes back glowing with excitement. The IOC felt like one big family, he tells me. Sven even got to sit next to IOC President Thomas Bach at lunch. They chatted about Germany and about refugees, about the idea and inspiration for the team. President

Bach told Sven he supported Germany's decision to help us, that there was no other humane choice. The team was his way of helping.

Our plans are coming together now. We'll fly to Rio at the end of July. Sven and I will stay with the rest of the team and the other athletes in the Olympic Village. I grin when Sven tells me this. I wonder if I'll get to meet my childhood hero Michael Phelps. Then Sven frowns, the way he does when he's got something to say. He hesitates a few seconds, choosing his words.

'I've been meaning to ask you,' he says at last. 'The team sponsors are asking if you want them to fly Sara to Rio.'

'What?' I say. 'That's amazing! Of course I do.'

Sven raises his eyebrows.

'Are you sure?' he says.

I frown.

'Why wouldn't I want her there?' I say.

Sven shrugs. He knows me going to Rio is a sensitive subject with Sara and that she has other plans for the summer. But I'm sure she'll want to go. At least, I hope she will. And it would mean so much to have her there with me. We did it all together. We swam together as kids, left our home together, battled the waves together. Together, we found a safe place for our family to begin a new life. Now we'll stand together in front of the whole world. I can't wait to tell her. That evening I get home to find Sara hanging out in our room. I grin.

'You want to go to Rio?' I say. 'Because the sponsors are offering to pay for your flights and hotel.'

Sara frowns and puts down her phone.

'Wait. What?' she says. 'But I'm going to Greece to volunteer in August. My friend has bought me my flight already.'

Come on, I tell her. It's Rio. There will be plenty of time to do her own thing in Greece afterwards. I want her there with me. We can do it together. At last, she grins.

'Ok,' she says. 'I'll be there, if that's what you want.'

July passes in a blur of swimming and TV interviews. Sven has me abandon our Tokyo schedule of aerobic training. We focus on speed training, at race pace. He has me do eight 50m races as fast as I can with long recovery rests in between. And it's working, I'm getting faster. I can now do 100m butterfly in 1:08. I still dream of a miracle result at the Games, but I remind myself of Steven's words in Luxembourg. For now, it's all about the story, Yusra, the voice. Not the swimming.

The shift in focus from swimming to speaking affects Sven, too. After Rio, we agree, I'll need a different coach. Sven and I can't go on like we have been, with him taking on so many different roles in my life at once. It's not easy to be an effective coach when you're also a close friend, a mentor, and a manager of sorts. We need to be able to discuss the important things, all the plans, the speeches, the media work, without swimming getting in the way.

Sven's work with me is also beginning to interfere with his coaching job at the club. Some of the parents of the kids in our group don't understand. They think he neglects their kids because he's focusing on me. Sven has to keep explaining that he does the same job with all the kids. I know he deals with me in the same way as all the others in training. It's only out of the pool that he helps with the extra stuff. Sven speaks to Reni and agrees someone else on the club's coaching team should take me on after Rio.

It takes ages for Sara's travel visa for Brazil to come through, so we decide Sven and I will go ahead and she'll join us there whenever she can. The night before we leave, I pack my case in a whirlwind of happy and excited thoughts. A whole month in exotic Brazil. Mum, Dad and Shahed come to the airport to see me off. Shahed's too young to really get what's happening, but Mum and Dad are both in tears.

'Just remember how hard you worked for this,' says Dad, hugging me.

'Yes,' says Mum. 'God is rewarding us for everything we went through. You deserve it. I always knew you'd do something big.'

On the plane, Sven and I sleep, eat, and watch movies. We both try to relax, we know there will be a lot to do once we get to Rio. Somehow it feels like the work is already over, but we're excited for what is coming next. For the moment, I'm not nervous about my races. We're just going to have fun and focus on the serious part, the competition. We land in Rio early in the morning. We're met at the airport by Sophie Edington, the team press attaché and former world-class swimmer, and Isabela Mazao from UNHCR. We take a bus transfer from the airport. Sven spots IOC President Thomas Bach in the vehicle behind us. It seems he arrived with us on the same plane. I stare out of the bus window at the tightly packed, pink houses. On the horizon, a collection of strangely shaped green mountains rises above the city. We arrive at the Olympic Village, a cluster of beige concrete high-rises near a big lake out of town. We're shown the way to one of the fifteen-floor apartment blocks. The top couple of floors have been assigned to the refugee team, the ROT athletes. As we walk up the path to the entrance I hear someone shout my name. I look up and see my old friend Rami waving out of one of the top windows. He holds out his phone to get a picture.

'Smile for your sister!' he shouts down.

I grin and make the peace sign with two fingers. We step inside the block and Sven and I split off to find our apartments. I'm sharing with the other female athletes on the team. There are four of us in all, two to each sparse, functional bedroom. I find the apartment empty; the other team mates aren't around. I leave my luggage in my room and go upstairs to find Rami in the apartment he's sharing with our male team mates. He opens the door. I grin and hold my hand out for a high five. It's surreal. Us. Here. In Rio. At the Olympic Games.

We find Sven again and wander outside into the Village to explore. We walk along the path that runs around the outside of the complex. We pass a fitness centre, a recovery area with hot tubs, tennis courts, basketball courts, swimming pools. Everything an athlete could want. On the edge of the Village is a barrier, beyond that a mixed zone with a row of shops and fast-food outlets. Accredited broadcasters and journalists are allowed into the mixed zone, but no further. The Village is a private haven just for us. The best thing in the complex is a colossal dining-hall tent. It must be about the size of three football fields. Inside, athletes from all over the world are sitting at long trestle tables. We wander past five different buffets laid out with every type of food I could imagine. Each buffet is themed: Brazilian, Asian, international, halal and kosher. My eye falls on the last buffet, a pasta and pizza stand. Bingo.

'Is this all for free?' I ask Sven.

'Yes,' he says and grins. 'It's all you can eat.'

I gaze at the tables of exotic fruits, yoghurts, and cereals. To one side runs a series of fridges packed with soft drinks, energy drinks and water. Sven hands me a card to open the fridges and tells me to help myself. I stare wide-eyed at the array of food, stretching on into the distance. I couldn't try everything here if I was here for a whole year.

Back in the apartment, I find my female team mates already settled in. I'm sharing a room with Yolande, a Congolese judoka now living in Brazil. In the other room are Rose and Anjelina, both Sudanese runners living in Kenya. I've read short summaries of their stories and I'm a bit daunted. They all had it very hard. My roommate Yolande grew up in the Democratic Republic of Congo. War was all she knew. As a kid, she was separated from her family and learned judo at an orphanage. Yolande competed for Congo in international competitions, but training conditions were extremely difficult. A few years before, she and Popole, another ROT team mate, had sought asylum in Brazil while competing in the World Judo Championships. The others, Rose and Anjelina, along with three male team mates, Yiech, Paulo and James, are all runners from South Sudan. They fled the civil war when they were kids and grew up in Kakuma, a huge refugee camp in the north of Kenya. Rose tells me the whole Kakuma camp is rooting for the team. They're all watching. I think of my friends still living in the *heim* in Berlin, about the coaches and other swimmers from the club. I wonder if they'll be watching my races, rooting for us too.

We don't talk about the refugee team. It doesn't seem like the time for deep discussions. I'm too shy to ask Rose about life in Kakuma and I'm not sure if she'd be insulted. I decide to stick to a safe subject: sport. It's overwhelming enough just to be here, at the

Olympics, living out every athlete's dream. But later, lying in bed, I think about my team mates and what they've been through. I realize how much I've missed while I've been busy telling my own story. Now I'm part of something much bigger. With the team, I'm representing sixty million displaced people across the world. It's a huge responsibility, but I know my job. I have a message to spread: that being a refugee is not a choice. That we too can achieve great things.

The next morning, Sven meets with Sophie Edington, the ROT press attaché, to discuss my schedule for the following four weeks. My first heat is scheduled for Saturday, the opening day of the Games. I will train every day with Sven until then. For the remaining time, Sophie has drawn up an ambitious timetable. It feels like every free minute of the week before my heat will be taken up with press conferences, interviews, meetings, and speeches. Sven is doubtful we'll be able to fit it all in. He suggests asking Sophie to boil it down to the essential meetings. But I'm here to tell my story, for the ROT team, for the IOC. I tell him we should do all of it.

The next day, we have our first public outing as a team. We take a train up Corcovado mountain to see the Christ the Redeemer statue. At the top, a crowd of journalists and photographers is waiting for us. They pounce on me for a comment.

'We're so happy to be here,' I tell them. 'We all have the same strong feeling about never giving up. We did a lot to get here.'

It's only the beginning. The next three days are taken up with long press conferences. At each one, the situation gets more embarrassing. It seems I'm the story. Journalists ask my team mates one or two polite questions, then they turn to me and ask another fifty. After each event, Sophie helps me prioritize four or five back-to-back interviews with the biggest broadcasters and press. I talk to journalists from Australia, Germany, Japan, and South Korea. All of them are after the same story. Always the boat. I do my duty and tell them what happened with a smile, my heart shut down, my head working. The reporters seem happy. But even the press conferences and the extra interviews aren't enough. Journalists and photographers follow me wherever I go. I'm mobbed as soon as I set foot outside the Village. Camera teams show up at the pool while I train with Rami. They wait to grab me on the way in and out of the press conferences. At one event, a Brazilian journalist tries to follow me into the bathroom. Another British journalist gets my number from somewhere and messages me constantly, asking where I am and what I'm doing. I show Sven the messages.

'Does she want to be my friend, or what?' I say.

'Just ignore her,' says Sven.

I can't wait to see Lam, Magdalena, and Steven, who are also in Rio covering the Games. They might be journalists, but there's no pressure around them, they're my friends. Lam and Magdalena will be at our team's welcome ceremony in a few days' time. Steven is busy reporting on other stories out in the city, but we'll see him after my races.

By the end of the third day I'm already exhausted by all the press work. Sven, Rami, and I are eating in the cavernous dining hall in the Village. All three of us are on the lookout, scanning the crowds for famous athletes. We've already spotted Rafael Nadal and Novak Djokovic, but Rami and I are holding out for the big one, our ultimate hero, Michael Phelps. Sven reaches into his bag and gets out his printed version of Sophie's schedule.

'So tomorrow is another full day of interviews,' he says.

'My God,' I say. 'How many more?'

He flips the pages.

'A few,' he says. 'I told you it was a lot.'

I shake my head.

'It's too much,' I say. 'You've got to tell Sophie I can't do it all.'

Sven shakes his head. No way, he says. I have to tell Sophie myself. He's going to send her to see me and I have to say no to her face. I squirm at the thought, but I'll have to do it. I feel bad about letting Sophie down, but I can't keep on spending every waking moment with journalists, the stress is just too much. I have to swim in a few days' time.

'There!' says Sven, pointing to his right.

I stand up to get a better look. I catch my breath. There, a few tables away to the right, sit Ryan Lochte and the rest of the American swimming team. I scan the small crowd around them. Then I see him, those massive shoulders, that thick-set neck. Michael Phelps. My childhood hero. My stomach lurches. I'm suddenly full of nerves. Rami grins and claps his hand on the table.

'Let's ask him for a selfie,' says Rami.

'No,' I say. 'He's focused. He's in the middle of a competition. If I were him I wouldn't want people coming over to ask for photos.'

Rami watches wistfully as Phelps turns and walks out of the tent.

The next day our official ROT Olympic apparel, designed by swimming brand Arena, arrives. There's a tracksuit, a warm-up jacket and best of all, a white swimming cap with my name in bold, black lettering under the Olympic Rings: 'R.O.T. Mardini'. I squeal with excitement and pride. It's unreal. A Mardini, here, at the Olympics.

Later that day the team is scheduled to appear at the opening day of the IOC session, an annual meeting a bit like a parliament. I've been asked to say a few words. Sven and I are waiting for a taxi outside the Village to go to the session when a Korean journalist jogs up to us. He wants to ask me some questions. He seems nice, so I start chatting to him.

'No, Yusra,' says Sven and grabs my arm to pull me away.

Sven scowls at the journalist and tells him to leave us alone. The man shuffles off. I'm shocked.

'What did you do that for?' I say to Sven. 'He seemed ok.'

'Don't talk to them,' says Sven. 'You have to tell them no. Believe me, if the others see they can just walk up to you and get an interview, we won't be able to go anywhere without being mobbed.'

Maybe it's just all the stress, but I can't help feeling annoyed. Since when does Sven decide who I talk to? Isn't it up to me? The taxi pulls up. I get in, slam the door, and sit in angry silence all the way to the hotel where the event is being held. We arrive and wait backstage until it's time for the team to appear on stage. As I calm down, I realize Sven is right, I have to be careful with all this media attention. He's only looking out for me.

After a short introduction, I step on stage with the rest of the team. The IOC members session gives us a standing ovation. My eyes flit around the crowd and I think back to the press conference in Berlin. Stay calm, focus on the message. I walk up to the lectern together with my team mate Yiech, one of the Sudanese runners living in Kenya. He's first to speak.

'We are ambassadors for the other refugees,' says Yiech into the microphone. 'We cannot forget this chance that you gave us. We are not bad people. It's only a name to be a refugee.'

That's right. Only a name. A name given to us by circumstances beyond our control. Now we have to reclaim it. Yiech and I swap places and I step up to the lectern.

'We are still humans,' I say. 'We are not only refugees. We are like everyone in the world. We can do something, achieve something. We didn't choose to leave our homelands. We didn't choose the name refugee. We promise again that we are going to do what it takes to inspire everyone.'

I feel a rush of energy as I step away from the microphone. It feels good to say these words out loud in front of so many powerful people. To be telling the world who we really are. But exciting as it might be, it's clear I can't do everything on the press schedule. I speak with Sophie later that day. We agree to scale down the interviews and postpone some until after my second heat the following Wednesday.

Next on the schedule is the welcome ceremony. All the Olympic teams are officially welcomed to the Village in a ceremony held in the mixed zone. It's a short, symbolic gesture, lasting only about ten minutes. The welcome ceremonies have already been going on for days, running through the teams in alphabetical order. Ours is scheduled to take place in the evening, just before the Russian team. By pure chance, that means journalists can turn up at one time and cover the two big stories of the week: the Russian doping scandal and us. As a result, the mixed zone is crammed with hundreds of reporters, camera teams, and photographers. We wait on the edge of the mixed zone and take pictures of the chaotic scene.

When it's time for our team's ceremony, we have to battle our way through the waiting journalists. They jostle towards us as we approach. Sven, Lam, Rami, and I fight our way in. After the ceremony, the scrum is even worse. Reporters crowd around me, shoving microphones and cameras into my face. I can hardly move. Lam and Sven squeeze in either side of me and bat the press out of the way. As we battle our way out, Sven raises his hand to alert a nearby security guard. The man drags me out of the crush and takes me back to our apartment block. Along the way we're joined by Pamela Vipond, Deputy Director of Olympic Solidarity. She's been in touch with Sven for months, ever since he sent that first email about me to the IOC. She grins and chats to us, helps to calm things down and put me at ease. Later I climb into bed, shaken and completely exhausted.

The next day at breakfast, Sven brings up the opening ceremony. It'll be held the night before my first heat and we have to decide whether to go.

'Normally, if an athlete had a race the next morning, they wouldn't go to the opening ceremony,' says Sven. He grins. 'But, well, this is different, right?'

It's obvious, I tell him. We have to be there. It might be a once-in-a-lifetime chance.

'Who's carrying the flag for the team?' I ask Sven.

'I spoke with the IOC people about that,' he says. 'I told them you're not the only member of the team and that someone else should do it. They decided on your team mate Rose.'

I smile. He's right. And anyway, I think the rest of the team would want to kill me if I carried the flag. I've been doing all the interesting things, the speeches, the interviews. I've had enough attention. It's right that someone else gets to be in the spotlight for once.

The day of the opening ceremony, Rami and I train in the morning and then go back to the Village to get ready. In the apartment, I find clothes laid out for us to wear. A navy jacket with gold buttons, a pair of beige trousers, a white shirt and a spotty necktie. I change and meet Rami, Sven, and the others outside to catch a bus to the Maracanã stadium.

We're taken into a nearby indoor arena to wait our turn with the other athletes. Our team will go in second to last during the Parade of Nations, just ahead of host team Brazil. We sit in the arena and watch the glitzy ceremony on huge screens. At one point, hundreds of samba dancers flood the stadium floor and reconstruct a carnival. Backstage in the arena, the athletes get up from their seats and dance along in the aisles. The parade begins, and the teams file out in alphabetical order. At last, it's just us and the Brazilians left. The host team's party is in full swing as our tiny ROT team exits the arena with them. Outside, we're mobbed by hundreds of wild Brazil fans, dancing and singing with us all the way into the stadium. Inside, we are ushered towards the stadium entrance. I step onto the walkway as a deafening roar rises from the crowd.

22

'Refugee Olympic Team.'

The announcement echoes around the stadium. Tens of thousands of people jump to their feet at once, cameras flashing, arms waving in excitement. I catch my breath. It's the largest crowd I've ever seen. The packed aisles around us reach all the way to the rooftops.

A mounted camera whirls past. I grin and wave my tiny white flag. Ahead, Rose sways the Olympic flag high above her head. I spot IOC President Thomas Bach and UN General Secretary Ban Ki-moon, standing, clapping, cheering us on. My heart pounds in my ears as we walk down the central aisle. Either side, stewards dressed in neon tabards dance under flashing lights to thumping carnival music. We melt into the crowd of athletes. The ring-shaped roof towers around us. Directly above in the gap, stars twinkle between low clouds.

I stare at the rings on the flag in Rose's hands. I close my eyes and see the Damascus skyline at dusk as the call to prayer rings out. I smell the rain in the olive orchards in Daraya. Syria. My lost country. What's a flag anyway? In my heart, I'm no less Syrian. I know I'm still representing my people. All the millions of us forced to flee, all those who risked the sea for a life without bombs.

Behind us, an even bigger roar goes up as the Brazilian team enters. The stadium erupts with music, singing, cheering, and dancing.

'Ladies and gentlemen, the athletes of the Rio 2016 Olympic Games!'

The thousands roar again. I watch on giant screens as dancers move tall mirrored boxes into the centre of the stadium and spin them round until they make the shape of the Olympic rings from above. Green plants erupt from the top and confetti shoots up towards the roof. Fireworks explode over the stadium in the shape of five rings. Streams of golden fire shoot into the night sky above our heads. The flames fade, and the stadium darkens until it's a twinkling cavern, lit only by a soft blue light. Cameras flash in the darkness.

Sven taps me on the shoulder.

'We'll wait until after the speeches,' he whispers. 'Then we'll leave.'

First up to the lectern is Carlos Arthur Nuzman, Chairman of the Rio 2016 Olympic Committee. He welcomes the guests and the athletes to the Games.

'The Olympic dream is now a wonderful reality,' he says. 'We never give up our dreams. We never give up.'

The words hang in the air. A wonderful reality. I'm in my living room in Daraya, vowing to make it to the top. I'm staring in horror at the bomb in the pool. I'm diving into the sea, desperate prayers ringing in my ears. I'm falling asleep in a Hungarian prison. I'm pushing myself harder than ever in the pool in Berlin. This is my gift to my six-year-old self: young and determined and idealistic. It seemed so far away then. Now I'm here. The moment my whole life has been leading up to. The Olympic Games.

IOC President Thomas Bach is speaking now at the lectern.

'We are living in a world where selfishness is gaining ground,' he says. 'Where some people claim to be superior to others. Here is our Olympic answer. In the spirit of Olympic solidarity and with the greatest respect, we welcome the Refugee Olympic Team.'

The stadium erupts again with cheers as a camera pans past us. I wave the little flag and grin.

'Dear refugee athletes,' says the IOC President. 'You are sending a message of hope to all the many millions of refugees around the globe. You had to flee from your homes because of violence, hunger or just because you were different. Now with your great talent and human spirit, you are making a great contribution to society.'

I remind myself I'm not alone in this. Each of my team mates stands for millions of people, many of them with stories harder and more harrowing than mine. And here we are, showing the world what we can achieve.

IOC President Bach's speech draws to a close. Sven taps me on the shoulder again. It's time, he says, we should go. I have to be up early the next morning for my race. Sven and I leave my team mates behind, find our way out of the stadium, and climb onto the shuttle bus back to the Village.

Back in my room, I sit on my bed. My mind is a whirlwind. I think of Sven and what he's done for me. I think of the other team coaches, of the dedication and generosity they've shown us. And now, the Olympics, their reward. I think of my team mates. Each of them standing strong for their communities, shouldering the responsibility of millions. I remember the message from the young guy struggling to survive in Syria. My life is hard, he wrote, but you've inspired me to go on.

'*Ya Allah*,' I say out loud to the blank, white wall. 'There is no God but you. God is the greatest. Forgive me, for I am one of the sinners.'

I sit for a moment in the silence of the empty apartment. Then I stand and pack my goggles, cap, swimsuit, towel, and flip-flops into my swimming bag. I lay out my clothes for the next day. At last, as I lie down to sleep, my mind is still.

The alarm goes. My eyes flick open. Today. It's today. I shower and pull on my clothes. I find Sven in the dining hall.

'Morning,' he says. 'How are you feeling?'

I manage a grin.

'Good,' I say automatically.

I get up and walk along the buffets. The sight of food makes my stomach squirm. I take an apple and a cupcake and sit back down opposite Sven. He raises his eyebrows.

'You're going to eat more than that, I hope?' he says.

I frown.

'No, please,' I say. 'I can't.'

Sven stands and wanders off towards the food stands. Five minutes later he's back, carrying a box full of pasta.

'Not for breakfast,' I say. 'Really I can't.'

He puts it down in front of me.

'I'll leave it there,' he says. 'You should eat some carbs.'

I look away. My stomach flits with a whole swarm of butterflies. Sven clears his throat.

'So there are just four others in your heat,' he says. 'Remember, you're up against yourself. You've been swimming very well in training over the last few days. Those short-distance butterfly sprints, 25m in thirteen seconds, you're the fastest I've ever seen you.'

My legs feel weak. I take a few deep breaths. Sven looks at his watch.

'Ok,' he says. 'It's time to go.'

I leave the pasta untouched on the table and walk with Sven to the bus stop. We climb onto the shuttle bus in silence. I stare out of the window at the high-rise concrete towers, and breathe. With each breath I feel my mind quieten, my stomach settle. By the time we arrive at the Aquatics Stadium, I'm not afraid, only determined. I warm up, swinging my arms loose at the pool edge, then I swim to warm up in the pool. The movement does me good. The water lulls me into a state of alert calm. I put on my racing suit, training jacket, swimming cap and goggles, and go into the call room to wait. I meditate. No thinking now. All I need is my muscle memory. They call my name. The first swimming race of the 2016 Olympic Games is about to begin. As I step out into the pool, I pray again.

'Nothing is easy except what you have made easy,' I mutter. 'If you wish, you can make the difficult easy. Please God, make my race easy.'

It's cold. The spectator seats are less than a third full. There's a patter of applause as I walk out towards the start blocks with the four other swimmers. I take off my training jacket. An announcer reads out our names.

'Yusra Mardini, Refugee Olympic Team.'

Slowly, gradually, the applause swells from the spectator seats. My nerves crescendo suddenly as the cheers grow louder. I turn down the volume in my head, fight to keep my mind still. If I think, I'll be lost.

Time speeds up. I step onto the block at my feet. I put my right foot forwards, wrap my toes around the steel edge and grab it with both hands. My mind is blank. All I see is the water in front of me. All I hear is the rhythmic beat of my pulse. The echoes in the pool slow to a heartbeat.

Take your marks.

I tense and rock back.

Beep.

I dive into the glinting water.

The Voice

I met Steven in Rio one night not long after my second and final race. He, Rami, Sven, and I drove along the beachfront at Copacabana, laughing at how strangely things had worked out. We flicked through pictures from Belgrade on Steven's phone.

'Did you think when you were taking those pictures that Yusra would be famous one day?' said Rami.

'I had a feeling that she was perhaps special,' said Steven.

I stared into my phone, embarrassed.

'Not that special,' I said.

Sara's travel visa finally came through and she flew out to join us in Rio. We struggled through an emotional joint press conference. When the inevitable boat questions started, Sara beckoned to me. I leaned in and she whispered in my ear. Exactly a year ago, she said, we were in the sea. I leaned back and stared at her. Both our eyes filled with tears. A year since we nearly lost that desperate gamble. And now what shore had we washed up on? We hugged as the cameras flashed in our faces.

Sara took me aside afterwards and told me her plans for Greece. She had decided to go back to the island, Lesbos. A young volunteer there called Eric had written to let her know that our story was inspiring to the Syrian kids on the island. Eric worked with ERCI, an organization rescuing migrant boats at sea. He told Sara they could use an Arabic speaker to help guide in the boats. I stared at her in admiration. What a brave thing to do.

The remaining days in Rio passed in a whirlwind of meetings, interviews, and photo shoots. Sara left for Greece just after we got back to Berlin. There was no time for me to rest either. Leaving Brazil marked the beginning of another chapter. I had a new job. I had a message to spread. Just a few weeks later I flew to New York to address the United Nations General Assembly's Leader Summit on Refugees. I was given the great honour of introducing US President Barack Obama. I can't say I wasn't nervous stepping on stage. It was my first chance to deliver my message to world leaders.

'This experience has given me a voice and an opportunity to be heard,' I told the summit. 'I want to help change people's perceptions of what a refugee is, for everyone to understand that it is not a choice to flee from your home, and that refugees are normal people who can achieve great things if given the opportunity.'

Afterwards I met President Obama. I was nervous, but he put me at ease right away. It was amazing to meet this powerful leader and for him to treat me as someone special, someone worth talking to. The night after my speech, I went to a United Nations event celebrating those advancing women's rights across the world. There I first met Queen Rania of Jordan. I was completely star-struck. Here was this woman, so beautiful and strong, wanting to talk with me about my life. We got on well, and later she nominated me for *People* magazine's list of 25 Women Changing the World.

A few months later, in November 2016, I flew to Rome to visit Pope Francis and presented him with a Bambi, a German media award. He was kind and gracious, and it was humbling to meet another great man changing the world for the better. Later that month, Sara and I received Bambi awards ourselves at a glitzy, star-studded ceremony. In January 2017, I addressed world leaders once more at the DAVOS World Economic Forum. In April, I became a Goodwill Ambassador for UNHCR. My message has been the same throughout: a refugee is a human being like any other.

For all the travel and speeches, my life still centres around swimming. Sven is no longer my coach, but he's still my close friend and mentor. He now works for me full-time as a sports director. Sven's job includes supporting my new manager Marc in staying on top of my crazy schedule. My new coach at Wasserfreunde, an upbeat, no-nonsense Cuban called Ariel, is a big advocate of power training. He pushes me hard to increase my speed. Overcoming pain barriers, he tells me with a grin, is all in the mind.

Sven, Marc, and Ariel. My team. All three know I'd do anything for swimming and they're working hard to keep my Olympic dream alive. Last July, Sven and Ariel came with me to Budapest where I swam in the World Championships. I dreaded going back to Hungary. It was hard not to feel hate for the people there and the place itself. Unsurprisingly, everyone was very welcoming this time around. But I stayed well clear of the train station.

A few weeks after the Worlds, Marc and I flew to Japan with UNHCR. I met with the Japanese Olympic Committee there and told them I'm training hard for the Tokyo Games. That autumn I signed a sponsorship deal with sportswear manufacturer Under Armour. Nothing is certain, but I hope more than anything to become an Olympian for a second time in 2020.

Olympian or not, as long as I can't go home, I'll still wear that other name tag. Refugee. After Rio, I learned to embrace that word. I don't see it as an insult. It's just a name for ordinary people who were forced to flee their homes. Like me, like my family.

Mum, Dad and Shahed now have refugee status too. We all want to stay in Berlin. We've been told we can stay in Germany until 2019. After that, we hope our residency permits will be extended if necessary. I trust Germany to do the right thing. We're happy to be living in peace. But it's tough to start over again and build a new life from scratch. Our lives are very different here. Each one of us has to find their own way.

Shahed has it easiest because she's the youngest. She's now ten years old and is growing into a tough, clever young girl. She's adapted quickly to her new home and she babbles away in fluent German with her many native school friends. We're all happy for her, of course. But sometimes we worry about her losing her Syrian identity if we stay in Germany long-term.

Life is harder on my parents. Mum is learning German, but has found it difficult to make friends. Many of the other refugees on her German course are depressed, and the language barrier stops her from reaching out to locals. She misses family back in Syria, my Grandma, aunts, uncles, and cousins still in Damascus. But she'll be ok. Mum's a fighter.

Dad is learning German too, but progress is slow. He often gets frustrated about not being able to coach. Last year he did a six-month training programme and got a German lifeguarding certificate. But his German isn't good enough yet to work. He used to talk sometimes about going back to Syria and I'd tell him we're better off where we are for now. Now he's more settled, and bit by bit things are getting better for us all.

For me, going back isn't an option until the war stops. It's easier for me, I've been very lucky to find such amazing friends in Germany to support me in my new life. Others, including some of the guys we travelled with, see things differently. They were so miserable in Germany they preferred to go back and face the risks at home in Syria. But most of them are still here, working hard to make the best of it. Nabih and Khalil are in Berlin, studying for their German *Abitur* school-leavers' qualification. Ahmad, Idris, Zaher and their families are now spread out across Germany. Many of them are engaged, married, or having kids.

Last autumn, Sara moved back to Berlin to study. Her year volunteering in Greece did us both good. The space brought us closer again. We both needed time to find our way without one another. Sara gives a lot of talks and speeches too. This is just as much her story as it is mine, and she has her own side to tell. We both feel a heavy responsibility to help others. But speaking isn't easy. The boat story haunts us wherever we go.

I struggle with that story. I struggle with why we survived the sea when so many didn't. I struggle to remember what made us take that terrible risk, what made us think our lives were that cheap. It was somehow worth that gamble. But from here, it's hard to imagine how.

I haven't swum in the sea since, mostly because I'm scared of what I might see in the water. I don't dwell on what happened. But I can't stop the waves marching now and then. Every time I hear that another boatload of desperate people drowned at sea, I picture us clinging to the rope, I hear the engine spluttering back to life. Each time, it hits me again how close we were to death. If the motor hadn't revived, we wouldn't have made it.

People often ask me if I'm the girl who pulled the boat, but it wasn't like that. Only superwoman could pull a boat full of people.

I know these are dark times and people want heroes. But I'm just an ordinary girl. A swimmer. I had a normal life before the war. I never dreamt of being a hero. But now, after the Olympics, I have a voice, I have a mission. I want to inspire people and I want to show people who refugees really are.

So who are we? We're human beings. I'm a refugee. So is Sara. So are Mum, Dad and Shahed. No one chooses to be a refugee. I didn't have a choice. I had to leave my home to survive, even if it meant risking death along the way. I have to keep spreading this message, because there will be more of us to come. I fled my country three years ago. But as you read this, other young people are chancing dangerous border-crossings, climbing into overcrowded, flimsy boats, or being locked up and thrown food unfit for animals. They, like me, were normal kids with ordinary lives until war split their worlds apart. They, like me, are searching for a future in which death doesn't fall from the sky. A place to live out calm days after the storm.

Now, with the storm behind me, I focus on that peaceful future. I don't believe the secret of being happy is living a life free of problems. It's about being able to smile despite the hardships. So I block out the negative voices and listen to those who believe in me. I surround myself with a team that has the same drive as I do. I've never been more certain that I'm meant to swim, my destiny lies in the pool. And overcoming the obstacles of the past years has only made me more determined. It's like my coach Ariel always says, limits exist only in your head. It's simple. I'm an athlete and I'll never give up. One day, I'll win.

It isn't easy. There are times when I give everything and it still isn't enough. Then I close my eyes and conjure that desperate moment in the sea when everything seemed hopeless. When the taunting voice told me to give up and get death over with. I remember how I fought, and won. How I kicked, kept my head above water, stayed alive. Then warmth surges through my whole body, bringing hidden reserves of power to my aching muscles. Opening my eyes, I know. Nothing can break me now. Whatever happens, I'll get up. I'll swim on. I'll survive. I'll emerge from the chrysalis as a butterfly.

Acknowledgements

I'd like to thank Sven and Sara, who made this book possible.

Back in the summer of 2017, when work on this book began, Sara left her life in Greece and flew to Berlin to help me capture her experience of our journey together. Later, she revisited many painful places on Lesbos Island to make sure no detail of how we washed up on the shores of Europe was missing. Thank you, Sara, my idol, my sister. I love you.

Thanks also to Sven, who gave me a home, a pool, and a future. Since the day we met he has been on my side, and I know he always will be. Sven spent hours poring over drafts of the manuscript, editing, tweaking, and helping make sure our story was as vivid and nuanced as possible. Sara and Sven, you are my foundation. And you are the backbone of this, our book.

Heartfelt thanks to all the others who contributed to my story. Deepest thanks to journalist Steven Decraene for his unswerving friendship and guidance and for donating his memories so generously to this book. I'm also indebted to Michael Schirp for his comments and for all the times he has gone beyond his job description on my behalf. Thanks also to my old friend Rami Anis for sharing his memories of the times our stories intersect.

Thanks to Josie Le Blond for her invaluable help. Thanks also to my publishers: Carole Tonkinson (Bluebird), Margit Ketterle (Droemer) and Karen Wolny (St Martin's) for all their editorial guidance and support.

Thank you also to the rest of my team. To my coach Ariel Rodriguez, for his tireless motivation and patience. And to my manager Marc Heinkelein for his vision, enthusiasm, and dedication to always fighting my corner.

I'm also deeply grateful to all the friends I met along the way for allowing me to share our story with the world. Thank you to Zaher and the others for guiding us, keeping us safe and letting us join your family and to Ayham and Bassem for showing courage and humour in the darkest waters. I also want to thank Mette, Elise, Katrin and her family and all my friends at Wasserfreunde Spandau 04 for their friendship, hospitality, and support. Also thank you to Reni, Gabi, and Michael for helping Sara and I settle in when we had lost our country, our family, and our home.

Many thanks to those worked so hard to see a Refugee Olympic Team at the Olympics. Special thanks go to IOC President Thomas Bach and Deputy Director Pere Miro for welcoming Sven and I so warmly into the Olympic family. Thanks also to Pamela Vipond and Sandra Logemann of Olympic Solidarity and to the ROT team press attaché Sophie Edington. And thank you to all my ROT teammates for their inspirational dedication to sport and to our cause.

I'd also like to thank everyone at UNHCR, the UN Refugee Agency, for their support and encouragement over the past years. Special thanks to Claire Lewis and everyone at the Global Goodwill Ambassador Program, for giving me the platform and opportunity to spread the truth about refugees to the world.

Finally, I'd like to thank the rest of my family: my sister Shahed who is so dear to me and especially my mother, Mirwat, and father, Ezzat, for teaching me that with determination, strength, and courage, I can reach the shore. All those times you sat at the poolside. It wasn't for nothing.